The Educator's Guide to REST

Burnout, stress, and emotional fatigue have become all too familiar in today's educational landscape. *The Educator's Guide to REST* offers a lifeline as a grounded, evidence-informed, and emotionally resonant guide for teachers who want to rediscover their purpose, find joy in their work, and create sustainable practices for resilience and well-being.

Developed from years of classroom experience and action research, REST (Resilient Educator Support Team) is a 12-module framework built around the idea that educators need practical, compassionate tools and supportive communities. The flexible 12-module format is suitable for individual, classroom, or professional learning community use. It addresses self-awareness and emotional intelligence; mindfulness and stress management; building strong relationships; purpose and passion; adaptive thinking and problem-solving; self-care and well-being; self-compassion; optimistic outlook; building resilience through play; celebrating educators; and sustaining resilience and moving forward. Interactive tools are throughout, including reflection prompts, resilience assessments, and mindfulness practices

Supported by data collected across the US, this guide weaves together personal stories and mindfulness, emotional intelligence, neuroscience, and practical strategies. It's not just theory; rather, it's a call to action to make teaching a more sustainable career.

Stephanie Letourneau is a veteran public-school educator, college adjunct professor, curriculum developer, and professional development leader with over two decades of experience spanning K–12 and higher education. She currently teaches high school health education while serving as an adjunct professor at Merrimack College, North Andover, MA.

"*The Educator's Guide to REST* is a practical, heartfelt resource for cultivating resilient learning communities. Stephanie Letourneau weaves adaptable mindfulness-based learning practices into an interactive experience with purposeful reflections, activities, and intentional pauses. She integrates her personal classroom experiences to show how joy and well-being can be embedded into the school day. This book is an asset for educators, teams, and schools seeking to build healthy, connected, and thriving communities."

Lindsey Frank, M.Ed., *President of Educating Mindfully, Author, Mindfulness-Based Learning Specialist*

"Stephanie Letourneau's *The Educator's Guide to REST* is a gift for educators and their students. With lived examples and data, practical tools and strategies, any educator starting out or with decades under their belt will find relief and restoration in these pages."

Christopher Willard, *Harvard Medical School, Author of* Alphabreaths *and* Feelings Are Like Farts

"At a time when teaching is becoming more and more stressful, *The Educator's Guide to REST* is a critical support. In it, Stephanie Letourneau provides teachers with important concepts and actionable strategies to help them build resilience and manage their mental health. And many of those ideas can be easily shared with students should the reader so-choose. This book will improve schools for both students and staff. Highly recommended!"

Brendan Mahan, M.Ed., M.S., *Author of* Overcoming the Wall of Awful©

"This book is a beautiful example of how one educator's lived experience and choices about her own well-being can inspire and support those who are looking for ways to NOT leave the profession. Letourneau gives educators hope and guidance through the tangible strategies that they can apply to both their personal lives and their professional roles. It was an honor to be a witness to the Action Research initiative that helped to prove that REST works!"

Dr. Kelli Sammis, *Founder of The Pranayama Group*

"Finally, a guide that speaks honestly to the real struggles that today's educators face! Offering practical, research-backed solutions, Stephanie Letourneau provides readers with a comprehensive toolkit grounded in a genuine understanding of what teachers face on a daily basis. The interactive format and data-driven insights make this essential reading for any educator seeking sustainable well-being while striving to remain in the profession they love."

Brent T. Wright, M.Ed., *Assistant Dean, Graduate Programs, School of Education & Social Policy, Merrimack College*

"The Educator's Guide to REST by Stephanie Letourneau is a compassionate, research-based resource that offers practical strategies grounded in personal experiences, mindfulness and neuroscience. This guide supports teacher well-being through accessible, restorative practices. It's not just professional development—it's personal development that empowers educators to create sustainable, mindful habits in and out of the classroom. A must-read—definitely five stars."

Dr. Kathryn Welby, *Educator, Author, and Researcher*

The Educator's Guide to REST

An Interactive Guide to Resilience, Emotional Wellness, and Sustainable Teaching

Stephanie Letourneau

Routledge
Taylor & Francis Group
NEW YORK AND LONDON

Designed cover image: © Ana Letourneau

First published 2026
by Routledge
605 Third Avenue, New York, NY 10158

and by Routledge
4 Park Square, Milton Park, Abingdon, Oxon, OX14 4RN

Routledge is an imprint of the Taylor & Francis Group, an informa business

© 2026 Stephanie Letourneau

The right of Stephanie Letourneau to be identified as author of this work has been asserted in accordance with sections 77 and 78 of the Copyright, Designs and Patents Act 1988.

All rights reserved. No part of this book may be reprinted or reproduced or utilised in any form or by any electronic, mechanical, or other means, now known or hereafter invented, including photocopying and recording, or in any information storage or retrieval system, without permission in writing from the publishers.

Trademark notice: Product or corporate names may be trademarks or registered trademarks, and are used only for identification and explanation without intent to infringe.

ISBN: 978-1-041-19689-1 (hbk)
ISBN: 978-1-041-19687-7 (pbk)
ISBN: 978-1-003-71286-2 (ebk)

DOI: 10.4324/9781003712862

Typeset in Palatino
by Apex CoVantage, LLC

Contents

Acknowledgments ix
Meet the Author xi
Preface xii
    The Science Behind an Interactive Approach   xiii
    How to Use This Book   xiv
    You Hold the Pen   xiv

1 Introduction to Resilience   1
    So What?   1
    What Is Resilience?   3
    Establishing Relevance: Why These Chapters Matter   4
    Overview of Chapters   4
    Educator's Guide to Resilience: Self-Evaluation Tools   6
    Using the Resilience Wheel   15
    You Can Quote Me on That   19
    Find Your Focus: Words for Motivation and Growth   20
    Guided Meditation: Building the Foundation of Resilience   21
    Key Takeaways   22
    Closing Message   22

2 Developing Self-Awareness and Managing Emotions   26
    Teaching During COVID: My Meltdown Moment   26
    What Is Emotional Intelligence?   27
    Establishing Relevance   28
    Emotional Intelligence: The Key to Better Self-Awareness
    and Relationships   30
    Classroom Application   33
    Co-Regulation: Helping Students Manage Big Emotions   34
    Facing Feelings: Overcoming Emotional Avoidance   44
    Guided Meditation: Building the Foundation of Resilience   47
    Key Takeaways   48
    Closing Message   48

3 Mindfulness and Stress Management   52
    Zen and the Art of Bumper Cars   52
    Establishing Relevance   53
    What Is Mindfulness, Really?   54

Formal vs. Informal Mindfulness Practices   55
Mindfulness Strategies and Breathing Techniques   57
Everyday Mindfulness: Small Reminders Make a Big Difference 62
Guided Meditation: Embracing Mindfulness   65
Key Takeaways   66
Closing Message   66

4 Building Strong Relationships   **70**
Jake's Second Favorite   70
What Builds Strong Relationships?   72
Establishing Relevance   73
Student Relationships: The Heartbeat of the Classroom   74
Using "I" Statements to Foster Positive Communication   76
Building Strong Relationships Through Effective Communication 82
What Would You Do?   84
Activities to Build Strong Relationships   87
Boundaries: The Bridge Back to Yourself   91
Games to Build Trust With Students, Colleagues, or Families 97
Guided Meditation: Cultivating Connection   103
Key Takeaways   104
Closing Message   104

5 Professional Purpose and Passion   **108**
The Year Everything Changed   108
Establishing Relevance   110
Addressing the Overuse of "Find Your Why"   111
Purpose Statement Activity   112
Core Values   115
Strategies for Keeping Your Passion Alive in Your Work   115
Reconnect With Your Purpose: Vision Collage Activity   122
Manifesting a Purpose-Driven Teaching Life   123
Guided Visualization: Your Ideal Teaching Life   127
Guided Meditation: Reconnecting With Your Purpose   130
Key Takeaways   131
Closing Message   131

6 Adaptive Thinking and Problem-Solving Skills   **135**
The Late-Work Problem   135
Establishing Relevance   136
Decision-Making   138
Applying Problem-Solving Techniques to a Common Classroom
Challenge   145

Keeping Your Brain Active: A Key to Resilience	153
Mental Agility	154
Guided Meditation: Enhancing Flexibility and Creativity	156
Key Takeaways	157
Closing Message	157

7 Self-Care and Well-Being — 161

Creating My Eight Daily Factors of Self-Care	161
Acknowledging the Complexity of Self-Care	163
Establishing Relevance	164
Eight Daily Factors of Self-Care	164
Nutrition	164
Hydration	165
Sleep	166
Mindfulness	168
Time Management	168
Movement	172
Emotional Awareness	172
Joy	173
The Different Types of Tiredness and How to Rest	175
Guided Meditation: Prioritizing Self-Care	184
Key Takeaways	185
Closing Message	185

8 Self-Compassion — 190

Resolving to Embrace Enoughness	190
Establishing Relevance	192
What Is Self-Compassion, Really?	193
Practices for Moments of Struggle	194
Take a Self-Compassion Break	194
The High Five Habit: A Simple Practice to Reclaim Your Resilience	196
Guided Meditation: Self-Compassion Break	199
Key Takeaways	200
Closing Message	200

9 Optimistic Outlook — 204

Trust the Evidence	204
Establishing Relevance	206
Shift Happens: Reframe the Story	208
Guided Meditation: Cultivating Optimism	211
Key Takeaways	212
Closing Message	212

10 Building Resilience Through Play — 216
- From Panic to Play: Finding Fun in the Unexpected — 216
- Establishing Relevance — 218
- Why Play Matters in REST — 222
- What's Your Play Personality? — 223
- Guided Meditation: Rediscovering Play — 230
- Key Takeaways — 230
- Closing Message — 231

11 Celebrating Educators — 235
- We Show Up — 235
- Establishing Relevance — 237
- Ways to Celebrate Your School-Year Achievements — 237
- Guided Meditation: Appreciating Your Journey — 241
- Key Takeaways — 242
- Closing Message — 242

12 Sustaining Resilience and Moving Forward — 246
- Clearing Out My Closet — 246
- Establishing Relevance — 247
- Creating a Resilience Action Plan for Sustaining Resilience and Moving Forward — 248
- Example Resilience Action Plan for Jane Doe — 263
- Dream Big: A Vision-Based Approach to Goal-Setting — 265
- Guided Meditation: Committing to Long-Term Resilience — 268
- Key Takeaways — 269
- Closing Message — 269
- Continuing the Journey — 271

Acknowledgments

This book is the result of countless hours of reflection, creativity, and growth that would not exist without the support of some very important people.

To my daughters, Ana and Allie: Thank you for giving me the space to dream and create and for being my greatest inspiration. Your light, humor, and strength keep me moving forward every day. Your capacity for love and kindness blows me away. I will love you forever.

To my parents: Thank you for being my emotional anchors, for believing in me, and for reminding me that resilience is built on love. Thank you for reminding me that I needed to practice what I preach. Taking the time to sit and chat with you both has been a saving grace.

To my partner, Rodrigo: Your encouragement, laughter, and unwavering belief in me made this journey possible. You have been my biggest cheerleader (you literally bought me pom-poms), and I am endlessly grateful. To CC and Josie: Thank you for allowing me to be a part of your family and for graciously joining ours.

To the Merrimack College Institute for New Teachers: Thank you for giving me the opportunity to present, collaborate, and evolve this program into what it is today. Your belief in this work helped it grow beyond what I first imagined. Kathy, I would not be this far in my career without you. Amanda, and Brent, you trusted me and gave me space to do my thing. To all of the MINTS attendees: Know that you showing up for me means so much.

To my colleagues, every teacher needs to find their people, and I found mine in so many of you. Colleen, Mark, Mandy, Liz, Ali, Andrew, and all my fellow Rangers. Thanks for bringing joy into my workday.

To Chris W., Kathy W., and Brendan M.: Writing a book is hard. You made time for me. I will never forget that.

To Beth G.: I have put in the work during our years together. Thanks to you I realize I have something to offer. I trusted the evidence (and your advice).

To Breathe for Change: My journey through the master of education program deepened my understanding of data collection, research, and practical application. Through thoughtful study, action research, and reflection, I was able to refine and strengthen this program based on real-world feedback and measurable outcomes. Kelli, thank you for providing me with the tools to bridge passion with evidence-based practice.

Thank you to all the educators, dreamers, and change-makers who continue to inspire the work within these pages. This book was once just a dream, but because of you, it became something real.

Meet the Author

Stephanie Letourneau has been a passionate public school educator since 2001 and has served as an adjunct professor at Merrimack College since 2019. She holds three Massachusetts teacher licensures, along with specialized certifications in *Transformational Teaching and Leadership* through Breathe for Change and *Brain Longevity Education* through the Alzheimer's Research and Prevention Foundation.

Stephanie recently completed her second master of education degree in social-emotional learning, mindfulness, and yoga (RYT 500), where she developed and researched *The Educator's Guide to REST: Resilience, Emotional Wellness, and Sustainable Teaching Workshop Series*, which became the basis of this guide.

Drawing on more than two decades of classroom experience, Stephanie combines her love of teaching with a deep understanding of mindfulness, resilience, and brain health. She is dedicated to helping educators strengthen both their professional skills and personal well-being, empowering them to thrive in today's educational landscape.

Preface

As educators, we understand the importance of self-care. However, if you're anything like me, you may feel frustrated every time you hear that phrase. At times, it seems like school districts and state education departments sidestep addressing critical issues in education by shifting the responsibility onto us ("Just do some yoga!")

Now, don't get me wrong. Yoga is great. I'm a certified yoga teacher, and I'll be the first to tell you that breathwork and downward dogs have their place. But let's be honest: unless your yoga instructor is also the commissioner of your state's education department, they aren't going to fix the systemic issues that are burning teachers out.

So, what can we do? I firmly believe we *can* find greater happiness and fulfillment in our careers despite the chronic challenges like underfunding, overcrowded classrooms, and unrealistic expectations.

Here's the hard truth: There are so many things we can't control in this profession. The policies, the mandates, the staffing shortages. They're bigger than any of us. No one is coming to swoop in and save us. We can't wait for a magic fix. What we *can* do is choose how we care for ourselves and each other. We can do the work. that is, *our* work, to build the resilience and support we need, together.

That belief led me on a journey. I started asking questions. Lots of them. *How are educators really feeling? What's getting in the way of their well-being? What do they actually need to stay in this profession without losing themselves?*

I didn't just ask these questions, but I gathered data. Over the course of three years, I led year-long professional development for educators based on mindfulness and resilience, reaching hundreds of teachers in the area. For the 2024–2025 school year, I created and led a program called the Resilient Educator Support Team (REST) for educators across multiple schools and districts. Through surveys, self-assessments, exit tickets, interviews, and honest conversations, I listened deeply to the real experiences of teachers, looking for what was working, what wasn't, and what helped them hold on.

The data told a powerful story:

- ◆ 85% of participants reported feeling disconnected from their professional purpose and overwhelmed by stress before REST.

- After the series, resilience scores jumped by 15%, emotional well-being improved by 20%, and confidence in managing stress grew by 25%.
- And the most common post-session feedback? "I didn't know how much I needed this."

When I searched for a guide to help educators navigate challenges, I couldn't find one that had it all in one place, so I created the resource that was desperately needed for myself and my colleagues. I conducted action research, analyzed data, read many books and academic journals, and watched more TED Talks then I thought possible.

But, let's be honest, this isn't rocket science. It's not some groundbreaking formula or revolutionary system. These are things we *already know*. The problem is, when life gets busy and we get tired, the smallest, most important truths often get buried under the weight of to-do lists, meetings, and that never-ending pile of emails.

So no, this book isn't here to teach you something new. It's here to remind you of what you already know deep down: that you matter, that your well-being matters, and that taking care of yourself isn't selfish. Instead, it's necessary. I'll share personal stories to show you how I got to where I am and how I'm *still* learning and growing. I hope my stories help you see that I'm just like you. I'm not *only* an educator. I'm a parent, a child, a sister, a partner, a friend, and an aunt. We are all more than our profession.

I encourage educators, administrators, and support staff to use this guide to build resilience and reconnect with their purpose. While you can work through this interactive guide on your own, I encourage you to consider creating a REST professional learning community (PLC) with colleagues. Working together can deepen reflection, spark meaningful dialogue, and provide the mutual support we all need to not just survive the school year but to find joy and purpose in it. Think of this as your permission slip to pause, take a breath, and remember that you are enough, just as you are.

The Science Behind an Interactive Approach

Since educators are so busy, it's easy to read something, nod along, and then . . . forget it the next day. That's why this book is intentionally designed to be interactive, with reflection prompts, journaling exercises, and space to pause and process. This isn't just a feel-good idea, there's solid science behind it.

Research in cognitive psychology and neuroscience shows that expressive and reflective writing can lead to deeper learning and lasting change. Studies by Pennebaker and Smyth (2016) reveal that writing about experiences enhances emotional processing and helps integrate complex ideas. Neuroscience research also shows that writing activates multiple regions of the brain, strengthening pathways related to memory, attention, and self-regulation (Medina, 2014). Put simply: Writing helps us remember, stay focused, and make sense of our thoughts.

By taking time to reflect in writing, you're not just completing another task. Instead, you're wiring your brain for resilience, growth, and meaningful action.

How to Use This Book

This guide is here to meet you exactly where you are. There are no rigid rules, no pressure. Just a few thoughtful options for how to make it your own:

- **Sequential Approach:** Start at Chapter 1 and move through in order. You'll build a layered, comprehensive understanding of resilience and how to apply it over time.
- **Selective Approach:** Flip to the chapter that speaks to your current needs. Whether it's stress management or reconnecting with your purpose, trust your instincts. Come back to the others when you're ready. The self-evaluation tools in Chapter 1 can give you more direction.
- **Professional Learning Community (PLC):** Grab a few colleagues and use the book as a shared experience. The reflection questions and activities make great conversation starters for supporting each other. You can keep a journal if you prefer larger space for writing.

Each chapter concludes with a "Guided Meditation," "Key Takeaways," and a "Closing Message" from yours truly. To use the guided meditation, read through it first, then try it after reading. If you are working in a group, you can choose to have one person lead by reading it aloud. You'll also find mindful coloring pages with anchor words to help internalize the concepts.

This isn't a one-and-done workbook. It's something you can return to again and again. Each visit gives you fresh insight, deeper clarity, and stronger habits. So grab your favorite pen, a box of colored pencils, and maybe a good cup of coffee. Let's begin!

You Hold the Pen

For a long time, I didn't believe I could change my life.

After 20 years in education, I started to feel different about my work. I cared deeply about my students, my colleagues, and my community. I still loved teaching, but I was tired in a way that coffee and a pep talk could not fix. The pace, the expectations, the emotional labor, and the constant stream of teacher bashing on social media slowly piled up. Little by little, I stopped feeling like the joyful, confident teacher I once was. One day I finally stopped and acknowledged that my tank was not just low, it was completely empty.

Even feeling this way, the idea of change felt overwhelming. I told myself I didn't have options. I had invested decades into public education. What other jobs could I do? I was born to teach.

I thought about changing districts, but I love my community. Besides, I worried that my experience, something I valued, might be seen as costly rather than beneficial. Salary structures, budgeting, and hiring practices sometimes make seasoned educators feel like their expertise comes with a price tag instead of a gift.

Since leaving public education altogether wasn't something I wanted, (and the potential risk to my pension made that feel impossible anyway), I found other paths for change as I looked inward. I needed sustainability, meaning, and balance. I shifted to new roles, changed buildings, sold my house, went back to school, became a yoga instructor, and started leading professional development. None of it was easy. None of it came quickly. But each decision brought me a little closer to alignment with my values, my energy, and my purpose.

Eventually, all those choices brought me here. Writing this book.

And that's what I want you to know: *You are not stuck.* Even if the system is flawed. Even if there are risks. You still hold the pen. You still get to write the next chapter.

This isn't about overhauling your life overnight. It's about reflection and honestly looking at where you've been. It's about vision, that is, daring to dream about where you might go. And most of all, it's about presence, or learning to notice and appreciate the life you're already living, right here and now.

This book won't fix everything. But it might just help you rediscover your power to change *something*. And sometimes, that's where everything begins.

References

Medina, J. (2014). *Brain rules: 12 principles for surviving and thriving at work, home, and school* (2nd ed.). Pear Press.

Pennebaker, J. W., & Smyth, J. M. (2016). *Opening up by writing it down: How expressive writing improves health and eases emotional pain* (2nd ed.). The Guilford Press.

1

Introduction to Resilience

> **Focus:** Understanding resilience and its importance for educators.
>
> **Content:** Define resilience, explore its components, and discuss why it's crucial for teachers. Introduce the framework and goals of this guide.
>
> Let's start with the basics. Think of this as Resilience 101. Learning what resilience is and why it's essential is like laying the foundation of a house, because without it, everything else crumbles. This chapter sets the stage for everything that follows, giving educators the tools to begin their resilience journey.

So What?

Resilience is a word we hear all the time, but what does it *really* mean in the life of an educator? For a long time, I thought resilience was just a fancy word for "keep going no matter what." Stay late, say yes, push through the exhaustion, and hold it all together with a smile. That was my version of resilience . . . until it wasn't.

I'd spent years trying to do it all, at school, at home, in my relationships, but without ever stopping to ask myself, "At what cost?" I thought being a good teacher, a good mom, a good human meant showing up, no matter how much I was running on empty. But, eventually, it caught up to me.

That's when I remembered a little phrase from childhood, a phrase that once drove my parents up the wall but would eventually become a lifeline: *"So what?"*

Ah, the simplicity of this statement! *"So what!?"* I used to say it all the time as a kid. "Do your homework or you can't watch TV!" *"So what?"* Don't wear your good sneakers while riding your bike, or you'll ruin them. *"So what?"*

I'm sure it drove my mother and father bonkers to hear those words again and again when I was a young, rambunctious daughter not caring about the consequences of her actions. But that time didn't last long. By high school, I'd learned to be the "good girl." I never wanted to miss a day, even when I was sick. The consequences of falling behind in classes felt too big.

That pattern followed me into teaching. I wouldn't call out, wouldn't skip teaching a yoga class, wouldn't say no to extra work, no matter how exhausted I was. I pushed and pushed and pushed . . . until I finally hit a wall. That's when my therapist (thanks, Beth G.) reminded me of those long-ago words: *"So what?"* So what if I don't volunteer for that after-school activity? So what if I don't finish the project tonight? So what if dinner is frozen pizza? That little phrase cracked open something big for me. It helped me see that not everything is worth the mental load we carry. It helped me start letting go of the small stuff that clutters our minds and wears us down. *"So what?"* doesn't mean we stop caring. It means we get clear on *what* we care about and where we need to give ourselves permission to let go.

It also helps when I catch myself starting to judge others. "Janet didn't come to professional development." "Marcus is absent again today." I remind myself: *So what?* Neither of those things has anything to do with me. That phrase pulls me out of judgment and back into compassion. Maybe Janet is overwhelmed. Maybe Marcus is going through something. Maybe it's not my business and that's okay.

Of course, *"So what?"* doesn't apply to everything. Paying rent? Getting gas? Turning in your taxes? Yeah, those have real consequences. But the dozens of minor frustrations we carry each day? Those can often be dropped with a simple shift in mindset. *"So what?"* is my permission slip to let go of the unnecessary weight and reclaim a bit of peace.

At the end of the day, resilience isn't about being unbreakable or perfect. It's about knowing when to say, "This doesn't matter as much as my peace of mind." It's about giving ourselves (and others) grace. It's learning to pause, breathe, and focus on what truly matters. That's the heart of resilience and where our journey begins.

What Is Resilience?

Resilience isn't about pushing through no matter what. It's not about perfection, superhuman stamina, or pretending everything's fine. Resilience is the ability to bend without breaking. It's the capacity to recover from challenges, setbacks, and exhaustion and to keep showing up *in a way that honors your well-being*.

Research shows resilience isn't fixed; it's a learnable skill. It develops when we practice self-awareness, reflection, mindfulness, and healthy boundaries, and it thrives when supported by community (American Psychological Association, 2014; Southwick & Charney, 2018).

For educators, resilience is about holding space for others while also holding space for ourselves. It's about choosing how we respond to the chaos, the challenges, and the constant demands, and it starts with simple, small shifts. Like saying, *"So what?"*

Pause Here and Take a Moment to Reflect
Jot down your thoughts. Doodle. Let it be messy. There's no "right" way. This is your space.

When was the last time you felt overwhelmed, like you were just pushing through?

What are some small things you could start saying "So what?" to in your life?

What do you want resilience to look and feel like in your life?

Establishing Relevance: Why These Chapters Matter

For educators, resilience is more than a personal skill; it's a professional lifeline. Every day, you navigate challenges, support others, adapt to constant change, and continue to show up with heart. These chapters were designed to nurture that part of you. Think of it as more than just information but, rather, as an invitation to care for yourself, deepen your self-awareness, and build the inner resources you need to stay grounded in the midst of demands. Each chapter offers practical strategies, reflections, and tools you can integrate into your daily life so that resilience becomes part of who you are and not just something you reach for when things get tough.

Overview of Chapters

Here's how each chapter supports the essential elements of resilience:

Chapter 1: Introduction to Resilience
Resilience is the foundation. It's your ability to face adversity, recover from setbacks, and continue growing. In this chapter, we define what resilience really means for educators and why it's the heartbeat of sustainable teaching. You'll also find self-evaluation tools designed to help you identify your current strengths, uncover areas for growth, and pinpoint the specific strategies that will best support your journey. This is where your path to resilience becomes personal because understanding where you are helps you decide where to focus next.

Chapter 2: Self-Awareness and Emotional Intelligence
Awareness is where growth begins. Understanding your emotions, thoughts, and behaviors helps you recognize stress triggers and respond (not react) in ways that support your well-being. This chapter offers reflection questions, practical scenarios, and emotional check-ins to help you build a stronger relationship with yourself because self-awareness is the key to navigating challenges with more intention and less reactivity.

Chapter 3: Mindfulness and Stress Management
This chapter introduces techniques like breathwork, present-moment awareness, and nervous system regulation so you can meet stress with calm, not collapse. You'll find simple practices that can be done in just a few minutes a day, helping you create a personal toolbox for staying steady when the demands of the job feel overwhelming.

Chapter 4: Building Strong Relationships
Resilience is not a solo sport. Connection is one of your greatest protective factors. This chapter focuses on emotional support, empathy, trust, and communication with students, colleagues, and yourself. It includes practical tools for nurturing relationships, setting healthy boundaries, and building a support network that lifts you up when you need it most.

Chapter 5: Professional Purpose and Passion
When you reconnect with your "why," you reignite motivation, direction, and hope. Purpose isn't just fluffy. It's what helps us rise after a hard day and return the next morning with intention. This chapter encourages you to explore your unique contributions, remember what first drew you to this work, and honor the passion that fuels your impact as an educator.

Chapter 6: Adaptive Thinking and Problem-Solving
Mental agility helps you pivot instead of panic. This chapter focuses on flexibility, creativity, and seeing challenges from multiple perspectives. It's about shifting from "Why me?" to "What now?" You'll explore strategies for breaking through roadblocks, reframing obstacles, and approaching problems as opportunities for growth because your mindset is one of your most powerful tools.

Chapter 7: Self-Care and Well-Being
Self-care is more than bubble baths. (Though we love those, too.) This chapter looks at sustainable care practices, such as rest, boundaries, nourishment, hydration, and movement, that refill your tank not just empty your to-do list. You'll also explore the science behind self-care and create a plan that feels realistic for your unique life and work.

Chapter 8: Self-Compassion
Let's be honest: Teachers are often their own harshest critics. This chapter invites you to speak to yourself with the same kindness you give to your students. Through reflection, affirmations, and small daily practices, you'll learn how self-compassion can transform the way you handle challenges and foster a deeper sense of inner strength. Because healing begins with how we treat ourselves.

Chapter 9: Optimistic Outlook
Seeing the good doesn't mean denying the hard. It means holding space for both. In this chapter, we explore how cultivating optimism can fuel perseverance, creativity, and emotional strength. It's not about blind positivity. Rather it's about grounded hopefulness that keeps you steady through storms. You'll

learn how to reframe challenges, practice gratitude, and nurture a mindset that's both realistic and resilient.

Chapter 10: Building Resilience Through Play
Yes, play! Adults need joy, imagination, and laughter, too. This chapter reconnects you to curiosity, creativity, and spontaneity as essential tools for resilience and engagement. You'll find simple ways to infuse more playfulness into your life and work, even when time is tight, because joy isn't a distraction, it's a fuel source.

Chapter 11: Celebrating Educators
This journey deserves celebration. We close with reflection, appreciation, and joyful recognition of how far you've come, not because everything is perfect but because you kept going with heart. This chapter encourages you to pause, acknowledge your growth, and embrace moments of gratitude and connection.

Chapter 12: Sustaining Resilience and Moving Forward
Once you've learned these strategies, how do you keep them going? This chapter supports you in creating an action plan that's realistic, personal, and rooted in your daily rhythms. It includes prompts for reflection, accountability tools, and gentle reminders that resilience isn't a destination. It's a practice you can sustain, day by day, with intention.

Educator's Guide to Resilience: Self-Evaluation Tools

This journey isn't about checking boxes; it's about checking in with yourself, your purpose, and the kind of educator you want to be. Before you dive into the strategies and tools in this book, take a moment to pause and reflect on where you are right now.

The Self-Evaluation Tool and Resilience Wheel are here to guide that reflection. These tools are designed to help you identify your strengths, recognize areas for growth, and focus your attention on the practices that will most support your resilience.

You might choose to read this book from beginning to end, or you may prefer to jump to the chapters that feel most relevant to your current experiences. Your strengths and challenges will shift over time, so it's helpful to revisit the Self-Evaluation Tool and Resilience Wheel periodically. They're not static. They grow and change as you do.

Remember, there's no grade, no "right" or "wrong" here. Instead, there's just insight, honesty, and an opportunity to better understand your inner landscape.

Educator Resilience Self-Evaluation Tool

This tool is for personal reflection. It is *not* an evaluation of your job performance. Instead, it's a gentle guide to help you assess your current strengths, identify areas where you could use more support, and plan next steps for building resilience.

If you're working through this book with a group, you may choose to complete the self-reflection privately first, then come together to share general themes, insights, and strategies in small groups or pairs.

Return to this tool throughout the year to check in on your progress, revisit personal goals, and remind yourself that resilience is a dynamic, ongoing practice.

How to Use This Tool

1. Read each statement and think of related specific situations.
2. Rate yourself on the statement by marking the appropriate box (very difficult, difficult, easy, or very easy for you to do).
3. When you finish, search for patterns of strengths and challenges. This information is for you, so answer accurately without judging responses as "good" or "not as good."
4. Review your responses and take action in light of what you learn.

Introduction to Resilience

Statement	Very Difficult 1	Difficult 2	Easy 3	Very Easy 4
I understand what resilience means in the context of education.				
I can identify factors that contribute to my resilience.				
I recognize the signs of resilience in myself and others.				
I see the importance of community in fostering resilience.				
Total (_____/ 16) Notes:				

Self-Awareness and Emotional Intelligence

Statement	Very Difficult 1	Difficult 2	Easy 3	Very Easy 4
I can identify and name my emotions in the moment.				
I use self-reflection to understand the factors that contribute to my emotions.				
I recognize when my emotions influence my behavior and reactions.				
I understand my emotional triggers and have strategies for managing them.				
Total (_____/ 16) Notes:				

Mindfulness and Stress Management

Statement	Very Difficult 1	Difficult 2	Easy 3	Very Easy 4
I incorporate mindfulness practices into my daily routine.				
I use mindfulness to manage stress and maintain my well-being.				
I practice breathing exercises to reduce stress.				
I can stay present and focused in stressful situations.				
Total (_____/ 16) Notes:				

Building Strong Relationships

Statement	Very Difficult 1	Difficult 2	Easy 3	Very Easy 4
I connect meaningfully with colleagues and students.				
I listen actively and empathetically to others.				
I can navigate conflicts and maintain positive relationships.				
I build and maintain a supportive community.				
Total (_____ / 16) Notes:				

Professional Purpose and Passion

Statement	Very Difficult 1	Difficult 2	Easy 3	Very Easy 4
I feel connected to my professional purpose.				
I am passionate about my work as an educator.				
I set professional goals and work toward them.				
I reflect on my core values and align my work with them.				
Total (_____ / 16) Notes:				

Adaptive Thinking and Problem-Solving

Statement	Very Difficult 1	Difficult 2	Easy 3	Very Easy 4
I view challenges as opportunities for growth.				
I use creative problem-solving strategies.				
I stay flexible and resilient in the face of challenges.				
I encourage a growth mindset in myself and others.				
Total (_____/ 16) Notes:				

Self-Care and Well-Being

Statement	Very Difficult 1	Difficult 2	Easy 3	Very Easy 4
I prioritize self-care and maintain my well-being.				
I have a personal self-care plan with specific actions.				
I practice gratitude regularly.				
I engage in activities that promote my physical, emotional, and mental well-being.				
Total (_____/ 16) Notes:				

Self-Compassion

Statement	Very Difficult 1	Difficult 2	Easy 3	Very Easy 4
I speak to myself with kindness during hard moments.				
I understand the difference between self-esteem and self-compassion.				
I notice when I'm being self-critical and can pause to shift my tone.				
I practice self-compassion regularly.				
Total (_____/ 16) Notes:				

Optimistic Outlook

Statement	Very Difficult 1	Difficult 2	Easy 3	Very Easy 4
I can find positives even during challenging times.				
I maintain hope and motivation for the future, even when facing obstacles.				
I encourage a positive outlook in myself and others.				
I balance optimism with realistic action steps toward my goals.				
Total (_____/ 16) Notes:				

Building Resilience Through Play

Statement	Very Difficult 1	Difficult 2	Easy 3	Very Easy 4
I incorporate play, creativity, or humor into my routine.				
I recognize the value of play in adult learning and well-being.				
I feel re-energized by creative or joyful activities.				
I help create space for lightness and joy in my work community.				
Total (_____/ 16) Notes:				

Celebrating Educators

Statement	Very Difficult 1	Difficult 2	Easy 3	Very Easy 4
I recognize and appreciate my achievements as an educator.				
I celebrate the successes of my colleagues.				
I feel seen and valued in my professional community.				
I participate in or initiate appreciation activities that uplift others.				
Total (_____/ 16) Notes:				

Sustaining Resilience and Moving Forward

Statement	Very Difficult 1	Difficult 2	Easy 3	Very Easy 4
I have strategies in place to sustain my resilience over time.				
I regularly review and adjust my resilience action plan.				
I feel supported by my professional community.				
I am committed to continuous growth and resilience.				
Total (_____ / 16) Notes:				

Identifying Areas for Improvement in Resilience

Review Your Ratings

1. Go through each section (Introduction to Resilience, Self-Awareness and Emotional Intelligence, Mindfulness and Stress Management, Building Strong Relationships, Professional Purpose and Passion, Adaptive Thinking and Problem-Solving, Self-Care and Well-Being, Self-Compassion, Optimistic Outlook, Building Resilience Through Play, Sustaining Resilience and Moving Forward, Celebrating Educators) and look at your ratings for each statement.
2. Highlight or note down the statements where you rated yourself as "Easy" or "Very Easy."
3. Highlight or note down the statements where you rated yourself as "Difficult" or "Very Difficult."

Notes

Look for Patterns
1. Identify common themes or recurring areas of difficulty across different sections.
2. For example, if multiple statements about managing stress are marked as difficult, it suggests a need to focus on stress management.

Notes

Reflect on Impact
1. Consider how the areas marked as difficult impact your interactions with students, peers, and your overall effectiveness as an educator.
2. Ask yourself questions like: How do these challenges affect my daily work? How would improving in these areas enhance my professional and personal life?

Notes

Select Priorities
1. Choose one or two areas that you believe would have the most significant positive impact if improved.
2. Focus on areas that align with your professional goals or where you see the most immediate need for growth.

Notes

Using the Resilience Wheel

The Resilience Wheel (refer to Figure 1.1) is a visual tool designed to help you assess and reflect on various aspects of your resilience. For each category, rate your resilience on a scale of 1 to 10 (1 being the lowest and 10 the highest). Use the guiding questions provided to assist in your reflections. Shade in portions of the wheel corresponding to your ratings to create a visual representation of your resilience. Take a few minutes to reflect, considering your strengths and identifying areas where additional support may be beneficial.

Guiding Questions

Emotional: *How do I manage stress and emotions? What strategies do I use to stay emotionally balanced?*

Physical: *How do I take care of my physical health? What activities or routines help me stay physically resilient?*

Social: *Who are my key support people? How do I maintain and strengthen these relationships?*

Professional: *How do I stay motivated and passionate about my work? What professional goals am I working toward?*

Cognitive: *How do I keep my mind sharp and engaged? What learning activities do I enjoy?*

Community: *How am I involved in my community? How does my community support my resilience?*

Spiritual: *What practices help me find meaning and purpose? How do I nurture my spiritual well-being?*

Other: *Are there any other aspects of my life that contribute to my resilience? Cultural? Financial? Something else?*

Use your wheel as a living, breathing document. Revisit it, revise it, and remember: You're not behind. You're just building. One reflection at a time.

Pause Here and Take a Moment to Reflect

Notes

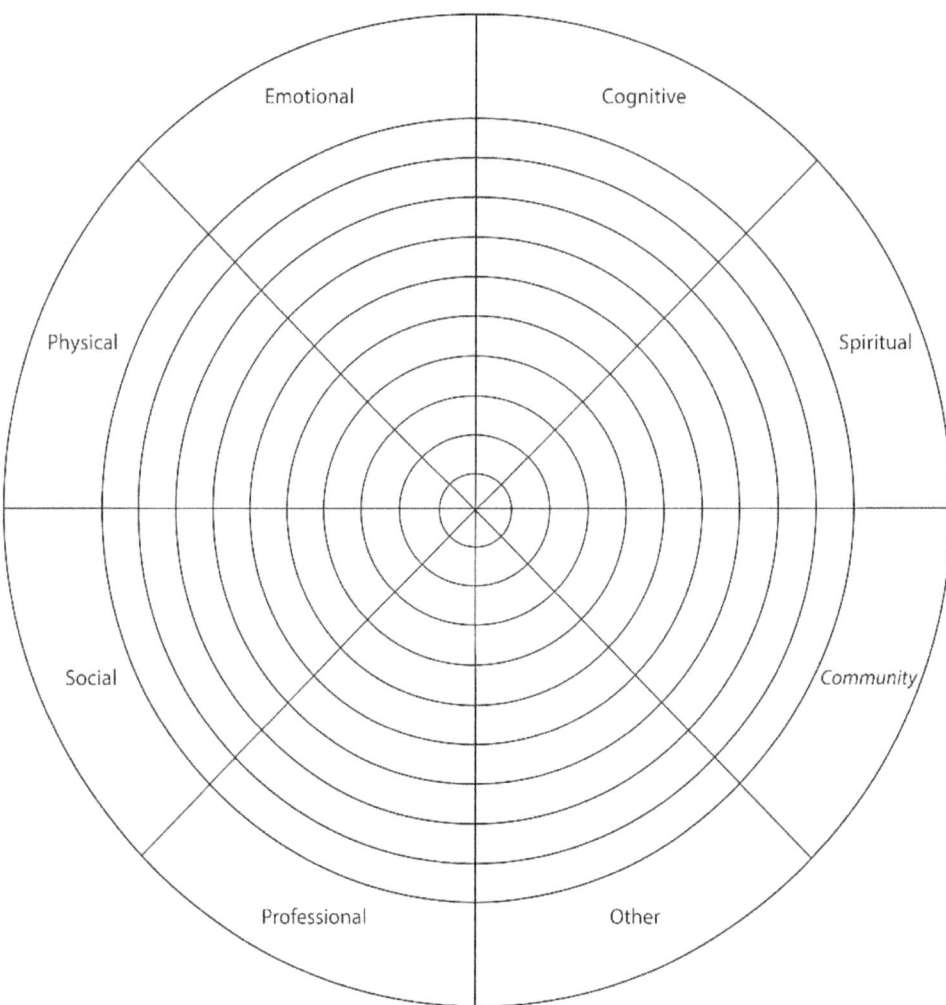

Figure 1.1 Resilience Wheel

You Can Quote Me on That

Read through the following quotes to find some inspiration. Find one that speaks to you? Consider writing it on a Post-it, dry erase board, or in your journal.

- "Our greatest glory is not in never falling, but in rising every time we fall."—Confucius
- "Fall seven times, stand up eight."—Japanese proverb
- "The bamboo that bends is stronger than the oak that resists."—Japanese proverb
- "Although the world is full of suffering, it is also full of the overcoming of it."—Helen Keller
- "In the midst of winter, I found there was, within me, an invincible summer."—Albert Camus
- "The difference between a strong man and a weak one is that the former does not give up after a defeat."—Woodrow Wilson
- "You must be the change you wish to see in the world."—Mahatma Gandhi
- "Difficulties strengthen the mind, as labor does the body."—Seneca
- "You have power over your mind—not outside events. Realize this, and you will find strength."—Marcus Aurelius
- "It's not what happens to you, but how you react to it that matters."—Epictetus
- "That which does not kill us makes us stronger."—Friedrich Nietzsche
- "What lies behind us and what lies before us are tiny matters compared to what lies within us."—Ralph Waldo Emerson
- "Into each life some rain must fall, some days must be dark and dreary."—Henry Wadsworth Longfellow
- "Permanent greatness and success come only to those who have a measure of resilience."—Thomas Carlyle
- "Great works are performed not by strength, but by perseverance."—Samuel Johnson
- "The gem cannot be polished without friction, nor man perfected without trials."—Chinese proverb

Pause Here and Take a Moment to Reflect

Notes

Find Your Focus: Words for Motivation and Growth

Take a look at the words in the list. Do any of these resonate with you? Circle a few that may help keep you focused and motivated this school year. Add any words you would like that are not on the list.

Resilience	Inspiration	Innovation
Growth	Transformation	Integrity
Balance	Success	Love
Empowerment	Hope	Peace
Courage	Joy	Vision
Perseverance	Abundance	Fortitude
Mindfulness	Optimism	Happiness
Clarity	Confidence	Kindness
Passion	Wisdom	Adventure
Gratitude	Compassion	Creativity
Purpose	Bravery	Energy
Strength	Ambition	Triumph

Pause Here and Take a Moment to Reflect

Notes

Guided Meditation: Building the Foundation of Resilience

Find a comfortable position, either seated or lying down. Let your hands rest softly on your lap, by your side, or wherever they feel at ease. Close your eyes and take a deep breath in, filling your lungs slowly, then exhale with a long, steady breath. Feel the air leave your body, releasing tension and letting go of what no longer serves you. Take a few more breaths like this, each one slower, each one more calming.

Allow your body to relax and your mind to settle. Feel the surface beneath you. Your chair, the floor, or the earth supports you fully. Let yourself sink into this support, knowing you are safe and held.

Now imagine a strong tree. Its roots reach deep into the earth, anchoring it with strength and stability. This tree represents your resilience. With each inhale, imagine drawing strength and stability from the earth, just like the roots of the tree. Feel this energy rise into your body, filling you with steadiness and calm. With each exhale, release tension, stress, and the weight of your worries, letting them flow down into the ground where they can be transformed. Visualize the trunk of the tree. It's solid, steady, unshaken. This trunk symbolizes your core resilience: your values, your purpose, and your ability to stand tall even in the face of challenges. Breathe into this strength.

Now, imagine the branches of your tree extending outward in all directions, reaching toward the sky. Each branch represents a different aspect of your resilience: emotional resilience, or your capacity to feel deeply and stay steady; physical resilience, or your body's strength, health, and ability to heal; social resilience, or the relationships that lift you up and hold you close; professional resilience, or your skills, knowledge, and ability to adapt; cognitive resilience, or your creativity, problem-solving, and wisdom; community resilience, or the shared strength of your networks and circles; spiritual resilience, or your connection to meaning, faith, or higher purpose; and any other unique aspects of your resilience that make you *you*.

With each breath, see these branches growing stronger, more vibrant, more alive. The leaves shimmer in the light, nourished by the energy flowing through the roots, trunk, and branches.

Take a moment to feel gratitude for the resilience you already have. Even in moments when you feel tired or stretched thin, remember: like the tree, you have weathered many storms and you are still standing. You are growing, evolving, and thriving.

When you're ready, take one last deep breath, feeling grounded and strong, like the tree. Gently wiggle your fingers and toes, reconnecting to the present moment. Slowly open your eyes, carrying this sense of strength and resilience with you into the rest of your day

Key Takeaways

- Resilience is not about "bouncing back." It's about growing through what you go through.
- Building resilience starts with awareness and intentional action, not perfection.
- REST is a community-centered approach, strengths-based framework designed by and for educators.
- You're not alone. Resilience is stronger when we cultivate it together.

Closing Message

Resilience doesn't mean being perfect or pushing through at all costs. It means knowing when to pause, when to ask for help, and when to say *"So what?"*

You get to create a life and career that feels good to you. One that is not just *doable* but *joyful*. You can't keep waiting for someone else to fix the system and save you from burnout. You have to do it yourself.

Let's take this one small step at a time, together.

Chapter 1 Notes

Engage and Reflect

What does resilience mean to you, and how do you define it in your own life?

Can you share an example of a time when you demonstrated resilience?

What are some factors that you believe contribute to your resilience?

How do you currently cope with stress and adversity in your teaching career?

What role do you think community and support networks play in building resilience?

What are some obstacles that prevent you from being more resilient?

How can you incorporate resilience-building practices into your daily routine?

How do you think building resilience can impact your professional and personal life?

References

American Psychological Association. (2014). *The road to resilience*. Brochure. https://www.uis.edu/sites/default/files/inline-images/the_road_to_resilience.pdf

Southwick, S. M., & Charney, D. S. (2018). *Resilience: The science of mastering life's greatest challenges* (2nd ed.). Cambridge University Press.

2

Developing Self-Awareness and Managing Emotions

> **Focus:** Developing self-awareness and managing emotions.
>
> **Content:** Techniques for increasing self-awareness and understanding emotional triggers, strategies for emotional regulation, and activities for reflective practice.
>
> This chapter dives into self-awareness and emotional intelligence. Imagine discovering your superhero powers! Understanding our emotions and those of others helps us navigate the ups and downs of teaching. Plus, it makes us less likely to lose our cool when the copier jams for the tenth time that day.

Teaching During COVID: My Meltdown Moment

I'll never forget the day I completely lost it during virtual teaching.

It was the middle of the COVID shutdown, and everything felt like a mess. There were tech issues, endless emails, a million demands that made it impossible to actually teach kids. I had a scheduling conflict with a colleague, and instead of taking a breath and talking it through, I snapped. I lashed out. I let my frustration boil over in a way that still makes me cringe.

And the worst part? I didn't fix it right away. For weeks, every time she popped into my virtual classroom, I felt a knot in my stomach. I avoided the issue, hoping it would just go away, but it didn't.

Eventually, I did the thing I should've done much sooner: I apologized. I owned up to my behavior, and the moment I said those two words—*"I'm sorry"*—the weight started to lift. My colleague, ever the gracious soul, forgave me. We moved forward, and I learned something important:

> Self-awareness and emotional intelligence aren't about never making mistakes. They're about *recognizing* when you've messed up, owning it, and doing the hard but necessary work to repair.

That experience didn't make me perfect, but it made me more human. And Lisa, thank you again for accepting my late apology.

What Is Emotional Intelligence?

Let's talk about it. Emotional intelligence, or EQ, is the ability to recognize, understand, and manage your own emotions and to recognize, understand, and respond effectively to the emotions of others.

Self-awareness is the foundation of emotional intelligence. It's the skill of noticing:

- How am I feeling right now?
- What's driving my reaction?
- How might my emotions impact my actions and the people around me?

Educators are human beings first. We get stressed, overwhelmed, frustrated, and sometimes, we snap. That's okay. What matters is that we notice it, take responsibility, and try to do better next time. Understanding your personal triggers can help you prepare for your responses. Emotional intelligence is what helps us pause before we react, breathe before we speak, and show up for others with compassion even on the hard days.

Pause Here and Take a Moment to Reflect

> *Think of a time when you reacted emotionally in a way you regretted. What happened? What triggered your reaction?*
>
> *What physical or emotional signs tell you that you're feeling stressed or overwhelmed? (Tight shoulders? Fast breathing? That "uh-oh" feeling in your gut?)*
>
> *What are your triggers at school? At home?*
>
> *What's one small thing you can do to pause and respond more mindfully the next time you experience one of those triggers?*
>
> *Who in your life could benefit from a little more emotional understanding or empathy from you?*

Establishing Relevance

Understanding and managing emotions is at the heart of building resilience. These skills are essential for navigating the rollercoaster of life, especially in a field like education, where every day brings new challenges and demands.

When we can recognize, name, and manage our emotions, we create space for calm, clarity, and compassion. This, in turn, supports not only our mental and physical health but also our ability to connect with others in meaningful, supportive ways. Let's take a closer look at why understanding emotions is such a critical piece of the resilience puzzle.

First, emotional regulation is key. When we're aware of our feelings, we can respond rather than react. This ability to self-regulate helps prevent overwhelm and fosters a sense of stability, even in the face of adversity. Instead of getting swept away by frustration, anxiety, or sadness, we learn to pause, breathe, and respond intentionally. That calm presence is the foundation for resilience.

Next, awareness of emotions helps us manage stress. By recognizing the sources of our stress, whether it's a looming deadline, a difficult conversation, or a feeling of self-doubt, we can take steps to cope more effectively. Whether it's using mindfulness techniques, asking for support, or simply taking a break, these strategies help us stay grounded during tough times. Managing stress isn't about avoiding challenges; it's about building the capacity to stay steady when challenges arise.

Understanding our emotions also leads to better decision-making. Let's face it, our feelings influence how we think and act. When we can step back and recognize what we're feeling, we can make choices based on what's best for us, not just what feels good in the moment. This allows us to respond with clarity and wisdom, even when emotions are running high.

Emotional awareness strengthens our problem-solving skills as well. When we're in tune with our feelings, we can approach challenges with a clearer head. Instead of getting stuck in frustration, we can see the bigger picture, consider different perspectives, and think creatively. This kind of flexible thinking is what helps us move forward instead of getting stuck in the same patterns.

Recognizing our own emotions also deepens our capacity for empathy. When we understand how we feel, we're better able to understand others' feelings, too. Empathy is the glue that holds relationships together, and it's essential for building strong support systems. We all need people who can hold space for us, and we become that person for others when we practice empathy.

Another benefit of emotional awareness is increased self-awareness. By tuning in to our feelings, we learn more about who we are, that is, our strengths, our growth areas, and what tends to trip us up. This kind of insight helps us leverage our strengths while working on the areas that need more care and attention. That's how we grow as both people and professionals.

Emotional understanding also improves communication. When we can name our feelings and express them clearly, we reduce misunderstandings and build trust. Good communication is especially important during hard times. When we're feeling stressed or overwhelmed, it's the bridge that helps us stay connected and supported.

Adaptability is another superpower that comes from emotional awareness. Life is full of unexpected twists and turns, and those who can acknowledge their feelings, adjust their mindset, and keep moving forward are the ones who stay resilient. Being emotionally aware helps us bend without breaking, finding creative ways to navigate change.

Strong relationships are the backbone of resilience, and they're built on emotional understanding. When we can manage our feelings, we're more likely to maintain healthy, balanced relationships that offer mutual support. These connections provide encouragement, perspective, and practical help when we need it most.

Finally, understanding emotions is at the core of resilience building itself. It's what helps us recognize when we're struggling, gives us the wisdom to seek help, and empowers us to use coping strategies that actually work. It's how we bounce back from setbacks and grow stronger through the challenges we face.

When we take the time to understand and work with our emotions, we create a foundation for steady growth. We build the inner strength to navigate challenges, the clarity to make thoughtful choices, and the compassion to support both ourselves and those around us. This is how resilience grows, one moment of awareness, one intentional step, one connection at a time.

Emotional Intelligence: The Key to Better Self-Awareness and Relationships

I used to think being "smart" was all about grades, degrees, or knowing the right answers. But, over time, through teaching, parenting, and just living, I realized that one of the most powerful forms of intelligence is emotional intelligence (EQ).

Emotional intelligence starts with tuning in to ourselves. Have you ever reacted in a way you later regretted such as snapping at someone when you were really just overwhelmed? I've been there. EQ helps us notice those moments *before* they spiral and gives us tools to respond instead of just react.

The best part? It's not fixed. Emotional intelligence is something we can build one honest reflection, one deep breath, one conversation at a time.

Psychologist Daniel Goleman identified five key components of EQ, and they've shaped the way I see myself and connect with others (Goleman, 1995):

> **Self-Awareness:** This means recognizing what you're feeling and why. I've learned to pause and name my emotions, whether it's "I'm feeling anxious because I'm stretched too thin" or "I'm excited because this project feels meaningful." That simple awareness changes everything.
>
> **Self-Regulation:** This is about managing your emotional responses. It doesn't mean suppressing your feelings; rather, it means honoring them without letting them control you. I'm still working on this (especially when I'm running late!), but when I can take a breath and choose a calm response, I feel more grounded and in control.
>
> **Motivation:** Motivation in the EQ world is about inner drive. It's that spark that keeps you moving toward goals, even when you're tired or discouraged. For me, that's often my "why". It's remembering the impact I want to have, the people I care about, and the purpose behind the work.
>
> **Empathy:** This one has deepened my relationships more than anything else. Being able to feel with someone, for example, to sit beside their pain or joy without rushing to fix it, has changed how I show up for friends, students, and even strangers. Perhaps that's why people chat with me in the grocery check-out line.
>
> **Social Skills:** Communication, collaboration, conflict resolution are the skills that build trust and connection. Whether I'm leading a meeting or listening to a student, I try to focus on being present, clear, and kind. It's not always easy, but it's worth the effort.

Emotional intelligence isn't about being perfect. It's about being *real*, being *aware*, and being *intentional*. And the more we practice, the more it becomes part of who we are.

Pause Here and Take a Moment to Reflect

> *Think about a recent situation where your emotions influenced your response, either positively or negatively. Take a few moments to write honestly. There's no right or wrong but just an opportunity to grow.*
>
> *What emotion were you feeling at the moment?*
>
> *How did that emotion impact your behavior or decision-making?*
>
> *If you could go back, would you respond the same way? Why or why not?*
>
> *Which component of emotional intelligence (self-awareness, self-regulation, motivation, empathy, or social skills) could help you navigate a similar situation in the future?*

Can Emotional Intelligence Be Measured?

So, can EQ really be "measured"? The short answer is: sort of. Unlike IQ, which is more straightforward to measure, EQ deals with emotions, behaviors, and relationships, which are much more nuanced. Some tools try to assess EQ, but they're more of a reflection or self-awareness prompts than a definitive score.

When you think about emotional intelligence, focus on the growth process instead of getting bogged down by a number. It's not about how you score. It's about how you evolve.

Pause Here and Take a Moment to Reflect

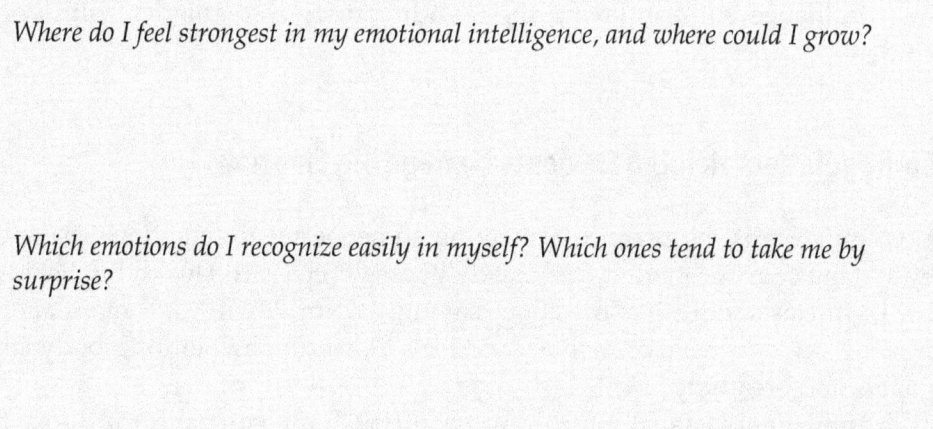

Where do I feel strongest in my emotional intelligence, and where could I grow?

Which emotions do I recognize easily in myself? Which ones tend to take me by surprise?

Classroom Application

Emotional intelligence isn't just a personal development tool. It's a powerful teaching strategy. In the classroom, your ability to manage your emotions and understand the emotions of others has a direct impact on the learning environment. When you stay calm in stressful moments and respond to students with empathy and awareness, you create a space where everyone feels safe, valued, and better equipped to learn.

Emotional intelligence also helps you interpret student behavior with greater insight. Instead of reacting to disruptions or disengagement as personal challenges, you begin to see them as signals, often rooted in stress, anxiety, or unmet needs. With this lens, you're better able to respond constructively and build stronger relationships with your students.

The good news? Emotional intelligence is not something you either have or don't have. It's a skill you can build. As you practice self-awareness, self-regulation, empathy, and social communication, you'll become more attuned to your emotional landscape and better able to support others through theirs.

The activities in this chapter will help you explore and strengthen your emotional intelligence. From understanding nonverbal cues to practicing mindfulness, you'll learn strategies that help you navigate challenges, reduce stress, and build authentic connections. These aren't just classroom tools, they're life tools.

As you build emotional intelligence, you're not only supporting your own resilience but also laying the foundation for co-regulation with your students.

Co-Regulation: Helping Students Manage Big Emotions

Co-regulation is the practice of helping someone regain emotional balance by staying calm, grounded, and steady yourself (Harvard Health Publishing, 2024). In classrooms, it's less about saying, "Calm down," and more about *showing* students what calm looks and feels like through your tone, body language, and breathing.

Young people (and many adults) often don't yet have the tools to self-regulate in stressful moments. Your calm presence can act as an anchor, signaling safety and helping them return to balance so they can cope and learn.

Here are a few practical ways to integrate co-regulation into your classroom:

- ◆ **Breathe together:** Invite students to take a few slow breaths with you before starting a lesson or after transitions.
- ◆ **Validate emotions:** Acknowledge feelings rather than dismissing them: "That test felt hard. It makes sense that you're frustrated."
- ◆ **Create connection points:** Use eye contact, a calm tone, or proximity to offer reassurance when a student is upset.
- ◆ **Stay steady in storms:** When students escalate, avoid matching their energy. Your role is to remain the anchor, not the storm.

Co-regulation isn't about solving the underlying issue on the spot; instead, it's about providing a safe, steady presence that helps students settle emotionally. Over time, as students repeatedly experience this modeled calm, they begin to internalize it and build their own capacity for self-regulation.

Pause Here and Take a Moment to Reflect

> *Think of a time when your students were at their best. How were you feeling before, during, and after this time? Were you regulated before your students came in? Were you teaching "in the moment"?*
>
> *Now think of a time when your students were not at their best. How were you feeling before, during, and after this time? Were you dysregulated before your students came in? Were you teaching "in the moment" or was your mind somewhere else?*
>
> *Reflect on those moments. What can you learn about yourself, your teaching, and your emotions?*

Let's Build Emotional Muscles Together

By practicing emotional intelligence and co-regulation, you're not just improving your own well-being, but you're becoming a model of calm, connection, and compassion for your students. These skills are essential for creating classrooms where everyone has space to learn, feel, and grow.

Ready to get started? Let's dive into the activities that will help you build your EQ and create a more emotionally intelligent classroom.

Emotions, Sensations, and Behaviors

Instructions: For each emotion listed, write down how it feels in your body and the behaviors you notice when experiencing that emotion. Consider what you can do for any of the emotions that you may find unpleasant. Examples for the first three are given; however, there is no one correct answer. This is personal to you.

Emotion	How It Feels in My Body (Sensations)	Behaviors	Coping Strategies
Happy	Warmth in the chest, lightness in the body, smiling	Laughing, increased energy, engaging with others	
Sad	Heaviness in the chest, lump in the throat, watery eyes	Crying, withdrawing from others, speaking softly	Journal, listen to music, talk with a friend or loved one
Angry	Tightness in the jaw, heat in the face, clenched fists	Raising voice, pacing, quick movements	Take a kickboxing class
Excited			
Nervous			
Scared			
Surprised			
Confused			
Bored			
Proud			

Emotion	How It Feels in My Body (Sensations)	Behaviors	Coping Strategies
Frustrated			
Relaxed			
Embarrassed			
Jealous			
Content			
Grateful			
Peaceful			
Lonely			
Energetic			
Disappointed			

Emotion	How It Feels in My Body (Sensations)	Behaviors	Coping Strategies
Hopeful			
Overwhelmed			
Curious			
Annoyed			

Understanding the connection between emotions, physical sensations, and behaviors is essential for emotional intelligence. This activity helps you identify how different emotions manifest in your body and influence your actions, providing valuable insights into your emotional responses. Recognizing these patterns can enhance self-regulation, communication, and resilience in personal and professional settings.

To deepen your understanding, share your reflections with a trusted family member, friend, or colleague. Comparing experiences can highlight how emotional responses vary among individuals, fostering empathy and connection. Extending the exercise to include coping strategies for unpleasant emotions equips you with tools to navigate challenges with greater awareness and confidence.

This awareness translates into a powerful tool for classroom management and student support. By recognizing your own emotional patterns, you model emotional intelligence and constructive coping strategies for your students. Adapting this activity for use with students helps them identify and articulate their emotions, improving communication, reducing conflicts, and fostering empathy. Additionally, understanding the connection between emotions and behaviors allows us to better interpret what might be driving a student's actions. For instance, a child's disruptive behavior may stem from nervousness or fear. Recognizing these underlying emotions enables us to respond with greater understanding and support.

Incorporating these practices into your classroom encourages a culture of respect, emotional safety, and resilience, creating an environment where both you and your students can thrive.

Pause Here and Take a Moment to Reflect

Were there any emotions that were particularly easy or difficult to describe in terms of sensations and behaviors?

Did you notice any recurring patterns in your emotional responses?

How do your emotional reactions align with or differ from those of others you discussed the activity with?

What coping strategies work best for the emotions you find most challenging?

How might this awareness of emotions improve your interactions with others?

How Would You Feel?

Instructions

Using the word bank, read each scenario and write the emotion that best fits your response. There's no single correct answer; people react differently. Afterward, compare your responses with colleagues, friends, or family.

You might notice, for example, that one person feels thrilled receiving a surprise gift, while another feels anxious or awkward because they didn't have something to give back. Recognizing these differences builds empathy and understanding.

Word Bank

Bored, Anxious, Happy, Content, Hopeful, Scared, Curious, Excited, Surprised, Proud, Confused, Relaxed, Embarrassed, Frustrated, Nervous, Sad, Overwhelmed, Energetic, Disappointed, Jealous, Angry, Peaceful, Grateful, Lonely, Annoyed, Silly

Scenarios

1. You received a surprise gift from a friend.
   You feel _____.

2. Your favorite team lost the championship game.
   You feel _____.

3. Someone cut you off in traffic.
   You feel _____.

4. You are about to go on a long-awaited vacation.
   You feel _____.

5. You have to give a presentation in front of a large audience.
   You feel _____.

6. You heard a strange noise in the middle of the night.
   You feel _____.

7. Your friends threw you a surprise birthday party.
   You feel _____.

8. You don't understand the instructions for a new task at work.
   You feel _____.

9. You have been waiting at the doctor's office for over an hour.
   You feel _____.

10. You completed a difficult task at work and were praised by your boss.
    You feel _____.

11. Your computer crashed right before you saved an important document.
    You feel _____.

12. You are lying on the beach, listening to the sound of the waves.
    You feel _____.
13. You tripped and fell in front of a group of people.
    You feel _____.
14. Your friend got a promotion at work, and you believe you deserved it more.
    You feel _____.
15. You are sitting by the fireplace, reading a good book.
    You feel _____.
16. Someone helped you out of a difficult situation.
    You feel _____.
17. You are waiting for the results of a medical test.
    You feel _____.
18. You moved to a new city and haven't made any friends yet.
    You feel _____.
19. You just finished a great workout and are full of energy.
    You feel _____.
20. You didn't get the job you really wanted.
    You feel _____.
21. You are applying for your dream job and think you have a good chance.
    You feel _____.
22. You have multiple deadlines approaching and don't know where to start.
    You feel _____.
23. You found your old diary in your attic and want to read it.
    You feel _____.
24. Your neighbor is playing loud music late at night.
    You feel _____.
25. You are meditating in a quiet room, focusing on your breath.
    You feel _____.

This activity is designed to boost emotional awareness and help you better connect scenarios with the emotions they can trigger. Being able to recognize and label emotions, both your own and those of others, is at the heart of emotional intelligence, and it plays a big role in how we communicate, support, and collaborate in both our personal and professional lives.

As an educator, this exercise can be eye-opening. Recognizing that specific situations don't land the same way for everyone helps us better empathize with our students and colleagues. For example, some people light up when they get a surprise gift, while others feel awkward, caught off guard, or even stressed because they don't have something to give in return. The same event can spark joy, discomfort, gratitude, or guilt depending on the person. When we recognize that, we can respond with more sensitivity and understanding.

Try doing this activity with colleagues, friends, or family. Compare your answers and talk about how and why your emotional reactions differ. You'll likely find that what feels exciting to one person can feel overwhelming to another. These conversations can deepen your understanding of the people around you and help you see that emotional responses are incredibly individual, and that's okay.

Practicing this skill can help you:

- **Recognize and validate emotions** (even when they don't match your own).
- **Respond more thoughtfully** to emotional situations instead of assuming everyone feels the same way.
- **Foster an environment of openness and empathy**, where students, colleagues, and even family members feel safe expressing how they truly feel.

Decoding Emotions: Building Awareness and Connection

Emotions don't just live in words. They show up in voices, faces, and bodies, often before we realize it. This activity helps you tune in to those cues to better understand yourself and others. You can do this with colleagues, students, friends, or family.

How It Works
1. **Speaker:** Describe a time you felt a strong emotion (anger, sadness, joy, fear, surprise, shame). Talk for five minutes about the situation, without naming the emotion. Stop if it feels uncomfortable.
2. **Face Observer:** Watch facial expressions and observe eyes, mouth, eyebrows. Take notes and guess the emotion afterward.
3. **Body Observer:** Watch posture, gestures, and movement or the head, shoulders, arms, hands. Note patterns and guess the emotion.
4. **Speech Observer:** Listen for tone, pitch, speed, and word choice. Take notes and make your best guess.

Reflect as a Group
- Which clues were easiest to spot?
- Did your interpretations differ?
- What did you learn about how *you* express emotions?
- How could these skills help you in the classroom, at work, or at home?

This isn't just about understanding others. It's also about understanding yourself. Becoming aware of how your emotions show up, sometimes before you even speak, can help you regulate your reactions and communicate with more intention. And when we do this with the people around us, we build more trust, empathy, and connection, which are qualities that make every environment, from classrooms to homes, feel more supportive and resilient.

Pause Here and Take a Moment to Reflect

What did you learn from this activity?

Did anything surprise you?

Is this something you could use, in some way, in your classroom? If so, how?

Facing Feelings: Overcoming Emotional Avoidance

Most of us, at one point or another, have tried to outrun our emotions. I know I have. There have been countless times when I buried myself in work, scrolled endlessly on my phone, or kept myself busy with any task that might distract me from that heavy, uncomfortable knot in my stomach. At the time, it felt like I was coping, but I eventually realized something important: Avoiding my emotions doesn't make them disappear. It just presses "pause," leaving them waiting in the wings and often building, intensifying, and demanding my attention later in a bigger, harder-to-ignore way.

Psychologist Sandra Parker (2023) writes about this in *Greater Good Magazine*, explaining that while emotional avoidance can feel like self-protection in the moment, it often chips away at our resilience and overall well-being over time. Her work made me reflect on my own patterns and recognize just how many ways I'd been sidestepping my feelings.

For instance, distraction, such as throwing myself into busywork or endless to-do lists, was my default move. It offered a temporary sense of control, but it kept me from processing what was really going on beneath the surface. Another pattern Parker highlights is cognitive avoidance, or getting stuck in your head instead of your heart. I've done this, too, replaying conversations, imagining every worst-case scenario, and convincing myself I was "problem-solving" when really, I was avoiding the raw discomfort of simply *feeling* the emotions underneath. It gave me the illusion of control but often left me mentally exhausted.

Then there's somatic focus, which is zeroing in on the physical signs of stress, like headaches, tight shoulders, or that sinking feeling in my gut, as if the body sensations are the "real" problem to solve. And, of course, numbing, which is checking out with food, screens, substances, or simply shutting down emotionally. While numbing can bring temporary relief, it often leaves us feeling disconnected from ourselves and from others who care about us.

Parker suggests a different path, one that's gentler but ultimately more effective:

- **Notice and Name Your Emotions:** Simply saying, "I feel anxious" or "I feel sad" can take away some of their power.
- **Practice Mindfulness:** Stay present, even if the feeling is uncomfortable, rather than fleeing the moment.
- **Slow Your Breath:** A few deep, intentional breaths can help calm your nervous system and create space to feel.
- **Reach Out for Connection:** Whether it's talking to a trusted person or journaling privately, sharing what you're feeling can keep you from feeling alone in it.

These practices don't erase hard emotions, but they make them easier to move *through* rather than getting stuck in cycles of avoidance.

What I appreciate most about Parker's perspective is that it isn't about perfection. It's not about "fixing" every emotion or trying to stay positive all the time. It's about showing up with curiosity and compassion for ourselves, even when things feel messy. In my own life, leaning in to my emotions, even the uncomfortable ones, has given me more clarity, deeper connections, and a sense of strength I never found by trying to outrun them.

Pause Here and Take a Moment to Reflect

Think about a time when you avoided an uncomfortable emotion.

Which strategy did you use—distraction, overthinking, somatic focus, or numbing?

How did that avoidance affect you in the short term? In the long term?

What might have been different if you had paused and simply allowed yourself to feel the emotion?

Of Parker's suggestions, that is, naming emotions, staying present, breathing, and connecting, which feels most doable for you right now?

How could practicing emotional awareness help you build resilience in the season you're in?

Guided Meditation: Building the Foundation of Resilience

Sit comfortably with your back straight and your feet flat on the ground. Close your eyes and take a deep breath in, feeling the air fill your lungs. Exhale slowly, releasing any tension.

Focus your attention on your breath, noticing the rise and fall of your chest. With each inhale, feel yourself becoming more aware of your body and your emotions. With each exhale, let go of any distractions.

Now, bring to mind a recent emotional experience. As you recall this experience, observe how it feels in your body. Notice any physical sensations or changes in your breath. Allow yourself to fully experience the emotion without judgment.

Silently name the emotion you're feeling. Is it joy, sadness, anger, or something else? Acknowledge it and then let it go, returning your focus to your breath. Remind yourself that emotions are temporary and part of your human experience. With each breath, feel a sense of clarity and calm. When you're ready, open your eyes, bringing this awareness into your day.

Pause. Breathe. Respond.

Your feelings matter. Your reactions shape your impact.

Take a moment. Notice what's happening inside you. Choose how you want to show up.

Key Takeaways

- Self-awareness is the foundation of all meaningful change and connection.
- Emotional intelligence helps us respond rather than react, especially under stress.
- Understanding your emotional triggers and patterns can unlock new choices.
- Naming your feelings can help you reclaim your power and purpose.
- Emotions aren't good or bad. They may be pleasant or unpleasant, but let's not label them in a positive or negative way.

Closing Message

Self-awareness is the first step in building emotional resilience. When we understand ourselves, we can better care for ourselves, and when we care for ourselves, we can care for others more fully.

You won't always get it right (trust me, I know), but every time you pause, notice, and learn, you're growing your emotional intelligence. This is the work. It's messy, it's human, and it's worth it. Keep on going!

Chapter 2 Notes

Engage and Reflect

How do you currently identify and manage your emotions during stressful situations?

What are some emotional triggers you have noticed in your teaching environment?

How does emotional intelligence affect your interactions with students and colleagues?

Can you share a recent experience where self-awareness helped you handle a challenging situation?

What strategies do you use to improve your emotional intelligence?

How can developing greater self-awareness improve your teaching practice?

What role does empathy play in your relationships with students and peers?

How can you create a more emotionally supportive classroom environment?

References

Goleman, D. (1995). *Emotional intelligence: Why it can matter more than IQ*. Bantam Books.

Harvard Health Publishing. (2024). *Co-regulation: How calm adults help kids manage big emotions*. Harvard Medical School. https://www.health.harvard.edu

Parker, S. (2023, September 14). Four ways we avoid our feelings—and what to do instead. *Greater Good Magazine*. https://greatergood.berkeley.edu

3

Mindfulness and Stress Management

> **Focus:** Incorporating mindfulness practices into daily routines.
>
> **Content:** Guided mindfulness exercises, stress reduction techniques, and practical ways to integrate mindfulness into the classroom and personal life.
>
> Mindfulness is like a mental vacation without the jet lag. This chapter explores ways to stay calm and collected, even when classrooms feel like circuses. A little mindfulness can go a long way in keeping us sane and centered, helping us handle stress with grace.

Zen and the Art of Bumper Cars

It was one of those nights where I felt like I was *finally* getting it all right. I had just led a packed yoga class: 30 people in the room, mats crammed like sardines, and the energy was electric. I felt *amazing*. Like I could float home on a cloud of post-yoga bliss.

And then . . . bam! I got into a fender-bender on the way home. My mind, still in savasana, wasn't exactly focused on stop signs and brake lights. And let me tell you, there's nothing like the sound of crunching metal to snap you right out of your Zen state.

Cue the self-talk spiral: *How could I be so careless? What kind of yoga teacher crashes her car after class? I'm supposed to be the one modeling mindfulness, for goodness' sake!*

But here's the thing: Mindfulness doesn't mean we're perfect. It doesn't mean we never mess up, never get flustered, never lose focus. It means we *notice* when we're caught in the swirl of stress and judgment, and we choose to respond with self-compassion instead of self-criticism.

That night, I realized I had a choice. I could beat myself up, or I could pause, breathe, and remember: *I am human. I make mistakes. I forgive myself. And I'll pay better attention next time.* That's the heart of mindfulness.

Pause Here and Take a Moment to Reflect

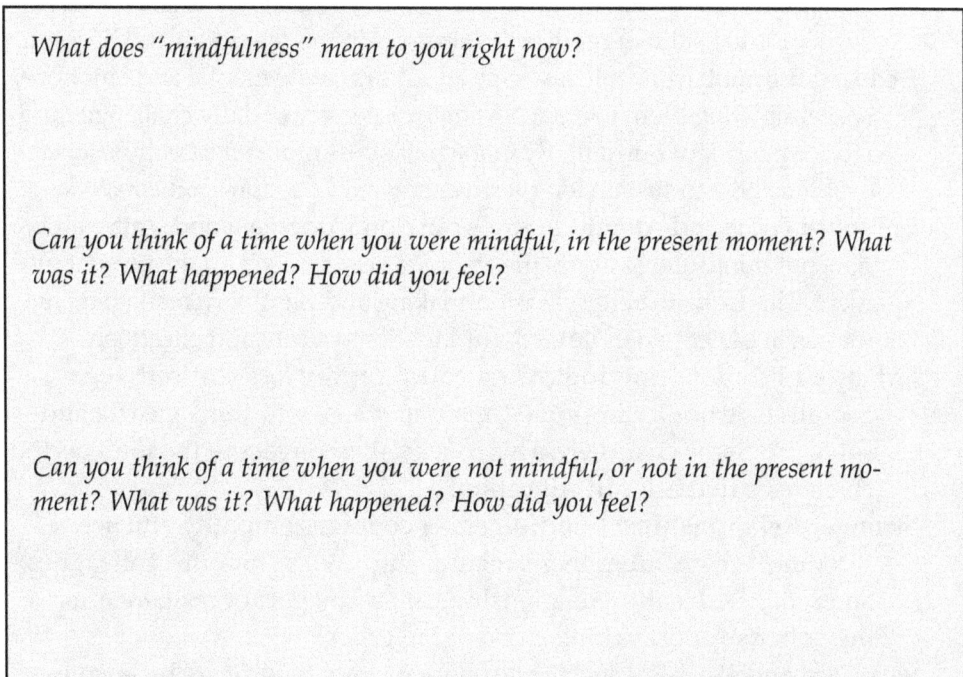

What does "mindfulness" mean to you right now?

Can you think of a time when you were mindful, in the present moment? What was it? What happened? How did you feel?

Can you think of a time when you were not mindful, or not in the present moment? What was it? What happened? How did you feel?

Establishing Relevance

In the whirlwind of teaching, where demands come from every direction, mindfulness serves as an anchor, helping us navigate the chaos with calm and clarity. Mindfulness isn't just a buzzword; it's a proven practice that enhances emotional regulation, reduces stress, and fosters resilience. By cultivating mindfulness, teachers can better manage the pressures of their roles while creating a more focused and positive environment for themselves and their students.

This chapter equips you with practical tools to integrate mindfulness into both personal routines and the classroom. These techniques empower you to respond to challenges with patience and intentionality rather than reacting impulsively or feeling overwhelmed. For educators, mindfulness can also serve as a powerful modeling tool, showing students the value of self-awareness and stress management.

By adopting mindfulness practices, you're not only improving your own well-being but also setting the stage for a more balanced, engaged, and thriving classroom. This chapter invites you to take a step back, breathe deeply, and reclaim your sense of calm even when life feels like a three-ring circus. Here are several reasons why:

> **Emotional Regulation:** Mindfulness practices help educators become more aware of their emotional states, which allows them to manage difficult feelings like frustration or anxiety before they escalate. This emotional balance leads to healthier reactions to stressors in the classroom and beyond.
> **Reduced Burnout:** Mindfulness helps educators create mental and emotional space, allowing them to detach from the intensity of daily challenges and reduce the risk of burnout. By managing stress more effectively, teachers are better able to sustain long-term energy and passion for their work.
> **Improved Focus and Attention:** Stress can cloud judgment and scatter attention, but mindfulness hones the ability to stay focused on the present moment. This leads to better decision-making and classroom management, making it easier to handle stressful situations calmly and effectively.
> **Enhanced Problem-Solving:** When educators are less stressed, their cognitive flexibility improves, making it easier to think clearly and solve problems creatively. This is crucial when facing the unexpected challenges that arise in education.
> **Stronger Relationships:** Mindfulness encourages empathy and active listening, which strengthens relationships with students, colleagues, and families. Healthy relationships are a key part of resilience, as they offer support during challenging times.
> **Self-Care and Well-Being:** Mindfulness promotes self-care by encouraging teachers to check in with themselves, rest, and recharge when needed. By managing stress levels, educators can sustain their well-being and avoid the exhaustion that diminishes their resilience.
> **Greater Job Satisfaction:** Educators who manage stress effectively and maintain mindfulness are more likely to feel positive about their work. A greater sense of satisfaction contributes to resilience by keeping motivation high and reducing the negative effects of job stress.

What Is Mindfulness, Really?

Jon Kabat-Zinn defines mindfulness as "the awareness that arises from paying attention, on purpose, in the present moment, and nonjudgmentally"

(Kabat-Zinn, 1994). It's not about achieving a perfect state of calm. It's about showing up for whatever is happening right now, with curiosity rather than judgment. Mindfulness invites us to observe our thoughts, feelings, and sensations as they are, helping us step out of autopilot and into the present.

That might sound a little "granola" to some of you, so let me break it down. Mindfulness isn't about clearing your mind or becoming a serene monk. Most people can't fully silence their thoughts, and that's okay. The goal isn't to eliminate stress but to notice what's happening with more clarity and less reactivity. Sometimes, you might even feel anxious while practicing mindfulness. That's normal. The practice is about noticing, not fixing.

Over time, regular mindfulness practice can lower stress, improve focus, and build emotional resilience. It helps you pause, breathe, and respond more thoughtfully instead of reacting automatically.

Mindfulness isn't just a technique. It's a way of being. It helps you stay connected to your own experience, offering a moment of stillness and self-compassion in the midst of everyday chaos. When we show up to life more fully, we bring more presence, calm, and care to ourselves and those around us.

Starting a mindfulness practice can feel intimidating, but it doesn't have to be complicated. You don't need a perfect body, special clothes, or to sit like a pretzel for an hour. You don't even need to clear your mind. All you have to do is focus on one thing at a time, whatever is happening in the present moment.

If you're washing your hands, you're simply paying attention to that experience: the temperature of the water, the scent of the soap, how the suds form, and the texture of the towel as you dry your skin. That is mindfulness.

Or maybe you're sitting at your desk, taking a moment to breathe. You intentionally notice each inhale and exhale, how your body moves with your breath, and how it feels. That's mindfulness, too.

Formal vs. Informal Mindfulness Practices

Formal mindfulness practice involves setting aside dedicated time to engage in structured activities, like meditation or yoga, with the goal of building focus, emotional regulation, and inner calm. These sessions are often scheduled and last from a few minutes to an hour, providing a deeper, more focused mindfulness experience. In contrast, informal mindfulness practice weaves awareness into daily life, like mindfully drinking coffee, walking, or washing dishes. This approach is flexible, without set times, and encourages a sense of presence in routine tasks, helping to reduce stress and foster a general sense of calm throughout the day. Both practices complement each other, supporting resilience and well-being in unique ways. Refer to the chart for more information.

Aspect	Formal Mindfulness Practice	Informal Mindfulness Practice
Definition	Dedicated, intentional time set aside to practice mindfulness (e.g., meditation, yoga).	Integrating mindfulness into everyday activities without specific set time.
Purpose	Develops a structured routine to build focus and calm over time.	Encourages mindfulness in daily life, fostering awareness in routine tasks.
Examples	Sitting meditation, body scan, mindful breathing, guided visualizations.	Being mindful while eating, walking, washing dishes, or listening.
Duration	Typically scheduled sessions (e.g., 5–60 minutes).	No set time because mindfulness is woven naturally into daily tasks.
Intensity	More focused and often deeper, building a dedicated mindfulness "muscle."	More flexible and adaptable to the moment, enhancing general awareness.
Goal	To deepen self-awareness and cultivate inner calm over sustained practice.	To bring awareness to the present moment throughout the day.
Benefits	Improves focus, stress management, and emotional regulation.	Reduces stress and brings presence to everyday experiences.

Mindfulness Strategies and Breathing Techniques

This section introduces simple, effective techniques to bring mindfulness into your daily life. Whether you're managing the chaos of a busy classroom or just trying to find a moment of calm, these strategies can help you feel more centered and less stressed.

5-4-3-2-1 Technique

The 5-4-3-2-1 technique is a grounding exercise that can help bring you to the present moment, especially if you are feeling anxious or overwhelmed. It involves using your senses to focus on your surroundings.

- **5 Things You Can See:** Look around and notice five things that you can see. These can be anything in your environment, such as a clock on the wall, a plant, a spot on the ceiling, or a picture frame. Take a moment to really look at each item and notice details you might usually overlook.
- **4 Things You Can Touch:** Notice four things you can physically feel. This might include the texture of your clothing, the feel of your chair, the floor beneath your feet, or the surface of your desk. Pay attention to the sensations and textures.
- **3 Things You Can Hear:** Listen carefully and identify three sounds in your environment. These can be as obvious as the sound of traffic outside or as subtle as the hum of an air conditioner. Focus on listening to each sound distinctly.
- **2 Things You Can Smell:** Identify two things you can smell. If you are in a place where there aren't many smells, you can move around to find something. Perhaps you can smell your coffee, the pages of a book, or a scented candle. If you can't find two things, think of your favorite smells.
- **1 Thing You Can Taste:** Focus on one thing you can taste. It might be the lingering taste of something you ate earlier or your current beverage. If you can't taste anything, think about your favorite taste.

Box Breathing

Box breathing, or *four-square breathing*, is one of my go-to techniques when I need to hit reset. It's simple, quick, and something I can do anywhere: in a busy hallway, during a staff meeting, or sitting in my car before heading into school. It helps slow everything down so I can feel a little more grounded and a lot less frazzled.

Here's how it works:

1. Inhale slowly through your nose for a count of four.
2. Hold your breath gently for a count of four.
3. Exhale slowly through your mouth for a count of four, emptying your lungs completely.
4. Hold again for a count of four before starting the next breath.

Repeat the cycle for a few minutes or even just a couple of rounds if that's all you have. Think of it as drawing an invisible square with your breath: in for four, hold for four, out for four, hold for four.

Why It Helps (and Why I Use It)

On the surface, it feels almost too simple, but there's a reason it works so well. The steady rhythm of box breathing helps regulate the autonomic nervous system, the part of our body that manages stress and relaxation (Schnieder et al., 2022). It signals to the body that it's safe to move out of high-alert mode, which can lower stress hormones like cortisol and help the mind feel clearer.

The equal counts of inhale, hold, exhale, and hold also give the brain something concrete to focus on. When I'm doing this, I'm not cycling through my to-do list or replaying a frustrating conversation; rather, I'm just counting and breathing. That shift alone can interrupt a stress spiral and bring me back to the present moment.

Box breathing is one of those tools I lean on when I need to feel centered fast. I've done it before presentations, while waiting for difficult phone calls, and even while standing in my kitchen on days when everything feels like it's moving too quickly.

It's not a magic fix, but it reliably creates a pause or space between the chaos outside and the calm I need inside. And most days, that space is enough to help me respond thoughtfully instead of reacting impulsively.

Mindful Check-In

Adapted from the everyday mindfulness strategies in *Growing Up Mindful* by Dr. Christopher Willard (2016), this check-in brings awareness to the present moment in just a few steps. A simple way to bring mindfulness into your daily rhythm. No mat, app, or incense required:

- **Pause.** Feel your feet on the ground.
- **Notice.** What do you see, hear, smell, or feel?
- **Breathe.** Take one slow, deep inhale and exhale.
- **Name.** What emotion is present right now.
- **Kindness.** Offer yourself a supportive phrase like:

This is hard, and I'm doing my best.

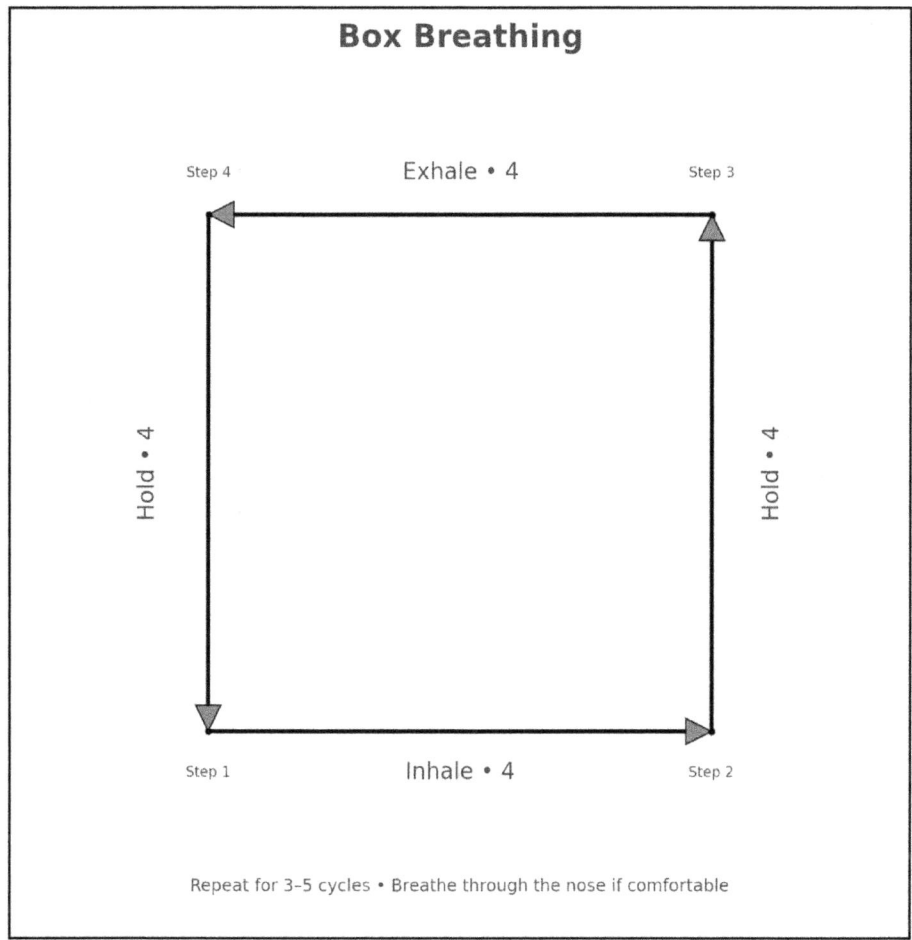

Figure 3.1 Box Breathing

Pause Here and Take a Moment to Reflect

What are three daily moments I could approach more mindfully?

What message of kindness do I most need today?

4-7-8 Breathing

The **4-7-8 breathing technique** (Figure 3.2), or *relaxing breath*, has become one of my favorite ways to reset when I feel overwhelmed. Developed by Dr. Andrew Weil, this practice is rooted in the ancient Indian tradition of *pranayama* but has been adapted for modern stress relief and overall well-being (Weil, 1997). It's deceptively simple:

1. **Inhale** quietly through your nose for a count of four, keeping the tip of your tongue resting against the ridge of tissue just behind your upper front teeth.
2. **Hold** your breath for a count of seven, staying as still and relaxed as possible.
3. **Exhale** completely through your mouth, making a soft whooshing sound, for a count of eight, emptying your lungs fully.

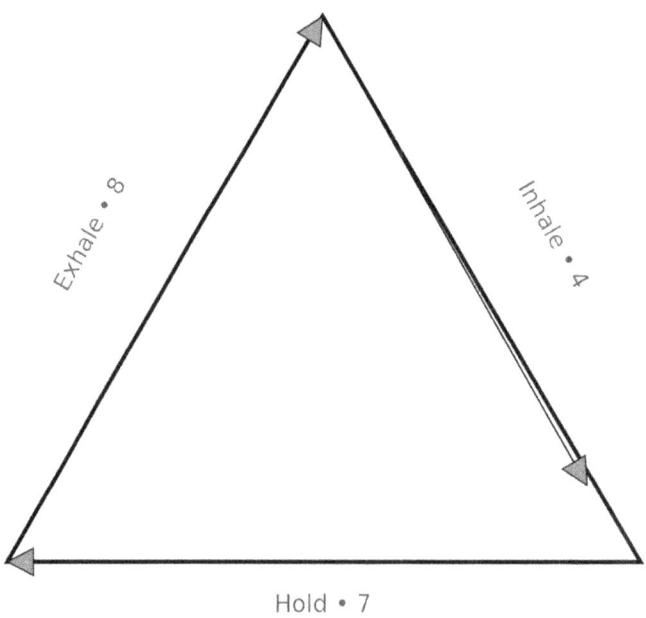

Figure 3.2 4-7-8 Breathing

Start with four breaths and, as it feels more natural, gradually work up to eight. I use this anywhere, such as before teaching, in my car before a big meeting, or during a stressful moment in the middle of the day. It doesn't require a mat, an app, or a quiet space, just a willingness to pause and breathe.

Why It Works (and Why I Trust It)

I'll admit, I used to roll my eyes when people told me to "just breathe" during stressful times. It felt far too simple for the heavy, complicated emotions I was experiencing. But the first time I actually tried 4-7-8 breathing, I noticed something shift.

There's real science behind that shift. The pattern activates the parasympathetic nervous system (the part of our body that handles rest and recovery) and downshifts the sympathetic nervous system (our stress and "fight-or-flight" response) (Weil, 1997). This gentle balancing act lowers the stress hormone cortisol and helps the body know it's safe to calm down.

The extended exhale (the "8") is especially powerful because it encourages the body to release carbon dioxide and bring in fresh oxygen, which creates a natural sense of grounding. Research also shows that slow, intentional breathing can improve heart rate variability (HRV), a measure of how resilient and adaptable our bodies are to stress (Lehrer et al., 2020).

My Experience With 4-7-8

For me, the benefit goes beyond biology. When I practice 4-7-8 breathing, my spiraling thoughts quiet. Counting my breaths pulls me into the present moment. I'm no longer replaying that awkward conversation or anticipating everything that could go wrong. I'm just here, breathing. That pause, which is the space between stimulus and response, is sometimes the most important gift I can give myself.

I've used this practice in school parking lots, before difficult conversations, and even in moments of self-doubt. Each time, it feels like flipping a switch from chaos to calm. And it's not about achieving perfection or instant peace; it's about carving out enough calm to meet what's next with more ease and clarity.

This technique isn't a passing trend. Its roots in *pranayama* give it depth, and Weil's work, through books like *Spontaneous Healing* and *8 Weeks to Optimum Health*, has made it accessible to anyone, anywhere. It costs nothing, takes only a few moments, and yet, for me, it's one of the most reliable ways to anchor myself when life feels overwhelming.

If you haven't tried it, I encourage you to practice a few rounds today. Not because it will erase every stressor but because it might create enough space for you to face what's in front of you with a little more steadiness. Sometimes, that pause is the most resilient thing we can do.

Everyday Mindfulness: Small Reminders Make a Big Difference

Mindfulness doesn't need to be one more thing on your to-do list. In fact, some of the most powerful practices happen in the middle of ordinary moments. As Dr. Christopher Willard (2016) reminds us, mindfulness is not just what we do in silence, but it's how we meet the moment we're in. He writes that "mindfulness isn't about clearing your mind. It's about focusing your attention—again and again, with kindness" (Willard, 2016). Whether you're standing in line at the copier, waiting for your class to settle, or driving home after a long day, you can take a mindful breath, tune in to your senses, and come back to yourself.

Most of us want to be more mindful, but then life gets loud, fast, and overwhelming. I've learned that building in small, consistent cues throughout the day makes a huge difference. Mindfulness doesn't have to mean sitting in silence for 20 minutes (though that's lovely, too). Sometimes it's a sticky note, a deep breath, or a simple pause before you pick up your phone. Next are practical ways to weave mindfulness into everyday moments. Check off one or two you'd like to try and notice how those small shifts can reset your mindset.

Morning Mindfulness
- ◆ **Wake Up Slowly:** Before reaching for your phone, take a moment to notice your breath, stretch gently, and set a calming tone for the day.
- ◆ **Begin With Breath:** Take three deep breaths or do a short stretch to center yourself.
- ◆ **Set an Intention:** Choose a simple focus for the day and how you want to feel or show up.
- ◆ **Eat and Drink Mindfully:** Savor your breakfast or morning beverage without distractions.
- ◆ **Refresh With Care:** Brush your teeth, shower, or wash your face with full attention.
- ◆ **Meditate Briefly:** Try a short 2–5 minute meditation to anchor your morning.
- ◆ **Scan Your Body:** Use a body scan or breathing exercise to check in before leaving home.

During the Day
- ◆ **Set Reminders:** Use your phone or computer to prompt mindful breaks.
- ◆ **Use Sticky Notes:** Place short prompts like "Pause" or "Breathe" in visible spots.
- ◆ **Create Breath Cues:** Take three deep breaths before transitioning between tasks.
- ◆ **Choose Daily Prompts:** Use activities (like doorways or handwashing) to cue mindfulness.

- **Try an App:** Use tools like Headspace, Calm, or Insight Timer to guide mindful moments.
- **Wear a Reminder:** Use a bracelet, ring, or necklace as a visual cue to return to the present.
- **Use Simple Tools:** Try a 1–3 minute sand timer or mindfulness bell for short breaks.
- **Check In With a Mirror:** Keep a mirror nearby to pause and reflect on your emotional state.
- **Observe Your Surroundings:** Take thirty seconds to look around and name five things you see, hear, or feel. It's a simple way to ground yourself in the present moment.
- **Take a Mindful Pause Before Responding:** When you feel triggered or rushed, pause for a breath before replying to an email, text, or conversation. That small space can shift your entire reaction.
- **Use Doors as a Cue:** Notice when you're entering a new room or leaving one behind. Let that simple act invite presence, awareness, and a moment to reset. As the environment is changing, invite your attention to shift with it.

In Motion

- **Walk With Awareness:** Focus on your steps, breath, and surroundings as you walk.
- **Stretch Mindfully:** Take a break to move and notice how your body feels.
- **Breathe Intentionally:** Use techniques like box breathing (4-4-4-4) or 4-7-8 to reset.
- **Exercise With Presence:** Tune in to the rhythm, sensation, and effort of your body in motion.

Mindful Eating and Drinking

- **Focus While Eating:** Choose one meal or snack a day to savor fully including taste, texture, smell.
- **Sip Slowly:** Notice the temperature, flavor, and sensation of your water or tea.
- **Express Gratitude:** Pause before eating to appreciate the nourishment in front of you.
- **Acknowledge the Journey:** Reflect on the effort and hands it took to bring your food to the plate.

Connection and Communication

- **Listen Fully:** Practice active listening without planning your response.
- **Be Present in Conversation:** Notice your tone, body language, and emotional response.

- **Use a Mantra:** Repeat a grounding phrase like "Be here now" during social interactions.

Reflection and Gratitude
- **Keep a Journal:** Use a mindfulness journal or tracker to note reflections or progress.
- **Practice Daily Gratitude:** Write down three things you're grateful for at morning or night.
- **Reflect at Night:** Revisit your day with curiosity. What felt mindful? What could shift tomorrow?

Home and Nature
- **Be Present in Chores:** Bring awareness to folding laundry, watering plants, or cooking.
- **Connect With the Outdoors:** Step outside to observe the sky, birds, or breeze.
- **Use Calming Scents:** Try essential oils or candles as sensory reminders to pause.

Evening Wind-Down
- **Unplug With Intention:** Turn off screens a few minutes before bed.
- **Slow Down Your Body:** Do a body scan or gentle stretching to release tension.
- **Create a Ritual:** Drink tea, take a bath, or breathe deeply as a nightly routine.
- **Ground Yourself:** Try the 5-4-3-2-1 technique to return to the present.
- **End With Reflection:** Consider one highlight from the day or something you're proud of.

Bonus Tips
- **Try One at a Time:** Choose one or two new mindful activities to explore each week.
- **Use Visual Cues:** Keep a small object like a stone, candle, or mirror in view as a reminder.
- **Track Your Habits:** Use a digital or paper tracker to mark your practice. Each check is a sign you're showing up for yourself and creating space for what matters.

Looking for more on mindfulness? *Happy Teachers Change the World* by Thich Nhat Hanh and Katherine Weare is one of my favorite books. It provides educators with mindfulness practices to foster a nurturing and joyful classroom environment. It integrates mindfulness techniques into teaching, aiming to enhance teacher well-being and improve student outcomes (Hanh & Weare, 2017).

Guided Meditation: Embracing Mindfulness

Find a comfortable position, either seated or lying down, and gently close your eyes. Let your hands rest easily and allow your shoulders to soften.

Take a slow, deep breath in through your nose . . . and exhale gently through your mouth. Feel the air move through you. Again, inhale deeply, and as you exhale, imagine letting go of any tension in your body. With each breath, allow yourself to sink a little deeper into stillness.

Bring your awareness to this moment. Notice any sounds around you, such as distant traffic, birdsong, the hum of a heater, without judgment. Just allow them to be part of your present. Feel the weight of your body supported by the chair or floor. Notice the rise and fall of your chest, the air entering and leaving your body.

Now, begin to imagine a peaceful, calming place. Maybe it's a quiet forest path where sunlight filters through the leaves. Maybe it's a warm, sandy beach with gentle waves rolling in and out. Or perhaps it's a cozy room with soft lighting, a blanket around your shoulders, and the scent of something comforting in the air.

Whatever peaceful place comes to mind, picture yourself there. Let the scene unfold around you. What do you see? Notice the colors, the light, the shapes. What do you hear: birds, wind, waves, silence? Is there a particular scent in the air: salt, pine, lavender? Let yourself fully enter this space. Feel safe here. Feel at ease.

As you breathe in, imagine you're filling your body with calm and clarity. As you exhale, release anything you no longer need, such as stress, tension, mental clutter.

If thoughts or worries begin to drift in, that's okay. Simply acknowledge them like clouds floating across the sky and gently return your focus to your breath and your peaceful place.

With each breath, feel a sense of peace expanding within you. Feel the stress gently melting away, the tension softening, your heart rate slowing. You are grounded. You are safe. You are present.

Take one final deep breath in . . . and exhale slowly. When you feel ready, bring your awareness back to the room. Gently wiggle your fingers or toes. And when it feels right, open your eyes, carrying this sense of calm and ease into the rest of your day.

Key Takeaways

- Mindfulness is about presence, not perfection. It's permission to pause.
- Small mindful moments (like breath or noticing) can interrupt stress spirals.
- Stress is inevitable; suffering is optional when we learn how to relate to it differently.
- You deserve tools that bring calm *within* your daily chaos, not just outside of it.

Closing Message

Let's end the chapter with a thought from *Zen and the Art of Bumper Cars*. "It's not about never getting hit, but how you steer and reset after each bump." Life, especially life in schools, is a bit like a bumper car ride. We're going to get jostled, surprised, and even frustrated at times. But we have choices. We can grip the wheel tighter and react with frustration, or we can loosen our hold, take a breath, and steer with curiosity and grace. When you feel overwhelmed, remember: pause, breathe, and come back to center. Your breath is always available as a grounding tool. Every moment is a fresh chance to reset your course. So the next time life bumps you, smile, adjust your grip, and keep moving forward.

Chapter 3 Notes

Engage and Reflect

What does mindfulness mean to you, and how do you practice it in your daily life?

Can you share a time when mindfulness helped you manage stress effectively?

What are some mindfulness techniques you find most useful?

How do you integrate mindfulness practices into your classroom or teaching routine?

What challenges do you face in maintaining a regular mindfulness practice?

How can mindfulness improve your overall well-being and resilience?

What are some simple mindfulness exercises you can do during the school day?

How can you encourage mindfulness practices among your students?

Pause and Breathe

References

Hanh, T. N., & Weare, K. (2017). *Happy teachers change the world: A guide for cultivating mindfulness in education.* Parallax Press.

Kabat-Zinn, J. (1994). *Wherever you go, there you are: Mindfulness meditation in everyday life.* Hyperion.

Lehrer, P. M., Eddie, D., & Yehuda, R. (2020). Respiratory regulation and its effects on stress and health. *Frontiers in Psychology, 11,* 486. https://doi.org/10.3389/fpsyg.2020.00486

Schnieder, S. C., Goessl, V. C., & Mychaskiw, A. (2022). Breathing techniques and the autonomic nervous system: Impacts on stress and anxiety. *Frontiers in Human Neuroscience, 16,* 853411. https://doi.org/10.3389/fnhum.2022.853411

Weil, A. (1997). *8 weeks to optimum health.* Knopf.

Willard, C. (2016). *Growing up mindful: Essential practices to help children, teens, and families find balance, calm, and resilience.* Sounds True.

4

Building Strong Relationships

> **Focus:** Cultivating supportive relationships and community.
>
> **Content:** Strategies for building and maintaining healthy relationships with colleagues, students, families, and the community.
>
> Strong relationships are the secret sauce in our teaching recipe. They're what keep us grounded even when the week feels heavier than we'd like. This chapter is all about building and sustaining those connections with colleagues, students, families, and the wider community. Because while test scores and standards matter, what people often remember most is how we made them feel (Pianta, 1999; Roorda et al., 2011).

Jake's Second Favorite

In education, relationships aren't just a "nice to have." They're the foundation for everything else. We talk a lot about test scores and standards, but at the end of the day, what students remember most is *how we made them feel*.

Let me tell you about Jake.

When we first met, it wasn't smooth sailing. I was focused on getting the work done; Jay was . . . well, *not*. Our early interactions were tense. He'd get frustrated. I'd get frustrated. We were stuck in a cycle with both of us trying to be heard but neither of us really *listening*.

But something told me to pause.

I started paying attention, not just to his behavior but to the *person*. I overheard him talking with a friend about how much he loved bananas. So, the next day, I brought him a banana. I heard him mention that he had a brother, so I asked him to bring his brother in to meet me. Small things. Quiet moments. That's where it started.

Slowly, Jake began to trust me. That's when I started to learn the *real* story, about his life in foster care, about the lack of food at home, about a foster mother who promised she'd keep him until he graduated but changed her mind at the last minute.

It wasn't easy. It wasn't fast. It took time . . . lots of time. It took *showing up*, again and again, with small acts of care: a banana, a fist bump, a safe space to talk.

By the end of the year, Jake called me his *second* favorite teacher. (I'll take it!) But the real victory wasn't the title. It was that Jay *graduated*. Despite the obstacles, he kept showing up because he knew someone believed in him.

That's the heart of building strong relationships.

It's not about fixing or saving. It's not about having all the answers. It's about paying attention. Listening. Being there.

That's how trust is built. That's how resilience grows. That's what makes the hard days worth it.

Let's dive into how we can build these kinds of connections with the students who need us and with the colleagues who walk alongside us every day.

Pause Here and Take a Moment to Reflect

> *When you were in school, who made you feel seen? Who believed in you?*
>
> *Think of a student, colleague, or family member you're struggling to connect with. What might they be experiencing that you don't see on the surface?*
>
> *What small, consistent actions could you take to build trust with this person?*

> *Reflect on a time when someone showed you compassion. How did it make you feel? How can you pay it forward?*

What Builds Strong Relationships?

Here's what I've learned over the years:

Presence: Be fully there. Put down the papers, stop multitasking, and focus on the person in front of you. Full attention says: *You matter. I see you. I'm here.* Presence doesn't mean perfection; it's about showing up in small, meaningful moments.

Consistency: Show up, even on the tough days. Trust grows when we're steady and reliable, not just when it's easy (Pianta, 1999). Relationships are built over time, through steady, repeated interactions. Consistency says, *You can count on me. I won't disappear when things get messy.* Whether it's a student struggling with behavior or a colleague facing burnout, they need to know you'll stick around, not just when it's easy, but when it's hard.

Curiosity Over Judgment: Instead of asking, "What's wrong with them?" ask, "What's going on for them?" Curiosity helps us see the story behind the behavior (Roorda et al., 2011). It invites us to look beyond the surface and wonder: *What's this behavior trying to tell me?*

Compassion: Small acts of kindness, such as a snack, a check-in, a simple "How are you today?," create psychological safety. Compassion doesn't fix everything, but it helps people feel seen and supported (Cohen & Wills, 1985).

Boundaries: Relationships thrive when there's mutual respect, not self-sacrifice. Boundaries protect our energy so we can keep showing up with patience and care (Aguilar, 2018; Ozbay et al., 2007).

Research is clear: Strong teacher-student relationships lead to higher engagement, better academic outcomes, and improved well-being (Pianta, 1999; Roorda et al., 2011). For educators, feeling supported by peers reduces burnout and boosts job satisfaction (Collie et al., 2012; Skaalvik & Skaalvik, 2011). But honestly, most of us don't need a study to prove it. Think back to your own school years, who made you feel seen? Who believed in you, even when you doubted yourself? That's the kind of connection research confirms and the kind we can intentionally create.

Establishing Relevance

It's no surprise that connection plays a powerful role in how we cope with life's challenges. Research consistently shows that individuals with strong, supportive relationships demonstrate greater resilience. In the face of adversity, those who can rely on a network of support, whether friends, colleagues, mentors, or family, are more likely not only to bounce back but to experience growth. Connection grounds us, gives us perspective, and offers stability when everything else feels uncertain.

In the world of education, connection isn't just helpful, it's vital. Teachers who feel supported by their peers report lower levels of burnout and greater job satisfaction. This guide focuses on reducing educator burnout and strengthening well-being, and at the center of that work is relationship-building. The reality is, we cannot do this job alone. Whether it's a passing conversation in the hallway, a trusted team that offers mutual encouragement, or simply knowing someone is in your corner, that sense of belonging matters. Deeply.

Connection is also one of the most powerful buffers against educator stress and burnout. Teachers who feel supported by their peers report lower stress and higher job satisfaction (Collie et al., 2012; Skaalvik & Skaalvik, 2011). Whether it's a trusted colleague, a supportive administrator, or just someone who makes you laugh on a hard day, these relationships keep us grounded and help us carry on.

Beyond stress reduction, strong relationships create a culture of empathy, kindness, and collaboration. When we model compassion and care for one another, it radiates outward, impacting the classroom, school climate, and student experiences. Students benefit from emotionally grounded teachers. When we feel supported, we show up with more patience, more presence, and a greater capacity to build the kind of classrooms where students feel valued and safe.

Connection also fuels professional and personal growth. Sharing ideas, brainstorming solutions, celebrating small victories are not just feel-good moments. They're integral to innovation and development. A connected team is not about competition but collaboration. When we lift each other up, we all rise.

Perhaps, most importantly, connection nourishes our emotional well-being. Having people in your life who understand your struggles, who can hold space for vulnerability, and who affirm your worth even on your hardest days is powerful. Emotional safety allows us to ask for help, to reflect, and to grow. Seeking and maintaining these relationships isn't extra, it's essential. Whether with a colleague, a mentor, or a friend, investing in connection is investing in your resilience.

Pause Here and Take a Moment to Reflect

> *Who is in your support system, both personally and professionally? Take a moment to list the people you turn to, count on, or simply feel safe around.*

Student Relationships: The Heartbeat of the Classroom

Equally important to educator relationships are the connections we build with students. Strong teacher-student relationships can transform the classroom. When students feel seen, safe, and supported by their teachers, engagement improves. Motivation increases. Risk-taking in learning feels safer. The classroom becomes more than a place of instruction. It becomes a place of belonging.

At the core of these relationships are mutual respect and trust. When we take time to learn our students' strengths, stories, and challenges, we affirm their value. It's not about just knowing their test scores but knowing who they are. When students feel that, they begin to show up more fully. And for educators, these connections deepen our sense of purpose. They remind us why we chose this path in the first place.

These relationships extend beyond academics. They shape how students develop socially and emotionally. In a connected classroom, students have a model for empathy, communication, and resilience. They learn how to handle disappointment, resolve conflict, and practice kindness. And importantly, they see that they are not alone in navigating the ups and downs of school and of life.

These connections benefit us, too. A kind note from a student, a lightbulb moment in class, or a heartfelt "thank you" on a hard day can refill a drained cup. These moments become reminders of impact and purpose, especially when the demands of the job feel heavy. They are anchors of joy and motivation.

What It Takes to Build Strong Relationships

Strong relationships don't come from grand gestures. They come from consistent, meaningful moments. A warm greeting. A genuine question. A shared laugh. Trust is built through honesty, reliability, and care. People feel safe when they know they can count on you to show up, to listen, and to follow through. Predictability in your presence and in your communication becomes a quiet kind of safety, and safety builds trust.

Listening is key. Real listening. The kind that isn't waiting to respond but simply holds space. Sometimes people don't need advice; rather, they need to feel heard. A gentle nod, a thoughtful pause, or a "that sounds really hard" can make someone feel seen. Feedback, when given with kindness and authenticity, lifts people up and fosters growth.

It's also important to recognize the value of small, daily interactions. A quick hallway check-in. A "how are you really doing?" A moment of shared joy. These are the threads that weave a strong community. And every interaction is an opportunity to create belonging, especially for those who often go unseen.

Names matter. Saying a student's name, and saying it correctly, sends a message: "You matter. I see you." Many students go an entire school day without hearing their name from an adult. For some, that small act of recognition may be the only affirmation they receive all day. We should never underestimate its power.

Creating emotional and psychological safety is the foundation of any lasting relationship. That means fostering an environment where vulnerability is respected, not punished. When someone shares something personal, how we respond matters. A supportive, compassionate response can strengthen trust and build lasting connections. Emotional safety is not just a nice idea. It's a practice of presence, empathy, and care.

Support doesn't always need to be big or loud. A kind word. A compliment. A gentle check-in. These are often the things people remember most. When we celebrate each other's wins and sit with each other in hard moments, we build community. These moments remind us that we are not alone and that matters deeply.

Shared values also strengthen connection. When we're working toward common goals, whether it's equity, inclusion, or simply doing our best together, it creates a bond. We find meaning in the work and each other, and that shared purpose drives us forward. Collaboration reminds us that we're in this together, and we don't have to carry the weight alone.

Kindness is never wasted. A note of appreciation. A thank-you. A moment of praise. These seemingly small gestures ripple far beyond what we see. When we create space to celebrate one another's strengths, we help each other thrive.

In the end, resilience grows in relationship. It's in the moments of connection, support, and shared humanity that we find the strength to keep going and to keep growing. When we feel seen, heard, and valued, we don't just survive. We flourish.

Pause Here and Take a Moment to Reflect

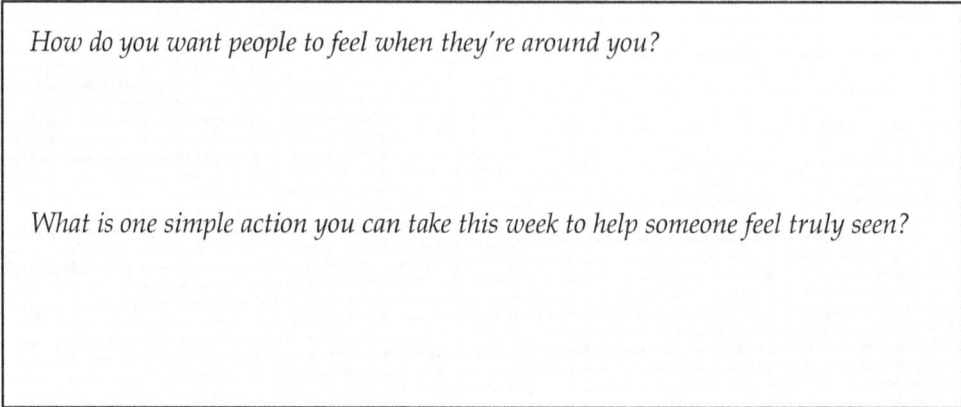

How do you want people to feel when they're around you?

What is one simple action you can take this week to help someone feel truly seen?

Using "I" Statements to Foster Positive Communication

Overview
"I" Statements are one of those simple tools that can completely change the way we communicate. Instead of blaming or pointing fingers, they help us speak from our own experience, what we're feeling, what we need, and what's not working, without putting the other person on the defensive. They're a way to be honest *and* respectful, even in tough conversations.

Why Use "I" Statements?
When we use "I" Statements, it lowers the emotional temperature. We're not accusing but sharing. That makes it easier for the other person to actually hear us, not just react. These statements help clarify our feelings, promote understanding, and lead to more respectful, solution-focused conversations. They're especially helpful when emotions are running high or when something's been building for a while.

How to Structure an "I" Statement
There's a basic structure that keeps things grounded and clear. Start by describing the behavior or situation without judgment or blame. Then, say how it makes you feel, as this helps the other person understand where you're coming from. Finally, share what you need or what you'd like to happen instead. It might sound like, "I feel frustrated when meetings start late because it throws off my whole schedule. I'd really appreciate starting on time." Simple, honest, and constructive.

Examples of "I" Statements for Different Audiences

Formula: "I feel [emotion] when [situation] because [reason]. I would appreciate it if [request]."

Speaking With a Colleague
Example: "I feel overwhelmed when our meetings run longer than scheduled because it cuts into my prep time for class. I'd appreciate it if we could find ways to stay within the planned time."

Speaking With an Administrator
Example: "I feel a bit uncertain when new policies are introduced without time for training because I want to ensure I'm implementing them correctly. It would be helpful to have a quick session or guide to support us."

Speaking With a Parent
Example: "I feel concerned when I don't receive updates about changes at home because it helps me support your child's learning. I'd appreciate it if you could let me know if there's anything affecting their school experience."

Speaking With a Student
Example: "I feel distracted when students talk during instruction because it makes it harder for everyone to focus. I need everyone's attention so we can make the most of our class time."

Practice using "I" Statements for each group listed. Think about how you might respond to each scenario constructively, using the steps outlined.

Formula: "I feel [emotion] when [situation] because [reason]. I would appreciate it if [request]."

Colleague Scenarios

A colleague frequently interrupts you during team meetings, making it challenging for you to share your ideas.

Your colleague tends to complete shared tasks at the last minute, affecting your ability to prepare for your shared responsibilities.

Administrator Scenarios

Your administrator sends out last-minute notices for mandatory meetings, disrupting your planning time.

You're given a new set of responsibilities without additional resources, and it's affecting your workload balance.

Parent Scenarios

A parent often reaches out with questions that could be answered in the weekly class newsletter but seems not to read it.

A parent has expressed frustration about their child's recent grades and questions your teaching methods.

Student Scenarios

A student repeatedly talks out of turn during group activities, disrupting the focus of others.

A student often forgets to bring necessary materials to class, impacting their ability to participate fully.

Emotion Words to Avoid in "I" Statements

"Abandoned"
- Implies that someone deliberately neglected or left you.
- Example to avoid: "I feel abandoned when you don't answer my messages."
- Better alternative: "I feel lonely when I don't hear back because I value our communication."

"Attacked"
- Suggests intentional harm or malice by the other person.
- Example to avoid: "I feel attacked when you criticize my ideas."
- Better alternative: "I feel hurt when my ideas are dismissed because I want to contribute."

"Ignored"
- Implies the other person is purposely neglecting you or your needs.
- Example to avoid: "I feel ignored when you don't respond right away."
- Better alternative: "I feel unimportant when I don't hear back because communication helps me stay on track."

"Betrayed"
- Suggests intentional dishonesty or violation of trust.
- Example to avoid: "I feel betrayed when you make decisions without consulting me."
- Better alternative: "I feel excluded when I'm not part of decisions that affect our work because I want to contribute meaningfully."

"Disrespected"
- Implies that the other person is deliberately devaluing you.
- Example to avoid: "I feel disrespected when you don't listen to my input."
- Better alternative: "I feel unheard when my input isn't acknowledged because I care about the team's success."

Why Avoid These Words?

These words imply intentional wrongdoing by the other person, which can derail constructive dialogue and make it harder to resolve the issue collaboratively. Instead, choose words that focus on your personal experience rather than the perceived intent of others.

Safer Emotion Words to Use
- Hurt
- Frustrated
- Overwhelmed
- Lonely
- Sad
- Confused
- Anxious
- Overlooked
- Upset
- Disappointed

By framing your emotions in a way that centers on your feelings rather than blaming the other person, you can foster understanding and avoid unnecessary defensiveness. Here's a set of examples illustrating how blaming emotion words can derail effective communication in "I" Statements and how to reframe them constructively. Each example includes an explanation of why the reframe works better.

Reframing Blame: A Guide to Constructive Communication

Blaming Statement	Why It Doesn't Work	Reframed Statement	Why It Works
"I feel abandoned when you don't include me in planning meetings."	Implies intentional neglect or rejection, triggering defensiveness.	"I feel excluded when I'm not part of planning meetings because I want to contribute to the team's success."	Focuses on your feelings of exclusion and emphasizes your desire to participate, encouraging collaboration.
"I feel attacked when you critique my lesson plans."	Suggests malice or hostility, escalating tension.	"I feel hurt when my lesson plans are critiqued without positive feedback because it makes me doubt my work."	Emphasizes how the critique affects you and invites constructive, balanced feedback.
"I feel ignored when you don't respond to my emails."	Implies deliberate neglect, which may make the listener defensive.	"I feel unimportant when my emails don't get a response because I rely on communication to stay aligned."	Centers on how the lack of response impacts you, avoiding assumptions about intent.
"I feel betrayed when you make decisions without consulting me."	Carries heavy emotional weight and suggests a breach of trust, escalating conflict.	"I feel excluded when decisions are made without my input because I value being part of the process."	Highlights your feelings of exclusion without assigning blame, fostering productive dialogue about collaboration.
"I feel disrespected when you talk over me in meetings."	Implies intentional devaluation, provoking defensiveness.	"I feel unheard when I'm interrupted in meetings because it makes it hard to share my ideas."	Focuses on the impact of interruptions (being unheard) rather than assuming intent (disrespect).

Why Reframing Matters

The key to effective communication with "I" Statements is removing the assumption of intent. When you focus on your feelings (e.g., hurt, excluded, unheard), the specific behavior (e.g., not responding to emails, interrupting), and your need/request (e.g., timely communication, the ability to share ideas), you open the conversation to solutions and understanding. The listener is more likely to engage constructively when they don't feel blamed or attacked.

Building Strong Relationships Through Effective Communication

At the heart of every strong relationship, whether it's with students, colleagues, or administrators, is communication that feels real, respectful, and rooted in empathy. When we take the time to listen deeply, respond thoughtfully, and speak with care, we strengthen the kind of trust that makes collaboration and growth possible. Three strategies I've found especially helpful are reaffirming feelings, mirroring, and sandwiching. These may sound simple, but when used with intention, they make a big difference in how people feel in conversation with us.

Reaffirming Feelings

One of the most powerful things we can do in a conversation is validate someone's emotions. When a student or colleague is struggling, it's not always about having the perfect solution. Rather, it's about saying, "I see you." Reaffirming feelings is about letting someone know that what they're experiencing is okay, and that they're not alone in it. For instance, when a student is clearly frustrated with a tough assignment, saying, "I can see this is frustrating, and it's okay to feel that way," helps them feel supported instead of judged. That simple act of acknowledgment can lower their stress and open the door to a more productive conversation (Cohen & Wills, 1985).

Mirroring

Mirroring is about listening with your whole attention and then reflecting back what you heard, either word-for-word or in your own phrasing, to show that you're tuned in. It's not just about parroting words; it's about creating a moment where the other person feels truly heard (Ozbay et al., 2007). I've used this a lot in team meetings or one-on-one chats with colleagues. If someone says, "I'm worried this new policy is going to pile more onto my plate," a mirrored response might be, "It sounds like you're concerned this will add to your workload. Did I get that right?" That moment of reflection shows respect, reduces misunderstanding, and helps both people feel more connected and grounded in the conversation.

Sandwiching

This is one of my go-to strategies when I need to bring up something that might be hard to hear, especially when speaking to someone I deeply respect. The sandwiching method means starting with something positive, offering the feedback or concern in the middle, and ending with a suggestion or another encouraging note. It keeps the tone constructive and preserves the relationship (Aguilar, 2018). For example, if I'm talking to an administrator about a new system that's been tough to navigate, I might say, "I really appreciate the new resources. It's clear a lot of thought went into them," followed by, "It's just taking more time than expected to get used to it," and then close with, "Do you think there's a way to simplify it or maybe offer a training to help us get up to speed?" It's honest, respectful, and solutions-focused.

None of these tools are about sugarcoating or avoiding hard conversations; instead, they're about creating space for honesty *with* kindness. When we lead with empathy and clarity, we build stronger relationships that can handle both praise and challenge. And in education, where so much depends on human connection, that kind of communication matters more than ever.

Pause Here and Take a Moment to Reflect

> Take a few quiet moments to reflect on your recent conversations with students, coworkers, or anyone in your professional world.
>
> As you reflect, ask yourself: *How do I want people to feel after talking with me? What small changes can I make to build more trust and connection in my daily conversations?*
>
> Consider the following prompts.
>
> Think about a time recently when someone shared something difficult or emotional with you. How did you respond? Did you acknowledge their feelings or try to jump into problem-solving? If you could revisit that moment, what might you say differently using an *"I see you"* kind of response?

Now think of a situation where someone misunderstood your intentions or you misunderstood theirs. How could mirroring have helped? Try rewriting a version of that interaction using a mirroring statement, such as: "What I'm hearing is . . ." or "It sounds like you're saying . . ."

Finally, recall a time when you had to bring up something that was challenging to say out loud, maybe to a colleague, administrator, or even a student. How did you frame it?

Now, try crafting a version of that same feedback using the sandwiching method. Start with something positive, gently insert your concern, and close with a constructive suggestion or affirmation.

Remember, communication isn't about being perfect. It's about being present, intentional, and human.

What Would You Do?

Try applying these techniques to these real-world scenarios. This activity reinforces how thoughtful communication can transform interactions into opportunities for collaboration and problem-solving. These strategies empower you to handle complex situations with confidence and build stronger, more productive relationships.

Communication With Colleagues

    Strategy: Practice active listening and empathy by using reflective techniques and acknowledgment. This approach helps build a supportive work environment and allows team members to feel valued.

    Example: Use "mirroring" to listen actively. When a colleague expresses a concern, summarize it back to them to ensure understanding. For example: "It sounds like you're concerned about the extra workload this new initiative might create. Is that right?" This approach fosters understanding and reduces miscommunication.

What Would You Do?

Scenario 1: A colleague feels overwhelmed by the number of meetings added to the schedule and expresses frustration to you. How could you respond to validate their feelings and encourage a constructive conversation?

Scenario 2: You've noticed that a colleague frequently interrupts during team discussions, making it challenging for others to share ideas. How could you use "I" Statements or mirroring to address this in a respectful, supportive way?

Communication With Parents

    Strategy: Establish rapport and maintain open, consistent communication with parents, focusing on student strengths and involving parents as partners in their child's education.

    Example: Start conversations with positive feedback before addressing any challenges. For example: "I've noticed that Sarah has been really enthusiastic in our recent projects, which is wonderful. I do want to discuss some challenges with her completing homework on time, and I'd love your insights on how we might support her at home and in the classroom." This helps create a cooperative tone and encourages a more collaborative relationship.

What Would You Do?

> Scenario 1: A parent frequently contacts you about their child's grades and asks why the student is not performing better. How could you acknowledge their concerns and work with them to support their child's progress?
>
> Scenario 2: A parent expresses frustration over their child being grouped with students who require more support, feeling it may hold their child back. How could you respond by validating their concern while emphasizing the value of collaboration and growth?

Communication With Students

Strategy: Use clear boundaries and empathy to establish a trusting environment where students feel respected. "I" statements and validation of students' emotions foster a supportive classroom dynamic.

Example: Use "I" statements to express needs and expectations clearly and respectfully. For example, "I need everyone's attention when giving instructions so that everyone understands the task." Additionally, validate students' feelings when they express frustration: "I can see this is frustrating, and it's okay to feel that way."

What Would You Do?

> Scenario 1: A student is frustrated and says, "This is too hard! I'll never understand it." How can you validate their feelings and encourage them to keep trying using "I" statements and empathy?
>
> Scenario 2: A student has been disrupting the class by talking out of turn. How would you use "I" statements to address the behavior while maintaining respect and encouraging cooperation?

Communication With Administrators

Strategy: Emphasize transparency and clarity in discussions. Administrators often manage multiple responsibilities, so direct, solution-oriented communication is appreciated.

Example: Use the "sandwich" technique to structure conversations with administrators: start with a positive observation, present the concern or request, and conclude with a constructive suggestion. For example, "I really appreciate the new resources we've received for our classrooms. I have noticed that the new system is taking more time to navigate, which impacts classroom time. Could we look at a way to simplify some steps or provide training?"

What Would You Do?

> Scenario 1: Your administrator has introduced a new online system for lesson planning that you find difficult to navigate. How could you use the "sandwich" technique to discuss the challenge while expressing appreciation and suggesting a possible improvement?
>
> Scenario 2: You have a request for additional resources in your classroom. How would you frame this request using transparency and clarity, while aligning your need with broader school goals?

Activities to Build Strong Relationships

The following is a list of different activities/strategies that may help build relationships with your colleagues, parents and families, students, the community, and administrators.

Building Relationships With Colleagues
- ◆ **Compliment Exchange:** One option is to write anonymous notes of appreciation for colleagues and read them together during a team meeting. You could also have staff members leave the anonymous

notes in bags on classroom doors. Staff could even tape the compliments right to the door so students could see. Perhaps the administration can dedicate a bulletin board where staff could post "shout outs" near an office.
- **Team Problem-Solving Challenge:** Collaborate on a school-related issue to share ideas.
- **Partner Walk-and-Talk:** Discuss personal wins and challenges while walking together.
- **Vision Collage:** Create a shared vision board to represent the team's goals and aspirations.
- **Speed Networking:** Quickly exchange teaching strategies or classroom tips in timed one-on-one rotations like speed dating!
- **Cross-Role Interviews**: Teachers and staff from different roles pair up to learn about each other's perspectives and challenges.
- **Chain of Gratitude:** Participants share thank-you notes for staff from various departments, creating a ripple of positivity.
- **Community Vision Collage:** Create collaborative artwork representing the school community's shared values and goals.
- **School Community Walk:** A casual group walk where staff get fresh air while sharing insights and hopes for the school culture.
- **Community Puzzle Challenge:** Staff work together to solve a puzzle that symbolizes the interconnectedness of the school community.
- **Breakfast or Snacks:** Once each month, different groups of staff volunteer to bring in food to share with everyone.
- **Movie Night**: Does your school have an auditorium? If so, project a funny movie and get those air poppers popping!
- **Dance Party**: During lunch, play some upbeat music. You may not feel like dancing, but the energy you all bring may help you get through the rest of your day!

Building Relationships With Parents and Families
- **Family Bingo:** Use this as an opportunity to spark conversations and identify commonalities during meet-and-greet events. This can even be done virtually! Consider playing more than just traditional bingo. What are the current topics you are teaching? Use the topics to create your game!
- **Family Showcase Night:** Parents share talents, hobbies, or cultural traditions to connect with teachers and other families.
- **Shared Goals Chart:** Work together to outline shared goals for their child's success and strategies to achieve them.

- **Gratitude Notes to Parents:** Teachers write personalized thank-you notes to express appreciation for parental support.
- **Parent Collaboration Brainstorm:** Host a session where parents and teachers brainstorm ideas for collaboration in the classroom.
- **Projects:** Invite parents to help with various projects, such as a STEM activity, art project, etc.
- **Bulletin Boards:** Get parents involved in decorating your classroom. Ask them to create a poster to introduce their child to the class and include a picture. Hang them up. Students love to see their pictures, and they love that the homework is for their parents, not for them! You can also do this with poetry and other writing assignments.
- **Local Library:** Advertise local library events to families and let families know which events you plan on attending. This makes it easier on you because you are not in charge. You don't need to provide anything or provide materials. All you have to do is show up and get to know your families.

Building Relationships With Students
- **Appreciation Circles:** Students share something they appreciate about their peers in a supportive, open setting.
- **Two Truths and a Lie:** A light-hearted game that encourages sharing and learning about each other.
- **Kindness Chain:** Students write compliments or kind words on paper links to create a visible symbol of connection.
- **Compliment Rocks:** Decorate smooth rocks with kind messages for classmates to take home or keep on their desks.
- **Team Challenges**: Engage in cooperative activities like building a tower out of marshmallows and toothpicks to promote teamwork.
- **Friendship Bracelets:** Gather materials such as embroidery floss or string, beads (optional). Create friendship bracelets to symbolize the supportive relationships built in the classroom. Share them with peers to reinforce community connections.
- **Compliment Cards:** Gather materials such as cardstock, markers, stickers. Make small cards with compliments or positive affirmations. Exchange these with students to build a positive and supportive atmosphere.

Building Relationships Within the Community
- **Community Service Projects:** Partner with local organizations for class-led initiatives like food drives, park clean-ups, or creating care packages for shelters. This encourages students to engage with and support their community.

- **Local Business Partnerships:** Invite local business owners to speak to the class about their roles in the community or work together on projects like designing posters or solving a community problem.
- **Community Scavenger Hunt:** Organize a scavenger hunt where students explore local landmarks, businesses, and historical sites, learning about their community in a hands-on way.
- **Pen Pal Program:** Partner with a nearby nursing home, community center, or another school to create a pen pal exchange, fostering intergenerational or intercommunity relationships.
- **Guest Speakers and Career Panels:** Invite community members, such as firefighters, artists, or scientists, to share their experiences and discuss how their work contributes to the community. This creates a bridge between the classroom and the world outside.
- **Utilize Your Local Newspaper:** This not only lets the community know some of the wonderful things happening in your classroom, it also makes the students and families feel special and more connected to you.

Building Relationships With Administrators
- **Leadership Appreciation Notes:** Provide teachers and staff with an opportunity to write thank-you notes or acknowledgments for administrators, highlighting specific leadership actions they value. Administrators can write thank-you notes to teachers, acknowledging the work that they do.
- **Collaborative Problem-Solving Session:** Organize a group meeting where teachers and administrators collaborate to brainstorm solutions to school-wide challenges. This fosters mutual respect and teamwork.
- **Administrator Q&A Roundtable:** Host an informal session where administrators answer questions from staff and share insights about their vision, challenges, and priorities.
- **Joint Vision Workshop:** Teachers and administrators work together to create a shared vision for the school's future, using brainstorming sessions or creative tools like mind mapping.
- **Leadership Walkthroughs With Feedback:** Pair teachers with administrators for classroom walkthroughs, where administrators observe and then invite feedback about their leadership style or school policies in action.

Boundaries: The Bridge Back to Yourself

Recently, a teacher friend I know and care about deeply reached out in frustration. She was at a breaking point. Amid yet another budget crisis, her department was being cut. She felt the emotional weight of it all, grieving for her colleagues and facing hard conversations. On top of that, she felt extremely overwhelmed with her workload. Despite all she was doing to support others, she felt invisible to many. She messaged me in a moment of exhaustion, wondering aloud if she could justify taking a mental health day so close to the end of the year. "What will happen if I don't go?" she asked. "Will anyone make me feel terrible about it?"

My response came easily because it's the same reminder I often need to hear myself: People can only make you feel terrible if you let them. You can let their words ruin your day, or you can let them go. What matters is that you took care of yourself. That you listened to what your body and spirit needed.

Her response? "God, I love you."

Of course, she already knew this. She just needed the reminder. Maybe even someone's permission. And the truth is, most of us still do.

I still catch myself asking my mom for permission (*"Do I have to do this?"*), and her answer is almost always the same: *"You don't have to do anything you don't want to do."* When I was younger and didn't feel brave enough to say no, I'd use her as a shield. If I didn't want to go to a party, I'd say, "My mom said I couldn't." Now, I just say: "No."

Recently, a colleague reached out to collaborate on a project during the final week of school. I originally said yes. But as the date got closer, I realized I didn't have energy. I sat with it, then revisited the conversation. I told him simply: "I gave it some more thought. I just don't have the energy for this. Maybe next year." He wasn't mad. He understood. School went on. And I made a boundary.

Setting boundaries doesn't make you selfish, it makes you sustainable. You do not need anyone's permission to take care of yourself. But if you do need a reminder, here it is:

You are allowed to protect your energy. You are allowed to rest. You are allowed to say no.

Pause Here and Take a Moment to Reflect

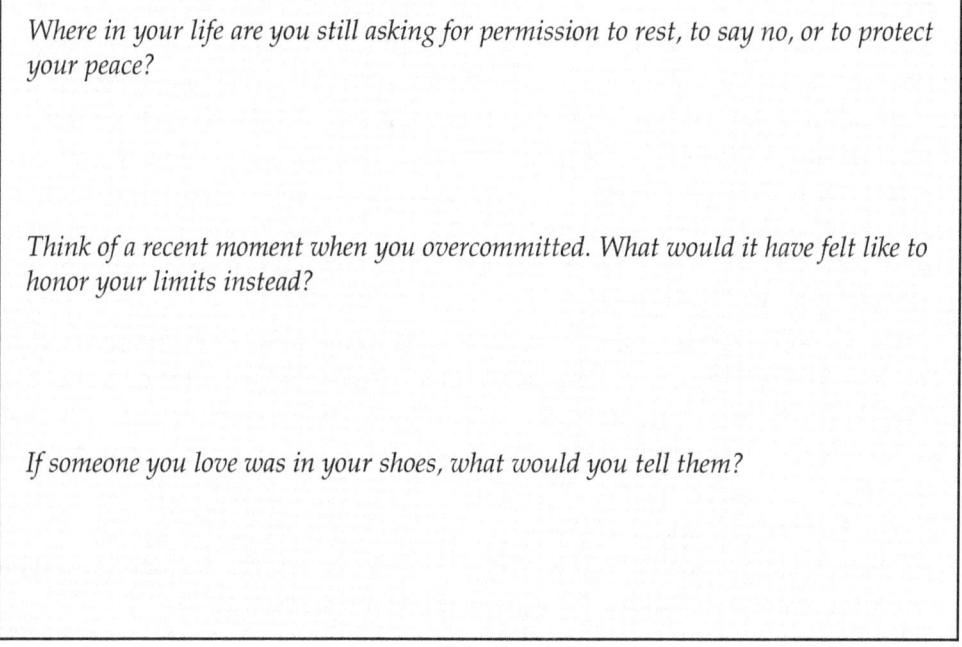

Where in your life are you still asking for permission to rest, to say no, or to protect your peace?

Think of a recent moment when you overcommitted. What would it have felt like to honor your limits instead?

If someone you love was in your shoes, what would you tell them?

Why Boundaries Matter in Resilience and Relationships

Let's talk about boundaries because they're not just a self-care buzzword. They're essential for resilience and for building healthy, lasting relationships. Boundaries aren't about shutting people out; they're about protecting your energy, honoring your limits, and showing up as your best self. When we don't set clear boundaries, it's easy to get stretched too thin, misunderstood, or even burned out. And when that happens, everyone loses.

Setting boundaries is an act of self-respect, and it's one of the most important tools we have for maintaining emotional well-being. Resilience depends on our ability to recharge, and that means we can't say yes to everything and everyone. Boundaries give us the breathing room we need to care for ourselves, focus on what really matters, and respond to challenges without running on empty. When we protect our time and energy, we're better equipped to show up fully for others and for ourselves.

They also help us avoid resentment. When we take on too much or constantly put others' needs before our own, it starts to wear on us. Over time, that can build frustration, even in the best relationships. Clear boundaries help prevent that. They create balance. They let both people in a relationship know where the lines are, which builds trust and a sense of fairness.

Boundaries are also about communication. When we say what we need kindly, clearly, and without apology, we make space for honest conversations. That kind of openness builds respect. It says, "I value you, and I also value myself." Relationships thrive when both of those things are true.

And finally, boundaries support growth. They give us room to reflect, adjust, and choose wisely where we invest our energy. Saying no to things that drain us allows us to say yes to things that help us grow. Whether that's a new opportunity, a needed pause, or just more time to breathe, boundaries help us live with more intention. Setting boundaries isn't always easy, but it's worth it. It's how we protect what matters most.

How to Set Boundaries

Elena Aguilar (2018) reminds us that setting boundaries isn't about pushing people away, it's about sustainability. Boundaries protect our energy so we can show up fully for others without burning out. They're not about saying, "I don't care about you," but rather, "I care about you and me, so I need to be clear about my limits."

Aguilar, author of *The Art of Coaching* (2013) and *Onward* (2018), takes a compassionate and grounded approach to boundary-setting. She emphasizes three essential tools, that is, mindfulness, self-awareness, and emotional intelligence, as the foundation for creating boundaries that are clear, kind, and sustainable. Her work reframes boundary-setting as a way to stay present and connected rather than distant or defensive.

It all starts with self-awareness. Aguilar (2018) encourages us to notice what drains our energy, what brings us joy, and where our physical, mental, and emotional limits lie. That reflection helps us recognize when we're edging toward burnout or resentment, which are two clear signals that boundaries are overdue. Self-knowledge, she explains, is what makes healthy boundaries possible.

Once we know what we need, the next step is communicating it clearly. Aguilar (2013, 2018) suggests we use language that's assertive but not aggressive. For example: "I need some uninterrupted time to focus on this project." Statements like this are calm, direct, and unapologetic. They honor our capacity without picking a fight or seeking permission.

Mindfulness also plays a big role. Aguilar (2018) notes that many of us only realize a boundary has been crossed when we feel it physically tight shoulders, a clenched jaw, a wave of irritation. Her advice: pause before reacting. Take a slow breath, notice how you're feeling, and give yourself a moment to respond intentionally rather than reflexively. That small pause can shift the entire dynamic of a conversation.

Most importantly, Aguilar (2018) reframes boundary-setting as an act of compassion, not selfishness. By preserving our energy, we're able to show up more fully for ourselves and for the people we care about. Feeling guilt, fear, or discomfort when setting a new boundary doesn't mean you're doing it wrong, rather it means you're stretching and growing.

She also reminds us that boundaries don't have to be a solo effort. Share them with people who support you. Trusted colleagues, friends, or mentors can help you hold the line when it feels difficult. And, like any skill, it gets easier with practice and support.

Practical Tips? Start Small

Try setting boundaries in lower-stakes situations so you can build confidence. Use "I" Statements that keep the focus on your own experience: "I feel overwhelmed when I'm interrupted during work hours, so I need quiet time from 9 to 12." Expect that some people won't love your boundary, but that doesn't mean it's wrong. Stay calm, stay kind, and stay consistent.

Finally, Aguilar (2018) encourages us to revisit our boundaries periodically. Ask yourself: *Are these still serving me? Do I need to adjust anything?* Boundaries, like we do, evolve over time.

At the end of the day, setting boundaries isn't about building walls. It's about creating healthy frameworks where connection, trust, and resilience can thrive. It starts with being honest about what you need and being brave enough to protect it.

Pause Here and Take a Moment to Reflect

> Boundaries are essential for maintaining emotional well-being, fostering respect, and building strong, healthy relationships. Use this worksheet to reflect on your needs, identify where boundaries are needed, and plan how to communicate them effectively.
>
> **Step 1: Reflect on Your Needs**
>
> *Think about the areas in your life where you feel overextended, disrespected, or overwhelmed. These are often signals that boundaries are needed. Where do you feel drained or stressed in your relationships or work? (e.g., "I feel overwhelmed when I'm expected to answer work emails after hours.")*

What would help you feel more balanced and respected in these situations? (e.g., "Setting clear work hours where I am unavailable for emails.")

Step 2: Identify Your Non-Negotiables

What values or priorities are most important to you, and how can boundaries protect them?

What are your top three priorities or values? (e.g., family time, self-care, professional growth)

What boundaries would support these values? (e.g., "I will not work on weekends to protect family time.")

Step 3: Communicate Your Boundaries

Effective communication is key to setting boundaries in a kind but firm way. Who do you need to communicate your boundaries to? (e.g., a colleague, supervisor, family member) Practice saying your boundary aloud using this formula:

- Start with "I feel . . ." *(Express how the situation impacts you.)*
- State your boundary. *(Clearly outline the behavior or limit.)*
- Offer a solution or alternative if appropriate.

Example

"I feel stressed when I receive work emails after hours. I need to set a boundary to only respond during work hours. If it's urgent, please call me instead."

Write Your Boundary Statement Here

Step 4: Honor Your Boundaries

Sticking to your boundaries is just as important as setting them. How will you reinforce your boundary if it's crossed? (e.g., "I will politely remind them of my work hours.")

How will you celebrate or reward yourself for maintaining your boundaries? (e.g., "Treating myself to a quiet evening with my favorite book.")

Remember, setting boundaries isn't about pushing people away; it's about inviting them into a space where mutual respect and understanding can grow. Be kind to yourself as you practice because it's a skill that strengthens over time!

Games to Build Trust With Students, Colleagues, or Families

Trust Walk

Blindfold Navigation Game

Overview: The Blindfold Navigation game is a team-building exercise that promotes communication, trust, and coordination. A blindfolded participant must navigate a passageway without stepping on colored dots on the floor, relying solely on verbal instructions from the rest of the group. One person stands closely to the blindfolded player to ensure their safety.

Objective: The goal is for the blindfolded participant to navigate from the start to the finish line without stepping on any colored dots, guided only by verbal instructions from their teammates.

Materials Needed
- Blindfold.
- Colored dots (or pieces of colored paper) to place on the floor.
- Clear start and finish lines marked on the floor.

Setup
1. Place colored dots randomly on the floor to create a passageway from the start line to the finish line. (You may need to use tape if the dots could cause slipping.)
2. Have one participant put on the blindfold.
3. Assign one person to stand closely to the blindfolded participant for safety.
4. The rest of the group will stand at a distance and give verbal instructions to guide the blindfolded participant.

   Starting the Game: The blindfolded participant stands at the start line. The safety person stands next to the blindfolded participant to provide physical support if needed. The rest of the group positions themselves at a distance where they can see the entire passageway.

   Navigating the Passageway: The group begins giving verbal instructions to guide the blindfolded participant from the start line to the finish line, avoiding the colored dots on the floor. Instructions should be clear and specific, such as "take two steps forward" or "move slightly to the right." The blindfolded participant listens carefully and follows the instructions.

Safety Measures: The designated safety person is responsible for preventing the blindfolded participant from tripping or losing balance. If the blindfolded participant is about to step on a dot or trip, the safety person can gently guide them to avoid the hazard.

Completing the Game: The game is completed when the blindfolded participant successfully reaches the finish line without stepping on any colored dots.

Rules
1. The blindfolded participant must keep the blindfold on throughout the game. The rest of the group can only give verbal instructions; no physical contact or non-verbal cues are allowed.
2. The safety person can only intervene to prevent tripping or falling.
3. The blindfolded participant should move slowly and carefully, following the verbal instructions.
4. The team wins if the blindfolded participant reaches the finish line without stepping on any colored dots.

Tips for Success
- Encourage the group to give clear, concise, and calm instructions.
- Remind the blindfolded participant to move slowly and listen carefully.

Debriefing: After the Game, Have a Discussion With the Participants
- How did the blindfolded participant feel relying solely on verbal instructions?
- What strategies helped in successfully navigating the passageway?
- How did the group ensure clear and effective communication?
- What challenges did they face, and how did they overcome them?
- How did the activity help build trust and coordination among team members?
- How can the skills used in this game be applied to real-life teamwork and problem-solving situations?

Human Knot Game

Overview: The Human Knot game is a classic team-building exercise that promotes cooperation, communication, and problem-solving skills. It's a fun and interactive activity where participants physically connect and then work together to untangle themselves without breaking the connection.

Objective: The goal is for the group to untangle themselves into a circle without letting go of each other's hands.

Materials Needed: No materials are required, just a group of participants.

Setup
1. Have participants stand in a circle, shoulder to shoulder.
2. Each person reaches out and grabs the hands of two different people who are not standing directly next to them.

How to Play
1. Once everyone is holding hands with two different people, the group is in a "human knot."
2. The challenge begins as the group works together to untangle the knot and form a single circle again, without letting go of each other's hands.
3. Participants may need to step over, duck under, and twist around each other to successfully untangle.
4. The game is completed when the group has untangled themselves and formed a circle.

Rules
1. No one is allowed to let go of the hands they are holding. If someone does, they must immediately reconnect with the same people.
2. If the group gets stuck, they can pause, discuss their strategy, and then try a different approach.

Tips for Success
- Encourage clear communication and patience. Suggest that participants take it slow and carefully consider each move. Remind them to be mindful of each other's comfort and safety.

Debriefing: After the Game, Have a Discussion With the Participants About Their Experience
- What strategies worked well for untangling the knot?
- How did communication affect the outcome?
- What challenges did they face, and how did they overcome them?
- How can the skills used in this game be applied to real-life teamwork and problem-solving situations?

The Human Knot game is not only fun but also a valuable exercise in teamwork, cooperation, and creative thinking.

Pass the Cup Game

A Team-Building Activity in Trust, Communication, and Coordination

Overview: Pass the Cup is a simple yet powerful team-building game that promotes trust, communication, and careful coordination. Participants stand in a circle and pass a cup of water around without spilling it. The challenge can be played with verbal communication or, for an extra twist, as a silent version using only non-verbal cues.

Objective: To pass a cup of water all the way around the circle without spilling, using either verbal or non-verbal communication to coordinate.

Materials Needed: One plastic cup ⅔ filled with water

Setup
- Have participants stand in a circle, shoulder to shoulder.
- Choose one participant to begin with the cup of water.
- Decide beforehand whether the cup will move clockwise or counter-clockwise.
- Choose whether the group will play with verbal communication or attempt the silent version.

How to Play
1. **Close Eyes:** All participants close their eyes and keep them closed throughout the activity. No peeking! This helps promote trust and heightens awareness.
2. **Begin Passing:** The participant with the cup carefully lifts it and begins to pass it to the person next to them, in the agreed direction. The cup should be passed slowly and steadily, using both hands.
3. **Communication Options:** *Verbal Version:* Participants may speak to coordinate using phrases like "I'm ready," "I have it," or "Here it comes." OR *Silent Version:* No talking is allowed. Instead, participants use gentle taps or touches to signal readiness to pass or receive the cup.
4. **Complete the Circle:** The cup is passed from person to person until it makes its way back to the original starting point. The goal is to complete the circle without spilling any water.

Rules
- All participants must keep their eyes closed until the activity is over.
- The cup must be passed carefully and securely to avoid spills.
- Everyone must stay fully engaged and respectful throughout the activity.

Tips for Success
- Move slowly and use both hands to pass and receive the cup.
- In the verbal version, encourage calm and clear communication.

- In the silent version, remind participants to use gentle, deliberate signals.
- Emphasize the importance of trusting one another and staying present in the moment.

Optional Challenge: After completing the verbal version, invite the group to try the silent version. It increases the difficulty and offers a great opportunity to explore non-verbal communication and deeper group trust.

Debriefing Questions: After the activity, bring the group together and reflect on the experience:
What strategies helped the group pass the cup successfully?
How did communication, or the lack of it, affect the outcome?
What challenges did you face, and how did you work through them?
How did this activity help build trust among team members?
How can the skills used in this game apply to real-life teamwork and problem-solving?

Counting Game

Overview: The Counting game is a team-building exercise that promotes coordination, non-verbal communication, and patience. Participants sit in a circle and must count from 1 to 10 in order, with only one person saying each number at a time, without making any body movements or verbal cues. If two people say a number simultaneously, the group starts back at 1. The first team to successfully count to 10 wins.

Objective: The goal is for the group to count from 1 to 10 in order, without any verbal or non-verbal communication, and with only one person saying each number.

Setup: Have participants sit in a circle, comfortably spaced.

How to Play

Starting the Game
- Participants sit quietly and cannot make any body movements or verbal cues to communicate.
- The game begins when one person starts by saying "1."
- The next person must then say "2," and so on, continuing in numerical order up to "10."
- Only one person should say each number. If two or more people say a number simultaneously, the group must start over from "1."
  - No communication! Participants are not allowed to speak or use any non-verbal communication (such as gestures, eye contact, or body movements) to indicate who will say the next number.

- The game relies entirely on the group's intuition and timing.
- Participants cannot count in a predetermined order (e.g., going around the circle) and cannot pre-plan who will say each number.

Restarting
- If two people say a number at the same time, the group must restart the count from "1."

Winning the Game
- The first team to successfully count to "10" without any overlaps or communication wins.

Tips for Success
- Encourage participants to stay calm and patient.
- Emphasize the importance of listening and intuition.
- Remind participants to avoid any form of communication other than saying the number.
  Debriefing: After the game, have a discussion with the participants about their experience:
- What strategies helped in successfully counting to 10?
- How did the lack of communication affect the group dynamic?
- What challenges did they face, and how did they overcome them?
- How did the activity help build trust and coordination among team members?
- How can the skills used in this game be applied to real-life teamwork and problem-solving situations?

The Counting game is an engaging way to build patience, coordination, and non-verbal communication skills within a group. It's a great icebreaker and team-building activity for various settings.

Pause Here and Take a Moment to Reflect

What are some activities that you already can do or will try to do to build relationships?

Guided Meditation: Cultivating Connection

Find a comfortable position, either seated or lying down, and gently close your eyes. Allow your hands to rest naturally and your shoulders to soften. Take a slow, deep breath in, filling your lungs completely . . . and then exhale slowly, releasing any tension you might be holding. Let your body begin to relax and your mind start to settle. There's nothing else you need to do right now. Just breathe and be here.

Now, bring to mind someone in your life with whom you share a strong, positive connection. This could be a dear friend, a family member, a student, or even a colleague Someone who brings a sense of warmth and trust into your life. Picture them in your mind's eye. See their face. Recall their voice, their laughter, their energy. Let yourself feel the sense of comfort and care that comes from being connected to them.

Begin to silently send this person kind and loving thoughts. You might say to them in your mind:

May you be happy. May you be healthy. May you be safe. May you be at peace.

Repeat these phrases slowly and gently, really meaning each word. Notice how your body responds as you do this. Maybe you feel a little more open, a little more grounded. Let yourself linger in that feeling for a moment.

Now, bring to mind someone with whom your relationship could use a little care. Someone you'd like to feel closer to or someone you've experienced tension or distance with. Picture this person in a neutral, compassionate light, not focusing on past challenges, but on the potential for understanding and connection. Imagine them receiving your positive thoughts just as fully:

May you be happy. May you be healthy. May you be safe. May you be at peace.

This isn't about fixing or forcing anything. Rather, it's about sending a quiet intention for healing, for clarity, and for kindness.

Feel the energy of these thoughts moving outward from you, like a bridge gently forming between you and the people you've visualized. Let yourself imagine what it feels like to be more connected, more at ease, more compassionate, not only with others but with yourself.

Take a few more deep breaths. Let your awareness expand to include all of the meaningful relationships in your life, including the ones that feel easy and the ones that may need time and care. Acknowledge the power of connection and the role your presence plays in nurturing it.

When you feel ready, begin to bring your awareness back to your body. Wiggle your fingers or toes. Feel the surface beneath you. Take one final, grounding breath. And when it feels right, gently open your eyes, carrying with you a renewed sense of connection, compassion, and calm.

Key Takeaways

- Connection is at the heart of resilience, and belonging builds strength.
- Strong relationships start with communication that is clear, kind, and curious.
- Healthy boundaries protect energy and preserve trust.
- Community care is just as vital as self-care. Ask for help and offer it, too.

Closing Message

As we wrap up today, I want to leave you with this: Relationships are built in the *small moments*. It's not about grand gestures or perfect words. It's about *noticing*: the student who loves bananas, the colleague who seems withdrawn, the quiet signals that someone might need you to lean in and care.

Building strong relationships takes time. It takes patience. It takes showing up, again and again, in the ordinary moments that, when you look back, were never so ordinary after all. Remember Jay. It wasn't one big conversation that built trust. It was many small ones. It was asking about his brother. Bringing him a banana. Listening when he needed to talk.

So as you go forward, keep your eyes and heart open. Look for the small opportunities to connect. Choose curiosity over judgment. Choose presence over perfection. And remember: The work we do in classrooms, staff rooms, and school hallways is about *people*. It always has been. It always will be. Let's keep showing up for one another, one small act of care at a time.

Chapter 4 Notes

Engage and Reflect

What strategies do you use to build strong relationships with your students?

How do you foster positive relationships with your colleagues and administrators?

Give an example of a time when a strong relationship helped you overcome a challenge.

What role does active listening play in building strong relationships?

How do you handle conflicts in your professional relationships?

What are some ways to create a supportive and collaborative classroom environment?

How can you improve your communication skills to strengthen relationships?

What are some activities or practices that can help build trust among students and colleagues?

References

Aguilar, E. (2013). *The art of coaching: Effective strategies for school transformation*. Jossey-Bass.

Aguilar, E. (2018). *Onward: Cultivating emotional resilience in educators*. Jossey-Bass.

Cohen, S., & Wills, T. A. (1985). Stress, social support, and the buffering hypothesis. *Psychological Bulletin, 98*(2), 310–357. https://doi.org/10.1037/0033-2909.98.2.310

Collie, R. J., Shapka, J. D., & Perry, N. E. (2012). School climate and social-emotional learning: Predicting teacher stress, job satisfaction, and teaching efficacy. *Journal of Educational Psychology, 104*(4), 1189–1204. https://doi.org/10.1037/a0029356

Ozbay, F., Johnson, D. C., Dimoulas, E., Morgan, C. A., Charney, D., & Southwick, S. (2007). Social support and resilience to stress: From neurobiology to clinical practice. *Psychiatry, 4*(5), 35–40.

Pianta, R. C. (1999). *Enhancing relationships between children and teachers*. American Psychological Association. https://doi.org/10.1037/10314-000

Roorda, D. L., Koomen, H. M., Spilt, J. L., & Oort, F. J. (2011). The influence of affective teacher-student relationships on students' school engagement and achievement: A meta-analytic approach. *Review of Educational Research, 81*(4), 493–529. https://doi.org/10.3102/0034654311421793

Skaalvik, E. M., & Skaalvik, S. (2011). Teacher job satisfaction and motivation to leave the teaching profession: Relations with school context, feeling of belonging, and emotional exhaustion. *Teaching and Teacher Education, 27*(6), 1029–1038. https://doi.org/10.1016/j.tate.2011.04.001

5

Professional Purpose and Passion

> **Focus:** Reconnecting with your professional purpose and passion.
>
> **Content:** Reflective activities to rediscover what drives you as an educator, goal-setting exercises, and ways to align your daily work with your core values and passions.
>
> Reconnecting with our purpose and passion reminds us why we became teachers in the first place. It's like rekindling an old flame but, this time, with our profession. Rediscovering our love for teaching can reignite that spark and keep us motivated and enthusiastic.

The Year Everything Changed

Let me tell you about 2023, the year I almost threw in the towel.

It had been 20 years. I knew every creaky floorboard, every closet where they hid the extra chairs, and every weird system for making the copier work (let's be honest, nobody *really* knows how that thing works). But, by the end, I felt stuck. Stale. Like I'd given everything I had to give, and the well was just . . . empty.

Nothing dramatic happened. There were no major changes or shocking announcements. We finally had the pandemic behind us, for crying out loud. I should have been dancing in the halls. But I wasn't. Something just felt... off. The priorities I was passionate about, like mindfulness and creative professional development, were not landing the way they used to. It was like telling your best joke and watching it roll across the floor like a sad tumbleweed while someone gives a single polite cough from the back row.

Suddenly, I found myself becoming more self-conscious than ever. And here is the funny part. I have always been a rule follower. I am the person who gets nervous returning a library book one day late. Yet somehow, I started to think that I would get in trouble for something. Every time the phone rang, I would worry it was someone calling to tell me I was being fired. It was just the story my tired, anxious brain decided to write on repeat. Eventually, my perception became louder than reality, and I began to question where I belonged.

And to make it even more fun? My youngest, Allie, was heading off to high school, and my oldest was already a junior. It felt like everything in my life was shifting at once.

Looking back, that year could have broken me. The burnout, the stress, the feeling of being scrutinized, misunderstood, and undervalued. It was enough to make me question if I even wanted to keep teaching.

But here's the thing: instead of giving up, I decided to *reset*. I packed up my classroom, my whole teaching life, and I moved to the high school to teach in the health department.

It was like a giant reset button. I gave myself permission *not* to have all the answers. I didn't stress (okay, I *tried* not to stress) over creating a brand-new curriculum from scratch. I just took it one step at a time. I focused on learning the building, figuring out who to ask when I had a question (because, every school has *that person* who actually knows how to fix the printer), and, most importantly, I focused on building relationships.

I started to rediscover myself as a teacher. I got to decide who I wanted to *be* in this next chapter.

I chose to lead with kindness.
I chose to create a curriculum with care but without obsession.
I chose to show up for students, one conversation, one connection at a time.

And you know what? That change brought me back to *why* I do this work in the first place. It gave me a new sense of purpose and, honestly, a new love for teaching.

That's what this chapter is all about: remembering your *why* or, maybe, rediscovering it after you've lost your way. This work is hard. It's messy, imperfect, and exhausting. But when we reconnect with our sense of purpose and we remember *why* we do this work in the first place, it becomes a little bit lighter. A little bit clearer.

I welcome you to take a breath, let go of what's not serving you and explore what it means to lead with heart, not fear. Let's tap back into the *why* that brought us here and the *why* that will carry us forward.

Pause Here and Take a Moment to Reflect

> *What's one thing you're holding onto that no longer serves your sense of purpose? What's one small step you can take this week to reconnect with your "why"?*

Establishing Relevance

When things get hard, and in education, they often do, your sense of purpose is what holds you steady. It's your anchor. When the pressure builds or everything feels chaotic, reconnecting with your "why" can bring clarity and calm. It helps you remember what really matters and reminds you why you chose this path in the first place.

Your purpose is also what helps you keep going. Passion doesn't mean every day is perfect, but it gives you the fuel to persevere through the tough ones, whether you're navigating challenging student behavior, juggling nonstop demands, or feeling the weight of criticism from the outside world. When you're connected to something bigger than the stress in front of you, it's easier to keep showing up with heart.

Feeling aligned with your purpose doesn't just help you push through, it feels good. It supports your emotional well-being. When you know your work has meaning, you're more fulfilled. You're less likely to burn out and more likely to trust in your own ability to make a difference. That kind of confidence and clarity is essential for resilience.

Purpose also shapes how we see things. It shifts us out of reactive mode and into something more intentional. Instead of focusing only on what's going wrong, we start asking, "What can I learn here? How can I grow?" That mindset shift helps us face challenges with more curiosity and less fear.

It keeps us learning, too. When you care about what you do, you naturally want to keep getting better at it. Passion fuels growth. And growth strengthens resilience because it arms you with more tools, strategies, and flexibility to meet whatever comes your way.

Purpose is also deeply relational. When you're grounded in your "why," you connect more deeply with the people around you, such as students, colleagues, families, your community. That connection creates a support system, and that support builds strength.

Passion also invites creativity. It helps us approach problems with fresh eyes and renewed energy. It makes us more willing to try new things, shake up the routine, and keep our work feeling meaningful and alive.

And maybe one of the most important things? Purpose helps you feel like your work *fits* with who you are. It bridges your personal values with your professional life so you're not constantly feeling like you're living in two different worlds. That kind of alignment reduces emotional strain and brings more ease into your day-to-day experience.

In the end, reconnecting to your purpose and passion helps you find joy, *real joy*, in the little things and the big picture. It helps you rediscover what lights you up, even when things are hard. And, for many educators, that sense of purpose becomes a quiet kind of leadership. When you live and work from your "why," people feel it. It inspires others and makes this work more sustainable, for you and for those around you.

Addressing the Overuse of "Find Your Why"

When we talk about professional purpose and passion, it's important to recognize how often educators are told to "find your why" but in ways that feel dismissive or even exploitative. Many of us have heard this from administrators or leaders, especially when they're asking us to do more with less. It's as if simply remembering "it's for the kids" should somehow make the increasing workload, lack of resources, and absence of recognition acceptable.

But that's not what this is about.

I want to challenge that narrative. Your purpose is not about justifying endless sacrifices or tolerating unsustainable demands. It's not a free pass for others to overlook your boundaries, needs, or compensation.

Instead, understanding your professional purpose is about *you*. It's about reclaiming your "why" as a source of strength, clarity, and fulfillment, not as a tool for guilt or burnout. Your purpose should inspire you, not exhaust you. It should help you focus on what matters most, prioritize your energy, and say no to things that don't align with your values.

When you connect with your true purpose, it becomes a guide, not a burden. It helps you navigate challenges with resilience, knowing that your work is meaningful and aligned with your values but also that you are more than your job. And that's the key: You can have purpose and still honor your boundaries. You can be passionate about teaching and still expect fair treatment, respect, and balance in your life.

Your purpose isn't permission to be exploited. It's a compass that's meant to guide you, not guilt you.

Purpose Statement Activity

In this chapter, we're going to focus on something foundational to resilience: our sense of purpose. Our purpose as educators is what fuels us, especially in challenging times. It reminds us why we started this journey and keeps us going.

When we are clear about our purpose, it gives us direction and helps us stay motivated. It's also a source of strength when we face obstacles, whether they're big or small.

This is a reflective and personal activity. There are no right or wrong answers. Your purpose statement is yours, and we're here to celebrate and support each other as we share.

Sharing our purpose can feel vulnerable, but it's a powerful way to connect with others and deepen our own understanding of what drives us.

Start by reflecting on a few guiding questions to help you think about your purpose. Then, you'll combine your thoughts into a concise statement that reflects what drives you as an educator. Finally, if you feel comfortable, you'll have the opportunity to share your purpose statement with a person/group.

To make this easier, we'll use a simple template to organize your thoughts. Feel free to adapt it so that it feels authentic to you. Your purpose statement will serve as a touchstone for you, a reminder of your why, and a way to refocus when things get tough.

Take some time to reflect on the questions and write your purpose statement. Remember, this is about capturing what matters most to you.

> **Instructions**: Reflect on your values, goals, and what drives you as an educator. Use the prompts to guide your thinking. Then, craft a clear and concise personal purpose statement. Once completed, be prepared to share your statement with the group.

Pause Here and Take a Moment to Reflect

Step 1: Reflect

Answer the following questions to explore your purpose

What inspired you to become an educator?

What do you hope to achieve through your work?

What brings you the most joy or fulfillment in your role?

What impact do you want to have on your students, colleagues, and community?

How does your work align with your personal values or passions?

Step 2: Write Your Statement

Combine your reflections into a purpose statement that:
- Is **clear** and **specific**.
- Reflects your **values** and **goals**. (Refer to the list provided.)
- Includes the **impact** you aim to create.

Template
"My purpose as an educator is to [what you do] so that [impact/result]. I am driven by [values/passions] and committed to [specific actions/goals]."

Example

"My purpose as an educator is to inspire curiosity and a love of learning in my students so that they become lifelong learners and critical thinkers. I am driven by my passion for equity in education and committed to creating a supportive and inclusive classroom environment."

Purpose Statement

Step 3: Share Your Statement

Take a moment to review and refine your purpose statement. When ready, share your statement with a colleague, friend, or family member.

Step 4: Reflect

How did you feel sharing your statement? Describe the experience.

Core Values

Here's a list of core values that can inspire self-reflection and help align personal and professional actions with what matters most:

Personal Core Values
1. Integrity—Acting with honesty and strong moral principles.
2. Compassion—Caring deeply for others and showing kindness.
3. Empathy—Understanding and sharing the feelings of others.
4. Authenticity—Being genuine and true to yourself.
5. Resilience—Bouncing back from challenges with strength.
6. Gratitude—Appreciating and being thankful for life's blessings.
7. Creativity—Using imagination and innovation to solve problems or express yourself.
8. Courage—Facing fears or challenges with bravery.
9. Humor—Finding joy and lightness even in tough situations.
10. Mindfulness—Being present and focused on the current moment.

Professional Core Values
1. Collaboration—Working effectively with others toward common goals.
2. Accountability—Taking responsibility for your actions and commitments.
3. Excellence—Striving to deliver high-quality work and continuous improvement.
4. Equity—Ensuring fairness and inclusivity in your work.
5. Innovation—Embracing change and new ideas to enhance processes or outcomes.
6. Service—Focusing on helping and serving others.
7. Growth—Committing to personal and professional development.
8. Leadership—Inspiring and guiding others to achieve their best.
9. Respect—Valuing others' opinions, rights, and contributions.
10. Work-Life Balance—Prioritizing well-being and harmony between work and personal life.

Strategies for Keeping Your Passion Alive in Your Work

Align Daily Tasks With Core Values

One of the most effective ways to stay connected to your passion is by aligning your daily tasks with what matters most to you. Think about your core values, whether it's creativity, connection, or making a difference, and find ways to infuse them into your day. For example, if creativity is a core value, look for opportunities to innovate in your lesson plans or classroom activities. This alignment can transform routine tasks into meaningful moments.

Examples
- If one of your core values is **collaboration**, you could prioritize team-building activities or intentionally include opportunities for collaboration in your daily tasks, such as scheduling time to co-plan lessons with colleagues or creating a peer-feedback loop for ongoing projects.
- If your core value is **helping others**, reframe even mundane tasks (e.g., grading or paperwork) by connecting them to the impact they have on student success or colleague support.

Set Professional Goals That Inspire Passion
Goals can be a powerful motivator when they reflect your deeper aspirations. Instead of focusing solely on external measures like test scores or administrative benchmarks, set personal goals that excite you. Perhaps it's building stronger relationships with your students, piloting a new teaching strategy, or advocating for positive change in your school. These goals remind you why you do what you do and give you something to look forward to.

Examples
- Set a goal to lead a workshop or training on a topic you're passionate about, such as resilience, mindfulness, or innovative teaching methods. This keeps you engaged and motivated while sharing your enthusiasm with others.
- Develop a goal to become a mentor to new educators, using your passion for teaching and leadership to support the next generation.

Here is a list of passions that people often identify as driving forces in their personal and professional lives. These can help inspire self-reflection and exploration.

Creative Passions
- Art (e.g., painting, drawing, sculpting)
- Writing (e.g., poetry, storytelling, journaling)
- Music (e.g., playing instruments, composing, singing)
- Photography or Videography
- Design (e.g., graphic, fashion, interior)
- Performing Arts (e.g., acting, dancing)
- Crafting or DIY Projects

Helping Passions
- Teaching or Mentoring
- Coaching or Guiding Others
- Volunteering for Social Causes
- Supporting Mental Health and Well-Being
- Advocating for Social Justice or Equity
- Community-Building or Organizing
- Providing Healthcare or Therapy

Intellectual Passions
- Reading and Literature
- Science and Discovery
- Technology and Innovation
- Philosophy and Critical Thinking
- History and Cultural Studies
- Problem-Solving or Puzzles
- Learning New Languages

Physical Passions
- Sports and Fitness
- Yoga and Meditation
- Outdoor Activities (e.g., hiking, camping)
- Travel and Exploration
- Gardening or Farming
- Cooking and Culinary Arts
- Martial Arts or Dance

Relational Passions
- Building Strong Relationships
- Raising and Supporting a Family
- Creating Safe and Inclusive Spaces
- Storytelling and Connection Through Shared Experiences
- Advocating for Children or Vulnerable Populations
- Networking and Building Professional Communities

Environmental and Global Passions
- Environmental Conservation
- Sustainable Living
- Animal Welfare
- Climate Advocacy
- Cultural Preservation
- Global Volunteering or Travel
- Wildlife Photography or Exploration

Spiritual Passions
- Practicing Faith or Spirituality
- Seeking Purpose and Meaning
- Meditation or Contemplative Practices
- Studying Sacred Texts or Philosophies
- Guiding Others on Spiritual Journeys
- Exploring Mysticism or Universal Connection

Miscellaneous Passions
- Entrepreneurship and Business
- Collecting (e.g., antiques, books)
- Gaming (e.g., video games, board games)
- Blogging or Podcasting
- Advocacy for Specific Groups or Interests
- Fashion and Personal Style
- Organizing and Productivity

Incorporate Hobbies and Interests Into Your Professional Life

One of the best ways to reconnect with your passion for teaching is to bring a little more *you* into the work. When your professional life reflects who you are outside of the classroom, everything feels more meaningful and, honestly, more fun. Your hobbies and interests aren't distractions from your role as an educator; they're powerful tools that can enhance your impact and keep you energized.

If you love storytelling, weave it into your lessons or share meaningful stories with your students or colleagues. If mindfulness or yoga is your thing, find moments to bring that into your day, whether it's a calming breath to start class, a short stretch break during a meeting, or just grounding yourself before a tough conversation. When we bring the things that light us up into our work, it shows and it's contagious.

If you're someone who loves art or crafting, think about designing interactive bulletin boards, inviting students or staff to create vision boards, or even leading a relaxed, after-school art night for staff. These small touches can brighten the environment and build connections.

If movement or fitness is something that fills your cup, you might start offering mini mindfulness breaks, movement moments during long meetings, or even model healthy habits in your classroom routine. These practices support well-being, for you *and* those around you.

It doesn't have to be complicated. Think of it as blending who you are with what you do. The more your work reflects the things that make you feel alive, the more sustainable and joyful it becomes.

Hobby-Driven Strategies
1. **Art and Design**
   - Create custom visuals for lessons, such as posters, infographics, or diagrams.
   - Incorporate student art projects that connect with your curriculum.
   - Use design apps or tools to make engaging presentations or classroom materials.
2. **Music and Performance**
   - Introduce songs or soundtracks that connect to your lessons or themes.
   - Write and perform educational songs or jingles.
   - Use rhythm or music breaks to energize or calm the classroom.
3. **Writing and Storytelling**
   - Share personal stories that relate to your lessons to make the material more relatable.
   - Encourage students to create their own narratives or write journals.
   - Create a blog or newsletter to share your teaching journey or classroom highlights.
4. **Cooking and Baking**
   - Integrate cooking or baking activities into lessons about culture, science, or math.
   - Use recipes to teach measurements, fractions, or chemistry.
   - Share healthy snacks with students or teach about nutrition.
5. **Photography and Videography**
   - Document classroom projects and activities with photos or videos.
   - Create short videos to introduce topics or concepts.
   - Teach students how to use photography or video for creative assignments.
6. **Sports and Fitness**
   - Include physical activities, stretches, or mindfulness breaks in your daily routine.
   - Organize team-building exercises or games related to your subject.
   - Promote sportsmanship and teamwork through class activities.

7. **Gardening and Nature**
   - Start a classroom garden to teach science, sustainability, or responsibility.
   - Use nature walks or outdoor activities as part of your lessons.
   - Decorate the classroom with plants or nature-themed elements.
8. **Mindfulness and Yoga**
   - Lead short mindfulness exercises or breathing techniques at the start of class.
   - Use yoga poses to teach balance, both physical and emotional.
   - Teach students strategies for managing stress and staying present.
9. **Gaming**
   - Design educational games based on your favorite board games or video games.
   - Gamify classroom activities to make learning more interactive.
10. **Travel and Culture**
    - Share stories, photos, or artifacts from your travels to inspire curiosity.
    - Incorporate cultural elements into lessons to broaden perspectives.
    - Create a classroom "passport" program to explore different countries and topics.
11. **DIY and Crafting**
    - Use crafting to make educational materials like models, maps, or props.
    - Offer hands-on projects for students to explore subjects creatively.
    - Host a "maker space" in your classroom for students to create and innovate.
12. **Technology and Coding**
    - Use coding activities or technology to teach problem-solving.
    - Incorporate tools like robotics or digital design software into your curriculum.
    - Teach students how to use apps or platforms to enhance their learning.
13. **Reading and Book Clubs**
    - Share your favorite books and how they shaped your thinking or teaching.
    - Start a book club with your students or colleagues.

- Use storytelling to create deeper connections with your subject matter.
14. **Comedy and Humor**
    - Use humor or improv games to make lessons more engaging.
    - Share funny anecdotes or create jokes related to your curriculum.
    - Teach students to use humor as a tool for resilience and connection.
15. **Volunteering and Service**
    - Organize service-learning projects that tie into your curriculum.
    - Share your passion for giving back by involving students in community work.
    - Use volunteer stories to illustrate real-world applications of classroom lessons.

Pause Here and Take a Moment to Reflect

Take a moment to think about what you already do, or what you could start doing, to keep your passion alive in your work. What's one strategy you use? For example, "I keep my passion alive by incorporating art into my lessons. I love creating visuals or hands-on projects that make learning come to life for my students." Jot down some ideas in the space provided.

Reconnect With Your Purpose: Vision Collage Activity

Looking for a creative way to get reconnected to your passion and purpose? Still feeling a little lost on your "why"? Need a creative pick-me-up to get back in touch with what lights you up? This activity is all about hitting pause, having a little fun, and making a visual reminder of what drives you. Whether you're feeling stuck or just want to recharge, a vision collage can bring your spark back.

Why It's Worth Doing

Resilience isn't about muscling through but about feeling grounded in what actually matters to you. When you're clear on your purpose, those tough days feel a little lighter. This activity helps you:

- **See Your "Why" Clearly:** Your goals and values, right there in front of you.
- **Boost Your Mood:** Focusing on what you want shifts your mindset toward the good stuff.
- **Chill Out:** Cutting, pasting, or clicking your way through this is surprisingly relaxing.
- **Stay Focused:** A visual of your goals keeps you on track when life gets hectic.
- **Reflect on Your Journey:** Where you've been, where you're headed, and what fuels you.
- **Create a Go-To Inspiration Spot:** Your collage becomes something you can return to whenever you need a pep talk.

What You'll Need
- **Digital Collage:** Canva, Google Slides, or PowerPoint
- **Handmade Collage:** Magazines, photos, doodles, scissors, glue/tape, and a board or big piece of paper

How to Do It
1. **Start by Reflecting (Yes, Before the Scissors Come Out)**
   Grab a notebook or just think it through:
   - What parts of your work make you feel alive?
   - Why did you choose this profession, and what still excites you?
   - What strengths do you bring to the table?
   - What does your "best self" look like at work (or in life) a year from now? Five years?
   - What kind of relationships, balance, and impact do you want?

2. **Gather Your Inspiration**
   Hunt down images, quotes, colors, and words that capture what matters most to you.
   - *Digital*: Search online or explore Canva templates.
   - *Handmade*: Grab magazines, print photos, or draw your own touches.
3. **Make Your Collage**
   - *Digital*: Drag and drop your images into Canva or Slides. Add words, colors, or notes.
   - *Handmade*: Arrange your pieces on your board or paper. Play with the layout until it feels like *you*. Add doodles or personal notes to make it pop.

There's no right or wrong way to do this. It's all about creating something that reminds you of your purpose and keeps you inspired. Hang it up, glance at it when you need a boost, and let it nudge you back toward what matters when things get messy.

Manifesting a Purpose-Driven Teaching Life

This chapter is about more than reconnecting with your "why." It's about giving you brain-based tools to move from feeling drained and reactive to teaching and living with intention. The strategies here aren't wishful thinking; they're rooted in neuroscience, showing why practices like visualization, gratitude, and manifestation can be powerful in helping us reset, realign, and sustain our resilience.

Why It Matters

Teaching can sometimes feel like you're spinning plates while riding a unicycle. Purpose is what keeps us from tipping over. When we reconnect with our "why," it grounds us and fuels our motivation, clarity, and emotional strength. And, as research shows, the way we think and feel doesn't just shift our mood, it literally reshapes our brain (Doty, 2016).

In this section, we'll explore the science of manifestation not as some "think it and it will magically appear" gimmick but as a way to train your mind and heart to align with the educator, leader, and human you want to be. What we focus on, believe, and emotionally connect to shapes how we see the world and how we show up in it.

The Science Behind It

Stanford neurosurgeon Dr. Jim Doty (2016), founder of the Center for Compassion and Altruism Research and Education (CCARE), reminds us that manifestation is really about mental conditioning, not magic. Here's what his research highlights:

- The brain can be rewired through intention, repetition, and compassion.
- Emotional connection, especially love and gratitude, is essential for a meaningful life.
- Success feels empty without purpose; when heart and purpose are aligned, life feels whole.
- Your brain is shaped by what you focus on. Visualization activates the same neural networks as real experiences.
- Repetition, emotional engagement, and belief strengthen neural pathways for lasting change.
- You don't manifest what you *want*; you manifest what you *believe* and deeply feel (Doty, 2016).
- Practices like gratitude, intention-setting, and service can shift your brain from fear mode into growth mode (Doty, 2024).

Your Brain on Manifestation

Manifestation works because our brains are plastic. They change in response to thought, experience, and emotion. When we ruminate on fear or self-doubt, we activate the amygdala, our fear center, which shuts down creativity, confidence, and problem-solving. Visualization helps reverse this.

When you vividly imagine your future self, that is, what you're doing, how it feels, and why it matters, and pair that with emotions like gratitude or excitement, your brain fires as if it's already happening. This not only boosts motivation but actually lays down the neural pathways that help you become that version of yourself (Doty, 2016).

Athletes, surgeons, and performers use visualization to build confidence, sharpen focus, and enhance performance. Educators can use it, too, to feel calmer before class, to connect more meaningfully, or to simply remind ourselves that we're more than our to-do lists.

Doty (2016) suggests starting simply:

1. **Find Stillness:** A few grounding breaths are enough.
2. **Visualize Your Future Self:** Focus on how it feels, not just the checklist of accomplishments.
3. **Feel Gratitude:** Imagine your goals as if they're already unfolding.

4. **Let Go of the "How":** Your job isn't to micromanage every step. It's to align your energy and actions.

Heart Mode vs. Fear Mode

Doty (2016) also describes two states we operate from: *Heart Mode* and *Fear Mode*. I've lived in both.

- **Fear Mode** feels like my chest is tight, my thoughts are racing, and I'm bracing for the next problem, almost like waiting for a bear to pounce. It's often triggered by stress or the pressure to control everything. That's my amygdala talking.
- **Heart Mode** feels like a deep breath. It's calm, open, and connected. This mode activates the prefrontal cortex and vagus nerve, allowing for empathy, creativity, and better decision-making.

I often ask myself: *Which mode am I in right now?* In Fear Mode, I'm reactive, snappy, or hyper-focused on small tasks. In Heart Mode, I'm smiling, connecting, pausing, and leading with intention.

Tools for the Shift

Here's what helps me and is backed by neuroscience (Doty, 2024):

- **Gratitude:** Boosts dopamine and serotonin, rewires the brain, and helps move us out of fight-or-flight.
- **Visualization:** Activates the same neural pathways as lived experience, helping us believe, and act on, new possibilities.
- **Service:** Helping others activates our brain's compassion systems, shrinking fear and boosting purpose.
- **Self-Compassion and Stillness:** Practices like loving-kindness meditation open the heart and reduce reactivity.

Why It Matters for Educators

These tools aren't just personal, they're contagious. We can model Heart Mode for students, colleagues, and our communities. Starting class with a gratitude check-in, leading staff meetings with an intention, or guiding students through future-self visualizations can shift the tone from "What's wrong?" to "What's possible?"

And maybe, most importantly, these practices help us remember: Resilience isn't about white-knuckling through. It's about rooting ourselves in something deeper, our heart, our purpose, and the belief that we can create a life and career that feel whole.

Pause Here and Take a Moment to Reflect

What does Fear Mode feel like for you (tight chest, racing thoughts, irritability, self-doubt)? What instances tend to put you in Fear Mode?

What does Heart Mode feel like for you (calm body, open thinking, empathy, aligned decisions)? How can you intentionally put yourself in Heart Mode?

Gratitude is one of the most powerful tools I use to help make that shift. Neuroscience backs this up. Gratitude increases dopamine and serotonin, rewires the brain, and helps move us out of fight-or-flight and into calm, creative presence (Doty, 2024). Even simple practices make a difference. I've started jotting down one thing I'm grateful for each morning and setting an intention like, *Today I will stay present* or *Today I'll give myself grace.* Sticky notes, journaling, even just repeating a mantra aloud in the mirror all help build those neural pathways. I've used a gratitude board with students and a "Three Good Things" practice with colleagues. These rituals don't just lift the mood. They anchor us in something deeper.

Visualization is another game changer. Doty (2024) talks about how imagining your ideal self or future activates the same neural pathways as actually experiencing it. When I picture myself walking into my classroom feeling calm, prepared, and respected, it gives me a roadmap. I think about what would need to change to make that vision real, both internally and externally. One of the most powerful exercises I've done is writing a note from my future self to my present self: encouraging, grounding, and full of love. That version of me has boundaries, purpose, and presence. She also reminds me that change takes time and intention.

Service is also central to this shift. When I focus on helping others, whether it's a student, a colleague, my own family, or the community, I notice that fear and scarcity shrink. Helping someone else taps into something bigger. Doty says that the brain is wired for compassion, and being of service actually supports our own growth and well-being. I often turn to a loving-kindness meditation when I'm struggling. I picture someone who's having a hard time and silently repeat: *May you be safe. May you be supported. May you find peace.* And then I turn that same compassion inward.

Although Doty's work is grounded in neuroscience, he also acknowledges something more: spirituality, meaning, and surrender. I've had those moments, too: when life brings clarity through stillness or when love shows up just when I need it. It reminds me that this work, that is, choosing the heart, isn't just brain science. It's soul work, too.

For educators, the implications are profound. We can model this shift in our classrooms, our staff meetings, and our relationships. Whether it's starting the day with a gratitude check-in or using visualization to help students imagine their future selves, we're creating environments where heart-centered leadership is the norm and not the exception. Instead of asking *what's wrong*, we can start asking *what's possible?* Instead of thinking about the *worst case scenario*, let's start thinking about the *best case scenario*!

Pause Here and Take a Moment to Reflect

> *How do these ideas resonate with you? Do you currently participate in gratitude, visualization, or service? If so, how? If not, are you open to trying?*

Guided Visualization: Your Ideal Teaching Life

Purpose
Visualization activates the same neural pathways as real experiences (Doty, 2024). It helps rewire the brain toward desired outcomes and builds emotional clarity around purpose. Visualization creates a mental blueprint. It primes your brain for what's possible.

Imagine
"You walk into your classroom. You feel grounded, prepared, and present. Your students greet you warmly. You feel connected, not rushed. Your boundaries are respected. You have time for planning, breathing, and connection. What does your ideal day look like? How do you feel? What supports are in place?"

Pause Here and Take a Moment to Reflect

What did you notice about your ideal environment?

What elements could be brought into your current routine?

What would need to shift, externally or internally, to make that happen?

What stood out to you?

What small element from your vision could you bring into tomorrow?

What internal shifts would make that more likely?

Future-Self Visualization

Future-Self Visualization encourages alignment with long-term goals and ideal identity.

Picture yourself one year from now. You're rested, centered, fulfilled. What habits helped you get there? How do you talk to yourself? Who are you surrounded by? What do you want to thank your present self for doing today?

Pause Here and Take a Moment to Reflect

Write a note from your future self to your current self, offering encouragement, clarity, and love.

Draw yourself sitting quietly outside. Add your face, your clothes, your hair . . . What surrounds you? How is the weather? Get creative with your artwork.

Figure 5.1 Draw Yourself Page

Guided Meditation: Reconnecting With Your Purpose

Sit in a comfortable position and close your eyes. Take a deep breath in and slowly exhale. Let your body relax and your mind become still.

Think about why you became an educator. Visualize a moment when you felt truly passionate and inspired in your teaching. Allow yourself to fully experience the emotions of that moment.

Focus on the positive impact you've had on your students and the difference you've made in their lives. Visualize their faces, their progress, and their gratitude. Silently affirm your purpose: "I am making a positive impact. My work is meaningful. I am passionate about teaching."

Feel the passion and purpose filling your heart, reigniting your motivation and enthusiasm. Know that every day, you are making a difference. When you're ready, open your eyes, carrying this sense of purpose and passion with you into your work.

Key Takeaways

- Your purpose is not your job title, it's the impact you create.
- Passion needs protection. Burnout isn't a lack of dedication; it's the result of sustained overload.
- Reconnecting to your "why" can help realign your "how."
- Purpose evolves, so give yourself permission to grow with it.

Closing Message

I know this work is *hard*. It's messy. It's imperfect. And some days, it's enough to make you question if you even want to keep going. I've been there.

But here's the thing: when we give ourselves permission to *reset*, to step back from the pressure of perfection and remember *why* we do this work in the first place, something shifts.

It's not about having all the answers. It's not about proving ourselves to anyone else. It's about showing up with heart, with care, and with a commitment to learning and growing alongside the people we serve.

You are allowed to let go of what no longer serves you.
You are allowed to evolve.
You are allowed to write your next chapter on your own terms.

So take a breath. Let go of the noise. And remember your *why*. Because when you lead with heart, not fear, you create the space for something truly extraordinary.

Chapter 5 Notes

Engage and Reflect

What inspired you to become an educator, and what keeps you passionate about teaching?

How do you stay motivated and connected to your professional purpose during challenging times?

Can you share a moment when you felt truly passionate and fulfilled in your teaching career?

What are some strategies you use to reignite your passion for teaching?

How do you set and achieve professional goals that align with your core values?

What role does personal growth and professional development play in maintaining your passion for teaching?

How can you create a balance between your professional purpose and personal life?

What are some ways to celebrate and acknowledge your achievements and progress in your teaching career?

Find your Purpose

References

Doty, J. R. (2016). *Into the magic shop: A neurosurgeon's quest to discover the mysteries of the brain and the secrets of the heart.* Avery.

Doty, J. R. (2024). *Mind magic: The neuroscience of manifestation and the art of changing your life.* Avery.

6

Adaptive Thinking and Problem-Solving Skills

> **Focus:** Enhancing adaptive thinking and problem-solving skills.
>
> **Content:** Techniques for developing creative problem-solving strategies and learning how to stay flexible and resilient in the face of challenges.
>
> Adaptive thinking and problem-solving skills are essential for navigating challenges. This chapter equips educators with creativity and flexibility, transforming unexpected situations into opportunities. It's like "Survivor: Classroom Edition" but with more solutions and less drama.

The Late-Work Problem

Let me tell you about a challenge that pushed me to think differently, even when my "brilliant" ideas did not go as planned.

Last year, I noticed a pattern with end-of-term classwork submissions. As deadlines approached, a wave of late work arrived all at once. Managing it took real time and focus. I was tracking missing pieces, grading, updating scores across systems, and trying to communicate clearly with students and other staff. It was a lot, and it also created an imbalance for students who had already turned things in.

So I tried something new. I set a clear boundary. Late work could be submitted for one week after the due date. After that, assignments would expire. I thought this would spread out the workload, encourage steady progress, and keep things fair.

Spoiler alert: it did not work.

Some students still needed more time, especially near graduation. School policies and timelines rightly aim to support students in meeting requirements, so flexibility was still needed. The reality is that everyone was working toward the same goal, and my single change could not account for all the moving parts.

Here is what I learned. Problem-solving is rarely about a perfect fix on the first try. It is about testing an idea, seeing what actually happens, and adjusting. My brilliant idea was not a failure. It was a data point.

I had to go back to the drawing board, but not alone. I invited students to help design a system that feels clear, doable, and fair. I am also checking in with colleagues and aligning with school expectations so the plan matches the support structures we already have.

That is adaptive thinking in real life. Try. Learn. Tweak. Repeat. And keep the door open for collaboration.

Pause Here and Take a Moment to Reflect

> *What's a problem in your teaching (or life) where your "brilliant" solution didn't quite work, and how can you adapt and try again?*

Establishing Relevance

Why Problem-Solving Matters

Problem-solving is a critical skill in every aspect of life. Whether in the classroom, workplace, or personal situations, challenges are inevitable. The ability to approach these challenges with creativity and adaptive thinking empowers us to find effective solutions, reducing stress and fostering a sense of control. In the context of education, problem-solving is especially relevant because of the dynamic nature of teaching, where unexpected situations arise daily.

Connection to Resilience

Resilience is the capacity to recover and thrive despite adversity. Problem-solving is a core component of resilience because it enables individuals to face challenges head-on, identify actionable solutions, and adapt to changing circumstances. When we practice adaptive thinking and problem-solving, we build the mental flexibility needed to stay calm under pressure, reframe obstacles as opportunities, and persist in the face of setbacks.

Mastering These Skills Ensures
1. **Better Student Outcomes:** Adapting teaching strategies to meet diverse learning needs.
2. **Workplace Harmony:** Resolving conflicts with colleagues or students effectively.
3. **Personal Well-Being:** Minimizing burnout by addressing stressors proactively.

This chapter's focus equips participants with strategies that can be applied immediately, such as practicing creative brainstorming. These tools are not just professional assets but life skills that enhance relationships, reduce stress, and foster a more positive and resilient outlook. In essence, problem-solving isn't just about finding solutions; it's about empowering yourself to thrive no matter what comes your way.

Pause Here and Take a Moment to Reflect

> *Teachers make an extraordinary number of decisions each day, an estimated 1,500–3,000. Take a moment to write down some of the decisions you make during your first 10 minutes after you arrive at school.*

Decision-Making

As teachers, we make thousands of decisions every day, with some big, some small, but all of them important. These decisions span across several categories, and recognizing them can help us reflect more intentionally on our practice.

We start with instructional decisions, which are often at the heart of our daily work. These include figuring out what content to prioritize, when to adjust the pacing of a lesson, and whether to reteach a concept or move forward. It's that constant dance between curriculum goals and student understanding.

Then there's classroom management, including the decisions that keep the room running smoothly. We decide how to handle disruptions, which seating arrangements work best for our group, and how to make transitions less chaotic and more meaningful. These choices shape the tone of the learning environment more than we often realize.

Student support decisions come into play when we notice a student is struggling, whether academically, emotionally, or behaviorally. We decide when to step in, how to adapt instruction to meet diverse needs, and what kind of support might make the biggest difference for a particular child. It's the human side of our job and often the most rewarding and complex.

On the more practical end, we're also responsible for a lot of administrative and logistical decisions, like taking attendance, managing paperwork, and coordinating with colleagues. These are often the behind-the-scenes decisions that keep everything moving, even when no one else sees them.

And finally, there are the relational and ethical choices we make every day. These might involve building trust with students and coworkers or navigating sensitive conversations with families. These decisions are rarely easy, but they speak volumes about our values and our ability to lead with empathy and integrity.

When we pause to recognize just how many decisions we make and how varied they are, it becomes clear that teaching isn't just about delivering content but about managing complexity with care, flexibility, and heart.

Impact of Decision-Making

Teaching isn't just about planning lessons or managing a classroom. It's about making numerous decisions every day, often on the fly and under pressure. From choosing how to respond to a student's question to deciding how to support a child in crisis, the mental load is real. This constant stream of choices leads to what researchers call "decision fatigue." It's the reason we sometimes feel completely drained by lunchtime, even if nothing major has gone wrong.

Decision fatigue can affect our well-being, our patience, and even our clarity. It wears down our ability to be creative, compassionate, and calm, which are all things we need in order to teach effectively. Over time, this can lead to stress, burnout, and that "numb autopilot" mode that so many educators know too well. And yet, even while juggling it all, we're still expected to stay focused on the big picture: supporting student growth, building relationships, and helping kids feel safe and seen.

That's why we need more than just grit or good intentions. We need strategies. We need tools that help us slow down our thinking, clarify what really matters, and make choices that align with our values and goals. The good news? Those tools exist. The next section offers a set of research-based problem-solving techniques designed to help you navigate both everyday challenges and the more complex ones that come with this work. They'll help you explore root causes, consider multiple perspectives, and generate meaningful, workable solutions without getting stuck in overwhelm or self-doubt.

We're not just decision-makers. We're solution seekers, caregivers, and leaders. And with the right tools, we can do all of that with a little more clarity, confidence, and heart.

The "5 Whys" Technique

One of my favorite problem-solving tools, because it's so simple but so powerful, is the "5 Whys" technique. It was originally developed by Sakichi Toyoda, the founder of Toyota Industries, and it's all about getting to the root of a problem by asking "why" over and over again. The idea is that most of the time, what we think is the problem is really just a symptom. If we keep digging, typically by asking "why" five times, we can uncover what's actually driving the issue. For example, let's say we're noticing that parent engagement is low. First why: Why aren't parents engaging? Because they don't attend events. Next why: Why don't they attend? Because they feel disconnected. Why? Because communication is inconsistent. Why? Because there's no system in place. Why? Because no one is assigned to manage it. Suddenly, we've moved from a surface-level complaint to a really clear root cause: We need a dedicated communication strategy and someone to own it. This method is so effective because it helps us stop chasing symptoms and, instead, solve the real problem. I use it with students, with teams, and even in my own life when something feels stuck. It's a tool that creates clarity, and clarity is something we all need more of.

Mind Mapping

Another great tool I turn to when I feel overwhelmed or stuck is Mind Mapping. It's a visual way to untangle complex issues and get everything out of your head and onto paper where you can actually see the big picture. Popularized by Tony Buzan (2018), mind mapping starts with a central idea or challenge in the middle of the page, and then you branch outward with related ideas, options, or strategies (refer to Figure 6.1). I love this method because it helps me organize my thoughts without the pressure of making them linear or "perfect." For example, if I'm thinking about how to improve classroom engagement, I might start by writing that phrase in the center. From there, I branch out. One branch for interactive activities like group projects or games, another for tech integration like using apps or virtual field trips, and another for feedback systems like student surveys. Each idea expands into sub-ideas, and before I know it, I've created a roadmap full of creative solutions. I've also used this for planning events, like a school open house. I'd write "Open House" in the middle, then branch out into categories like presentations, tours, parent engagement, and logistics, with details under each. What's great about mind mapping is that it gives you a bird's-eye view. You can spot gaps, find connections, and get clear on what matters most. Whether I'm lesson planning or brainstorming for a workshop, this tool always helps me move from scattered to structured.

The "Six Thinking Hats" Method

When I'm faced with a tough decision, ,especially one that involves multiple people or perspectives, I like to use Edward de Bono's Six Thinking Hats method. It's a playful yet powerful way to break out of one-track thinking and look at a problem from all angles. Each "hat" represents a different lens you can use to explore a challenge, and it's especially helpful in group settings where everyone tends to have a different take anyway.

Here's how it works:

- **White Hat:** Focuses on the facts and data. What do we know? What information is still missing?
- **Red Hat:** Brings in feelings, gut reactions, and emotions. What are people feeling, even if they can't explain why?
- **Yellow Hat:** Looks at the bright side. What are the potential benefits or reasons for optimism?
- **Black Hat:** Offers a reality check. What could go wrong? What are the risks?

- **Green Hat:** Sparks creativity. What new ideas, alternatives, or out-of-the-box solutions can we try?
- **Blue Hat:** Manages the process. Who's keeping us on track, summarizing ideas, and making sure everyone is heard?

Let's say we're debating a new grading policy. We might use the hats like this:

- **White Hat:** The data shows the current system is inconsistent.
- **Red Hat:** Teachers feel frustrated and burned out. Students are anxious.
- **Black Hat:** There's a risk that some students might exploit more flexible deadlines.
- **Yellow Hat:** Clearer expectations could lead to more fairness and trust.
- **Green Hat:** Maybe we can use an app or platform to streamline grading.
- **Blue Hat:** Let's collect these perspectives and build an action plan.

Or maybe we're trying to figure out how to boost community involvement at school events:

- **White Hat:** Past attendance has been low, especially at evening events.
- **Red Hat:** Families might feel disconnected or unsure if they're truly welcome.
- **Yellow Hat:** Increasing engagement could strengthen school-community ties.
- **Black Hat:** Timing, transportation, and childcare are possible barriers.
- **Green Hat:** Could we try hybrid events or offer food and raffles as incentives?
- **Blue Hat:** Let's prioritize one small pilot event and evaluate its impact.

What I love about this method is that it gives everyone a seat at the table: logic, emotion, creativity, and structure. It helps me slow down and really consider every layer of a situation before jumping to conclusions. And honestly, sometimes putting on a "hat" just makes a hard conversation feel a little more manageable.

SWOT Analysis

When I want to take a step back and look at the big picture, I turn to a SWOT Analysis. Originally developed by Albert Humphrey during a Stanford research project in the 1960s, this approach is still one of the most practical tools out there for evaluating a situation and making a solid game plan. SWOT stands for *strengths, weaknesses, opportunities*, and *threats*, and it's especially helpful when I'm making a strategic decision or trying to improve a program, project, or process.

Here's how it breaks down:

- **Strengths** are the internal positives. Consider what's already working in your favor? Think of resources, skills, or a strong culture.
- **Weaknesses** are the internal challenges or gaps that could get in the way.
- **Opportunities** are external positives, such as trends, partnerships, or new tools you could take advantage of.
- **Threats** are the external challenges, like competition, resistance, or limited support.

Let's say I'm trying to improve team collaboration at work. I might identify our strengths as having a skilled and supportive staff, while our weakness could be not having a consistent communication system. An opportunity might be new collaboration tools we could adopt, and a threat could be staff resistance to learning something new.

Another example: launching an after-school tutoring program. Our strengths could be passionate, qualified tutors and a central location. Weaknesses might include limited funding or a small team. As for opportunities, maybe there's growing demand in the community for academic support. But there could also be threats, like other competing programs that already exist nearby.

What I love about SWOT is that it gives structure to big decisions. It helps you see both what you're working with and what you're up against, so your action plan is grounded in reality, not just hope. It's a great way to make sure you're playing to your strengths while planning ahead for potential bumps in the road.

Brainstorming

Sometimes the best ideas come when we simply give ourselves permission to think freely, without judgment or pressure to be "right." That's the heart of brainstorming, a technique introduced by advertising executive Alex

Osborn in the 1950s. His idea was simple but powerful: If we stop criticizing ideas too early, we make more space for creativity and collaboration. Brainstorming is all about generating as many ideas as possible before narrowing them down.

To get started, you clearly define the problem or goal, then set a few ground rules: no criticism, all ideas are welcome, and the wilder the better. You can have participants speak their ideas aloud or write them down, whatever works best for your group. After the brainstorming session, take time to review and evaluate which ideas are most realistic or worth pursuing.

Let's say you're trying to boost participation in your after-school program. Some ideas might include offering free snacks, expanding the variety of activities, adjusting the hours, or even adding parent incentives. Or maybe you're planning a school fundraiser, and brainstorming might bring up everything from bake sales and book fairs to talent shows and car washes. After gathering all the ideas, the group could vote or rank which ones are most doable and appealing (like the book fair or talent show).

The beauty of brainstorming is that it opens up the conversation. It encourages fresh thinking, gets everyone involved, and builds momentum toward real solutions, especially when we follow up with thoughtful evaluation and action.

Role-Playing

Rooted in psychology and education, role-playing was pioneered by Jacob L. Moreno as a way to explore human behavior through action and perspective-taking. In a school setting, it becomes a powerful tool for building empathy and sharpening communication skills. When we step into someone else's shoes, even just for a few minutes, we start to understand the problem through a new lens.

The process is simple but effective: Assign roles based on the issue at hand (maybe a teacher, a student, a parent, or an administrator), act out a relevant scenario, and then reflect together on what was learned. For example, if you're trying to understand why students seem disengaged during virtual learning, you might have one person play a student, another a teacher, and a third a parent. Through the activity, you might realize students are overwhelmed by distractions and families could benefit from clearer guidance.

Another common use is practicing tough conversations, like parent-teacher conferences. One teacher takes the role of the parent, the other the teacher, and together they practice navigating concerns about a student's low grades. This kind of low-stakes rehearsal builds confidence and helps teachers develop strategies for real-life challenges.

Role-playing is more than acting. It's about pausing to ask, "What does this feel like for someone else?" It gives us space to think through problems, test out responses, and ultimately grow into more compassionate and effective educators.

SCAMPER Method

SCAMPER is a great tool for when I feel stuck and need a fresh perspective. Created by Bob Eberle, this strategy helps generate new ideas by tweaking or transforming something that already exists. Instead of starting from scratch, it nudges us to ask thoughtful questions that unlock creativity and innovation.

SCAMPER is actually an acronym where each letter stands for a different way to shift your thinking. Substitute asks, "What can I swap out or replace?" Combine invites us to merge ideas or elements for something better. Adapt encourages making adjustments to fit different needs. Modify helps us think about how something might be altered, enhanced, or exaggerated. Put to another use stretches us to repurpose an idea or resource. Eliminate asks what might be simplified or removed, and Reverse flips the whole thing on its head to consider the opposite approach.

Let's say we're trying to improve participation in the school lunch program. Using SCAMPER, we might substitute processed foods with locally sourced ingredients or combine a meal and a healthy snack into a combo deal. We could adapt recipes for allergies or cultural preferences, modify the cafeteria space to make it more inviting, or put it to another use like hosting nutrition education during lunch. Maybe we eliminate low-demand items and replace them with better options, or reverse the process entirely by offering pre-ordered, personalized meal plans.

SCAMPER helps break us out of the "this is how we've always done it" mindset. It's playful, practical, and a great way to problem-solve with a creative twist.

Reverse Brainstorming

Sometimes the best way to fix a problem is to first figure out how to make it worse. It sounds backwards, but that's the point. Reverse brainstorming turns traditional problem-solving on its head. Instead of immediately trying to come up with solutions, you start by intentionally identifying what would *intensify* the issue. Then, by flipping those "worst-case" ideas, you uncover creative and often overlooked solutions. This method is rooted in innovation strategies and outlined in Michael Michalko's *Thinkertoys*.

Here's how it works: First, define the problem you're trying to solve. Then ask a bold question: "How could we make this worse?" List out every possible way to tank the situation. Don't hold back. Once you've got a good list of worst-case strategies, reverse them to find constructive actions.

For example, if the goal is to improve student engagement, the reverse brainstorm might start with: "Make it worse? Easy! Lecture nonstop, ignore questions, eliminate all group work." Flip those around and you've got solid solutions: bring in more interactive activities, include movement, prioritize small group discussions, and use real-time feedback tools.

Reverse brainstorming is great when you're stuck or when the usual ideas just aren't cutting it. It allows for a little humor, a shift in thinking, and a chance to challenge assumptions, exactly what we need when we're trying to move from frustration to innovation.

Applying Problem-Solving Techniques to a Common Classroom Challenge

Let's take a challenge many of us have faced—students turning in assignments late—and apply several problem-solving strategies to it. These tools don't just help us find band-aid fixes. They offer structured ways to get to the heart of an issue, brainstorm meaningfully, and develop solutions that are realistic, creative, and sustainable.

The "5 Whys" Technique
This strategy helps us dig deep. By asking "Why?" five times, we move past surface-level assumptions and uncover the real root of a problem. For example, if students are turning in assignments late, we might discover that it's not laziness. Rather, it's a lack of time management skills. They weren't taught how to plan ahead or break big tasks into smaller parts. And we, as teachers, might not consistently teach these skills either. Once we identify that root cause, we can act: build time management into our lessons, hold mini-workshops, or guide students through planners and digital tools.

Mind Mapping
Mind mapping works when I need to untangle a problem that has a lot of layers. Starting with "late assignments" in the center, I might branch out into causes like procrastination or overwhelming workloads, then move into possible solutions such as rubrics, visual schedules, reminder apps. It's a way to

get all the messy pieces out in the open so we can spot connections, gaps, and easy wins. For me, seeing it laid out visually makes it feel less overwhelming and more actionable.

Six Thinking Hats

Edward de Bono's Six Thinking Hats helps us explore a problem from all sides, looking at facts, feelings, risks, benefits, wild ideas, and process. When I use this with colleagues, I'm often surprised by what emerges. For example, a student turning in work late might not be just a "red hat" (emotion = stressed) or "black hat" (risk = bad grades). The "green hat" might lead us to try peer accountability or creative reward systems, while the "blue hat" reminds us to step back and plan how we'll evaluate what works. It gives us a full, balanced view.

SWOT Analysis

Sometimes, I like to take a bird's-eye view. SWOT (strengths, weaknesses, opportunities, threats) analysis helps me assess what's working, what's not, and where the possibilities and roadblocks lie. If kids are turning in assignments late, our strength might be their motivation in other areas. The weakness? They don't have systems in place to manage tasks. The opportunity could be embedding executive functioning into advisory time. The threat? Resistance from students, or even parents, who aren't used to change. This analysis helps me plan intentionally, not reactively.

Brainstorming

This one's a classic for a reason. Gather your team, state the problem, and let the ideas fly, without judgment. When I've done this with colleagues, we've come up with everything from "assignment progress check-ins" to "flexible grace windows" to "letting students co-set goals." Once you've got the ideas, sort through them later to pick the most feasible. It's energizing and collaborative.

Role-Playing

When I've felt stuck, role-playing has helped me see the problem from the student's or parent's point of view. In a scenario about late assignments, playing the role of a stressed-out student made me realize how vague some of my directions were. As the parent, I noticed how hard it was to support my child without knowing what was expected. It's a powerful, low-stakes way to build empathy and uncover communication breakdowns.

SCAMPER Method

SCAMPER is like a creativity spark plug. You take the existing situation, for example, students submitting work late, and run it through prompts: What could I **Substitute**? Maybe smaller, more frequent tasks. **Combine**? Gamify deadlines with a fun reward system. **Adapt**? Use tech tools they already love. **Modify**? Change submission formats. **Put to another use**? Turn peer review into deadline motivation. **Eliminate**? Ditch harsh penalties. **Reverse**? Let students suggest due dates. This method reminds me that I can bend the rules of the system in thoughtful ways to better meet everyone's needs.

Reverse Brainstorming

When I really want to shake things up, I ask, "How could we make this problem worse?" It feels counterintuitive, but it's effective. For late assignments, I might say, "Let's eliminate all deadlines, remove structure, and never give feedback." Suddenly, the fixes are obvious: clear expectations, flexible structure, supportive check-ins. This strategy flips the pressure off perfection and invites humor, honesty, and clarity.

Each of these tools offers a different lens, but, together, they form a practical toolkit for tackling classroom challenges. And while no strategy is a silver bullet, using them consistently can help us move from frustration to action, and from stuck to solution-oriented.

Now It Is Your Turn to Practice

How would you solve one of the following problems? Do you have another problem that needs to be solved? You may want to use one of the blank templates on the following pages.

- Low parent engagement in school events.
- High levels of burnout among teachers or staff.
- Ineffective communication among team members.
- Lack of participation in professional development sessions.
- Resistance to new technology or teaching methods.
- A high turnover rate among staff in your workplace.
- Limited access to community resources for clients.
- Students struggling with focus during virtual learning.
- Conflicts between staff members over workloads.

The 5 Whys Technique

Problem Statement: _____
_____

Feelings Check-In (Optional): _____
_____

Strengths I Bring: _____
_____

The 5 Whys Reflection:

1. Why? _____
_____

2. Why? _____
_____

3. Why? _____
_____

4. Why? _____
_____

5. Why? _____
_____

Root Cause Identified: _____
_____
_____
_____

Action: _____
_____
_____
_____

Mind Mapping
   Problem Statement: _____
   _____
   Feelings Check-In (Optional): _____
   _____
   Strengths I Bring: _____
   _____

Possible Solutions:
   Action: _____
   _____

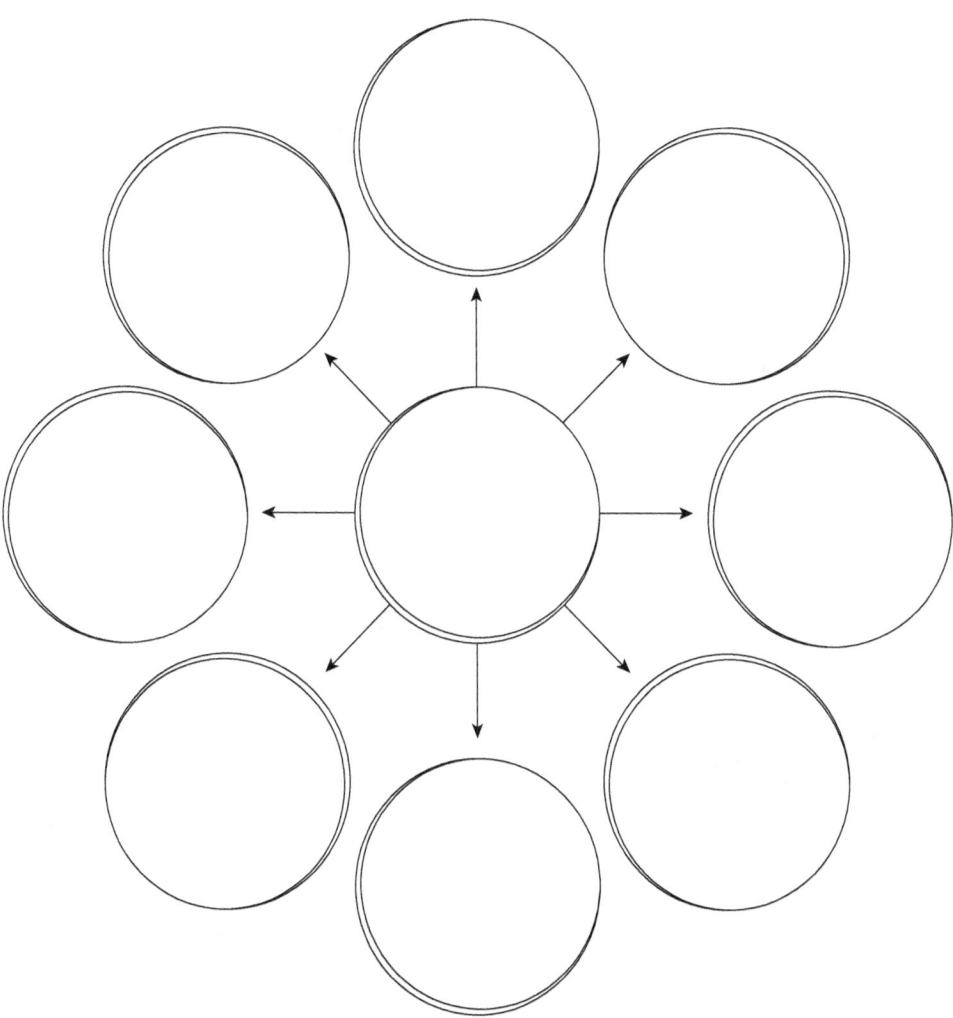

Figure 6.1 Brainstorm

Six Thinking Hats
   Problem Statement: _____
   _____
   Feelings Check-In (Optional): _____
   _____
   Strengths I Bring: _____
   _____

Hat	Perspective	Key Insights
White Hat	Facts and Data	
Red Hat	Emotions and Feelings	
Yellow Hat	Benefits and Positives	
Black Hat	Risks and Challenges	
Green Hat	Creative Solutions	
Blue Hat	Process and Reflection	

   Action: _____
   _____

SWOT Analysis
   Problem Statement: _____
   _____

Strengths	Weaknesses

Opportunities	Threats

   Action: _____
   _____

Brainstorming

Problem Statement: _____
_____
_____

Feelings Check-In: _____
Strengths I Bring: _____
Ideas and Solutions:

- _____
- _____
- _____
- _____
- _____
- _____
- _____
- _____
- _____

Action: _____
_____
_____
_____

Reverse Brainstorming

Problem Statement: _____
_____

How Could We Make This Worse?

- _____
- _____
- _____
- _____
- _____
- _____

Flip to Solutions:

- _____
- _____
- _____
- _____
- _____
- _____

Action: _____
_____
_____

SCAMPER Method

Problem Statement: _____
Feelings Check-In: _____

SCAMPER Technique	Ideas/Adaptation
Substitute	
Combine	
Adapt	
Modify	
Put to Another Use	
Eliminate	
Reverse	

Action: _____
_____

Keeping Your Brain Active: A Key to Resilience

What Do You Do to Keep Your Brain Active? Here Are Some Activities to Consider

- Solve a puzzle.
- Read a new word.
- Listen to a podcast or audiobook.
- Learn a new skill.
- Have a deep conversation.
- Write with your non-dominant hand.
- Sketch or doodle.
- Do a physical activity with coordination.
- Set and achieve small goals.
- Read something new.
- Play a strategy goal.
- Try a new recipe.
- Engage in mental math.
- Meditate or practice mindfulness.
- Challenge negative thoughts.
- Laugh and have fun.

A strong and resilient mind thrives on continuous learning and engagement. Keeping your brain active through games, problem-solving activities, and learning new skills helps build cognitive flexibility, enhances emotional regulation, and improves overall well-being. Activities like puzzles, strategy games, reading, and creative challenges stimulate neural pathways, reduce stress, and strengthen adaptability, which are all essential components of resilience. Just as we exercise our bodies to stay strong, we must challenge our minds to remain sharp and resilient in the face of adversity.

Pause Here and Take a Moment to Reflect

> *Make a list of things YOU enjoy doing to keep your brain active. What can you add to your list?*

Mental Agility

Mental agility helps you pivot instead of panic.

Think about the last time something unexpected knocked you sideways. Maybe it was a last-minute schedule change, a tough conversation, or one of those days where nothing seems to go right. Did you freeze up? Or did you manage to roll with it, even if it wasn't pretty?

Mental agility isn't about pretending everything's fine. It's about staying flexible, getting creative, and asking, "What now?" instead of, "Why me?" When you can shift your perspective, those frustrating roadblocks start looking more like speed bumps and, sometimes, like detours leading to something better.

Researchers have found that this kind of flexibility actually builds resilience. Genet and Siemer (2011) discovered that people who can switch perspectives and adapt quickly tend to bounce back faster from stress. Carol Dweck (2016) also reminds us that when we see challenges as lessons instead of personal failures, we don't just survive, but we grow. And when we practice reframing, that is, choosing to see a setback as a problem to solve rather than a dead end, it can lower stress and spark new ideas (Troy et al., 2018).

In short, your mindset is one of your strongest tools. By practicing these skills, you can train your brain to look for possibilities where others only see obstacles, and that shift can change everything.

Save Fred

> **Overview**: Save Fred is a fun and engaging team-building game that promotes problem-solving, communication, and teamwork. In this game, participants work together to save Fred, a gummy worm, who is stranded on top of a "boat" (a plastic cup) with his "life preserver" (a gummy lifesaver) trapped underneath the boat. The challenge is to save Fred by placing the lifesaver around him without directly touching Fred, the cup, or the lifesaver with their hands. I have enjoyed playing this game with students of all ages, as well as adults.
>
> **Objective**: The goal is for the team to successfully put the gummy lifesaver around Fred using only paper clips, without touching Fred, the cup, or the lifesaver with their hands.

Materials Needed

- 1 gummy worm (Fred) per team
- 1 gummy lifesaver (life preserver) per team
- 1 plastic cup (boat) per team
- 4 paper clips per team

> **Setup**: Place the plastic cup upside down on the table. Place the gummy lifesaver under the cup. Place the gummy worm on top of the cup.

How to Play

1. **Form Teams:** 2–4 people.
2. **Explain the Scenario:** Fred the gummy worm is stranded on top of his overturned boat, and his life preserver is trapped underneath the boat. The team's task is to save Fred by placing the life preserver around him without touching him, the cup, or the lifesaver with their hands.
3. **Using Paper Clips:** Each team member is given one paper clip. Teams must use the paper clips to move Fred, the cup, and the lifesaver.
4. **Rules for Saving Fred:** Team members cannot touch Fred, the cup, or the lifesaver with their hands. Only the paper clips can be used to manipulate Fred, the cup, and the lifesaver. You cannot puncture Fred, the lifesaver, or the boat. Fred must be placed through the hole of the lifesaver (life preserver) to be "saved."
5. **Completing the Task:** The team that successfully places the gummy lifesaver around Fred using only the paper clips wins.

Rules
1. Participants cannot touch Fred, the cup, or the lifesaver with their hands.
2. Each participant can use only one paper clip at a time.
3. Fred must end up with the lifesaver around him.
4. Teams must work together and communicate effectively to save Fred.
5. The first team to save Fred successfully wins, or if timing is used, the team that saves Fred in the shortest amount of time wins.

Tips for Success
- Encourage teams to communicate clearly and plan their strategy before starting.
- Emphasize the importance of patience and careful movements.
- Remind participants that teamwork and cooperation are key to success.

Debriefing: After the game, have a discussion with the participants about their experience:
- What strategies helped in successfully saving Fred?
- How did teamwork and communication impact the outcome?
- What challenges did they face, and how did they overcome them?
- How did the activity illustrate problem-solving and teamwork?
- How can the skills used in this game be applied to real-life situations?

Guided Meditation: Enhancing Flexibility and Creativity

Find a comfortable position and close your eyes. Take a deep breath in and exhale slowly. Allow your body to relax and your mind to become still.

Imagine a flowing river. The water moves smoothly around rocks and obstacles, always finding a way forward. Visualize yourself as the river, flexible and adaptable.

Think about a recent challenge you faced. Imagine the challenge as a rock in the river. Visualize yourself flowing around it, finding creative solutions and new paths.

As you breathe, feel a sense of flexibility and creativity filling your mind. Know that you have the ability to adapt and find solutions to any problem. Silently affirm: *"I am adaptable and creative. I can overcome challenges with ease."* When you're ready, open your eyes, feeling confident in your ability to navigate any situation with flexibility and creativity.

Key Takeaways

- Your mindset can be your greatest asset or your biggest barrier, so choose it intentionally.
- Adaptive thinking means shifting from "What's wrong?" to "What's possible?"
- Not every problem has a perfect solution, but every challenge offers growth.
- Resilience thrives when we approach obstacles with flexibility, creativity, and hope.

Closing Message

If this work has taught me anything, it's that no matter how "brilliant" we think our ideas are, some of them just won't stick, and that's okay. Problem-solving isn't about getting it right the first time. It's about staying flexible, learning from what didn't work, and being willing to *try again*. It's about asking, *"What can I learn from this?"* instead of *"Why did this happen to me?"*

The truth is, none of us has it all figured out. We're all just doing the best we can, learning as we go, and sometimes laughing (or crying) through the mess. Remember, you can adapt. You can solve problems. You can let go of what's not working and try something new. That's resilience. That's growth. And that's what will carry you forward, even on the hard days. Keep on going.

Chapter 6 Notes

Engage and Reflect

How do you approach problem-solving in your teaching practice?

Can you share an example of a time when you had to adapt to a challenging situation?

What strategies do you use to foster a growth mindset in yourself and your students?

How do you encourage creative thinking and problem-solving in your classroom?

What are some common obstacles you face in your teaching, and how do you overcome them?

How can you improve your flexibility and adaptability as an educator?

What role does collaboration play in effective problem-solving?

How can you create a classroom environment that supports adaptive thinking and innovation?

Keep on Going

References

Buzan, T. (2018). *Mind map mastery: The complete guide to learning and using the most powerful thinking tool in the universe*. Watkins.

Dweck, C. S. (2016). *Mindset: The new psychology of success*. Ballantine Books.

Genet, J. J., & Siemer, M. (2011). Flexible control in processing affective and non-affective material predicts individual differences in trait resilience. *Cognition & Emotion*, *25*(2), 380–388. https://doi.org/10.1080/02699931.2010.491647

Troy, A. S., Shallcross, A. J., Davis, T. S., & Mauss, I. B. (2018). History of cognitive reappraisal use predicts increased regulation effectiveness in the face of stressful events. *Journal of Psychopathology and Behavioral Assessment*, *40*(4), 611–619. https://doi.org/10.1007/s10862-018-9681-8

7

Self-Care and Well-Being

> **Focus:** Prioritizing self-care and maintaining well-being.
>
> **Content:** Identifying personal self-care needs, creating a self-care plan, and exploring various self-care practices that promote physical, emotional, and mental well-being.
>
> Self-care is not just bubble baths and chocolate (though those help!). It's about taking care of our physical, emotional, and mental health. This chapter reminds educators that it's okay to put themselves first sometimes. After all, we can't pour from an empty cup.

Creating My Eight Daily Factors of Self-Care

There was a time in my life when I felt completely overwhelmed, like I was spinning in circles, constantly doing *for everyone else* but not really sure how to care for myself. I knew I was tired, but I didn't know what to *do* about it. I didn't know what I *needed*. I just knew I couldn't keep going like this.

So I brought it to therapy. During a virtual session, my therapist listened, nodded, and then, like it was the most natural thing in the world, she gave me a list. A checklist, really. It wasn't fancy, just some basic reminders: drink water, eat meals, move your body, get enough sleep.

At first, I thought, *Really? That's it?* I felt like I was waiting for some magical solution, but instead I had this list that looked . . . simple. But as I started using it to check off water, food, sleep, movement, I realized that *simple* was exactly what I needed. It was like a basic maintenance plan for my human body. And then I realized: There were pieces missing.

The list didn't include anything about checking in with my emotions. And I knew, *deeply*, that my emotions impacted everything including my mood, my patience, my ability to be present with my kids or my students. I also knew that I could feel *all* the emotions, even frustration, sadness, anger, and still have a *good day*. So I added a line for emotional awareness as a reminder to pause, ask myself *"How am I feeling?,"* and just let that be okay.

Little by little, my checklist grew into what I now call my **Eight Daily Factors of Self-Care** (refer to Figure 7.1).

Figure 7.1 Self-Care

It's not about perfection. There are days when I don't check every box, and that's okay. But having this framework helps me stay grounded. It reminds me that self-care isn't about bubble baths or spa days (although those are great, too). Instead, it's about the *small, consistent habits* that support my well-being and help me feel like *me*.

That's what this chapter is about: building a realistic, personal self-care practice that nourishes your body, mind, and spirit. It's about getting honest about what you need and making space for it without guilt.

Pause Here and Take a Moment to Reflect

> *How do you currently take care of yourself?*
>
> *What small habit could you start this week to care for your well-being?*

Acknowledging the Complexity of Self-Care

Let's Get Real About Self-Care

We've all heard it before: "Take a bubble bath" or "Get a massage." As if that's going to magically fix everything. And sure, those things can help in the moment, but they barely scratch the surface of what real self-care actually looks like. The truth is, self-care isn't about checking off a to-do list of feel-good activities. It's about learning to listen to yourself. It's about recognizing when you're overwhelmed, setting boundaries without guilt, and giving yourself the kind of compassion you so often extend to others.

This chapter is about going deeper. We're not here for quick fixes or Pinterest-worthy routines. We're here to unpack what caring for yourself *actually* means, that is, physically, emotionally, and mentally, and how to build habits that are both sustainable and meaningful. Because self-care isn't just something you "do." It's something you live. It's how you remind yourself that *you* matter.

Establishing Relevance

Why Self-Care and Well-Being Matter

Here's the thing: When we don't take care of ourselves, everything starts to unravel. Our patience gets shorter. Our energy drains faster. Our ability to show up for ourselves, our students, and our families fades. Self-care isn't indulgent or selfish; it's the foundation that helps us keep going. When we make our well-being a priority, we show up differently. We think more clearly, communicate more effectively, and bounce back more quickly when life throws us off course.

Taking time to care for yourself means:

- **You recharge.** You don't run on empty and that makes you more present, focused, and grounded.
- **You model boundaries.** Whether you're leading a classroom, a team, or a family, you show others that it's okay to pause, breathe, and protect your peace.
- **You build resilience.** By meeting your needs consistently, you're more prepared to face the hard stuff without crumbling.

When we choose self-care, we're not choosing to "opt out." We're choosing to stay in the work, without losing ourselves in it.

Eight Daily Factors of Self-Care

These eight areas of nutrition, hydration, sleep, mindfulness, time management, movement, emotional awareness, and joy aren't about perfection. They're about making small, intentional choices that add up to something powerful. You don't have to master all eight every day. This isn't about pressure but noticing what you need and making one choice at a time that brings you closer to balance.

In the next section, we'll take a closer look at each of these factors and how they show up in real life because the goal isn't to do it all, it's to do what works *for you*.

Nutrition

I've realized that nutrition is a key pillar of self-care, not just for my body but for my mood and mental well-being, too. Research highlights how our diet influences the gut-brain axis, the communication link between the gut and brain, because our microbiome helps produce neurotransmitters and signaling molecules (Mindful Health Solutions, 2024). Stress in the gut often shows up as stress in the mind as mood swings, anxiety, or just feeling "off."

Studies show that diets high in refined sugars and processed foods can worsen depression and anxiety, while whole foods, such as fruits, vegetables, lean proteins, whole grains, legumes, and fish, can protect brain health by reducing inflammation and oxidative stress (Mindful Health Solutions, 2024). In other words, the food I eat can either drain me or help me feel grounded, resilient, and focused.

Even small shifts make a difference, like adding one new vegetable a week, swapping chips for nuts, or trying omega-3-rich meals or probiotic foods. Planning ahead helps, too, especially on busy weeks when my brain defaults to "grab whatever" mode (Mindful Health Solutions, 2024).

Of course, nutrition is just one piece of self-care. It works best alongside movement, sleep, stress management, and social connection, and while healthy eating can help with mood and resilience, it's not a replacement for therapy or medical support when needed (Mindful Health Solutions, 2024).

> **Tip**: Don't overthink it, just aim for variety. Try adding more colorful veggies to your meals, choose whole grains when you can, and listen to what your body needs. Simply put, when we nourish our bodies well, our minds function better, too.

Hydration

Don't underestimate the power of water. Staying hydrated is one of the simplest and most effective self-care habits, yet it's often the first thing we forget. Even mild dehydration, for example, as little as 1–2% of body weight, can impair mood, focus, memory, reaction time, and energy levels (Healthline, 2023; News Medical, 2020). Rehydrating quickly improves short-term memory, attention, reaction speed, and mood while reducing fatigue (PMC, 2019). This shows the link between hydration and cognitive performance is powerful and fast.

Hydration also supports key bodily functions: It regulates body temperature, aids digestion and circulation, lubricates joints, and helps eliminate waste (Real Simple, 2019; Health.com, 2023). In terms of mental health, dehydration can trigger brain fog and elevated cortisol, which is the body's stress hormone, while rehydration helps restore clarity and calm (Cleveland Clinic, 2025).

> **Tip**: A common guideline is about eight 8-ounce glasses per day (~2 L), but individual needs vary based on body weight, activity, climate,

and health. Experts recommend around ½ to 1 oz per pound of body weight (NY Post, 2025; EatingWell, 2025). To make hydration effortless, keep water within reach. Consider a bottle beside your bed or at your workspace to sip consistently throughout the day.

Sleep

Quality sleep is fundamental to both mental and physical restoration. It's not a luxury. It's a necessity. Deep sleep (slow-wave) and REM sleep allow your brain to consolidate learning, process emotions, form long-term memories, and clear waste from neural pathways (Walker, 2017). Without enough sleep, focus, creativity, decision-making, memory, and emotional regulation suffer.

Chronic sleep deprivation isn't just about feeling tired. It's associated with a higher risk of anxiety, depression, metabolic dysregulation, immune dysfunction, cardiovascular disease, weight gain, and inflammation (Walker, 2017). Consistently prioritizing sleep is one of the most effective forms of self-care.

Strategies for a Better Night's Sleep
- **Keep a Consistent Sleep Schedule:** Go to bed and wake up at the same time every day, even on weekends, to support your body's internal clock.
- **Practice Mindfulness or Meditation Before Bed:** Deep breathing, body scan, or gentle stretching helps ease tension. Notice simple sensations like your sheets or breath.
- **Journal or Brain-Dump:** Jot down worries, tasks, or gratitude to quiet your mind before going to sleep.
- **Limit Screen Time:** Blue light from devices interferes with melatonin production. Try to power down at least an hour before sleeping.
- **Create a Wind-Down Routine:** Dim the lights, sip herbal tea, stretch, or diffuse calming scents like lavender. Repeat a positive mantra like: "I worked hard today and deserve this rest."
- **Exercise Regularly (but not too close to bedtime):** Working out boosts sleep quality, but aim to finish at least a few hours before bed.
- **Optimize Your Bedroom Environment:** Keep your room cool, dark, and quiet. Use earplugs, eye masks, or white noise if needed.
- **Be Mindful of Food and Drink:** Avoid heavy meals, caffeine, and alcohol late at night. If you're a bit hungry, opt for a light, easy-to-digest snack.

In short: Your body needs sleep like it needs water, food, and air. Prioritizing rest isn't lazy. Actually, it's one of the most powerful forms of self-care.
Tip: Try using a sleep tracker, like the one described next.

Sleep Tracker

Use this tracker to observe your sleep patterns and reflect on how different habits affect your rest. Each day, fill in the following sections:

Bedtime: What time did you go to sleep?
Wake Time: What time did you wake up?
Hours Slept: Total hours of sleep you got that night.
Notes on Sleep Quality (1–5): Rate your sleep quality on a scale of 1 to 5 (1 = poor, 5 = excellent).
Evening Habits/Changes Tried: Note anything you did differently in the evening, such as no screen time before bed, stretching, journaling, or drinking herbal tea.

At the end of the week, review your patterns. Are there habits that help you sleep better? Any surprises? Remember, this tool is meant to help you build awareness, not to judge your sleep. Be honest, curious, and kind to yourself as you reflect.

Sleep Tracker

Day	Bedtime	Wake Time	Hours Slept	Notes on Sleep Quality (1–5)	Evening Habits/ Changes Tried
Monday					
Tuesday					
Wednesday					
Thursday					
Friday					
Saturday					
Sunday					

Pause Here and Take a Moment to Reflect

> *What habits or routines affect your sleep most?*
>
> *What's one change you're willing to try this week?*
>
> *How do you feel after a full night of rest vs. poor sleep?*

Mindfulness

Mindfulness is more than just a buzzword. It's the art of truly being where you are. In a world that's always pulling us in a dozen directions, mindfulness invites us to slow down, take a breath, and reconnect with the present moment.

Practicing mindfulness doesn't have to mean sitting cross-legged for hours. It can be as simple as taking a few deep breaths before a meeting, noticing the taste of your coffee, or checking in with how you're feeling. These small shifts can lead to big changes. A regular mindfulness practice reduces stress and anxiety, boosts emotional regulation, and helps us respond rather than react to life's challenges.

The more we tune in, the more we notice our needs, our patterns, and our capacity to pause before spiraling. It's a practice in presence, and a powerful tool for both calm and clarity.

For more ideas on incorporating mindfulness into your day, check out Chapter 3.

Time Management

Effective time management really can reduce stress and boost productivity when done right (Claessens et al., 2007; McLean Hospital, 2024). But it's not about stuffing your to-do list. Instead, it's about creating space for what truly matters. When you manage time with intention, life feels less chaotic and more grounded.

Breaking tasks into manageable steps and prioritizing thoughtfully can help dissolve that overwhelming "I'm drowning" feeling. It also gives you the mental margin to schedule in rest, movement, connection, and joy. Forget perfectionism. No color-coded planner or 5:00 a.m. wake-up is required. Whether it's a paper planner or a Post-it note list, find what works for you. In this section, we'll explore some specific strategies that can help.

Bottom line: Managing your time well isn't about doing more. It's about living better.

Time Management Strategies for Professionals

The Ivy Lee Method (Clear, 2014)
1. At the end of each day, write down the six most important tasks you need to complete tomorrow.
2. Rank them in order of importance.
3. The next day, start with task #1 and work on it until it's done, then move to the next.
4. At day's end, move unfinished items to tomorrow's list.
5. Repeat daily.

Why it works: It eliminates decision fatigue, encourages prioritization, and limits multitasking (Clear, 2014).

Prioritized To-Do List System
When life feels overwhelming, a simple running to-do list can actually add to your stress. This system helps you stay grounded by sorting everything into realistic timeframes and separating your work and personal priorities.

How to Do It (Step by Step)
1. Make two columns or sections: one for work tasks and one for personal tasks.
2. Write down all tasks, big and small, without worrying about order yet.
3. Sort each list into three categories:
   - Do Now—Needs to be done today or tomorrow.
   - Do Soon—Important but not urgent (within the next week).
   - Do Later—Can wait (within the next month or beyond).
4. Choose your top three priorities from the "Do Now" column and focus on those first.
5. At the end of the day or week, review and update your list, moving items forward, adding new ones, and crossing off what's done.

Why It Works
- Clears mental clutter by getting everything onto paper (or a digital app).
- Helps you focus on what truly needs your attention.
- Reduces the feeling that "everything is urgent."
- Gives equal space to both professional and personal life.

Tips
- Be realistic to keep each category manageable.
- Refresh the list weekly so it stays current.
- Celebrate small wins. Crossing off even one item counts as progress.

Brain Dump Strategy

When your mind feels like it has too many browser tabs open, a brain dump can reset your mental space. You write down everything such as tasks, worries, reminders, with no order or judgment.

When to Use
- Feeling overwhelmed with no idea where to start.
- A scattered to-do list.
- A racing mind that won't let you focus.

How to Do It
1. Grab paper or open a blank doc.
2. Set a 5–10 minute timer.
3. Write everything that comes to mind.
4. Pause, then sort items by urgent, later, delegate, ideas, etc.
5. Move what matters into your prioritized list.

Mindset Shifts and Planning Techniques

Managing your time well isn't about doing more. It's about doing what matters, with more peace and less panic.

- **Think in energy, not just time.**
  Instead of asking "What do I need to do at 10 a.m.?," ask "When do I feel most alert and energized?" Use your peak energy for high-focus tasks and save lower-energy times for emails (Times of India, 2025; McLean Hospital, 2024).
- **Done is better than perfect.**
  Perfectionism drains time and creativity. Set limits and move on once something is "good enough." Progress beats perfection.

- **Time = Priorities.**
  Check whether your time spent aligns with what matters most. If not, realign as even small adjustments can shift everything.

Focus Techniques
- **Pomodoro Technique:** Developed by Francesco Cirillo in the late 1980s, this method uses 25-minute work intervals (pomodoros) followed by 5-minute breaks; after four rounds, take a longer break. It boosts focus, reduces burnout, and enhances clarity (Cirillo, 1987; North Bay Counselling Services, 2022).
- **Two Minute Rule:** If a task takes under two minutes, do it now.
- **Task Batching:** Group similar actions (e.g., calls, grading) to maintain flow.

Prioritization Tools
- **Eisenhower Matrix:** Based on President Eisenhower's approach and popularized by Covey's *7 Habits of Highly Effective People: Powerful Lessons in Personal Change*, this matrix categorizes tasks by urgency and importance: do, schedule, delegate, eliminate (Covey, 1989; Times of India, 2025).
- **ABCDE Method:** Created by Brian Tracy in *Eat That Frog!*, this method ranks tasks A–E: must do, should do, nice to do, delegate, eliminate (Tracy, 2001).
- **MITs (Most Important Tasks):** Start your day with your top 1–3 priorities; everything else can wait.

Sustainable Habits and Digital Tools
- **Buffer Time:** Build in 5–10 minute gaps between tasks or meetings.
- **Tech Time Outs:** Limit scrolling and screen time.
- **Graceful "No":** Saying no isn't rude. It's necessary self-care.
- **Digital Tools and Apps:**
  - **Google Calendar/iCalendar:** Reminders and color-coding.
  - **Trello/Asana:** Visual task boards.
  - *Forest App:* Gamified focus by growing a tree while off your phone.

Pause Here and Take a Moment to Reflect

Which strategy speaks to your biggest time management challenge? Choose one to try this week. What's your plan to implement it?

Movement

Movement is powerful for both your body and your mind. Regular physical activity isn't just about staying fit; it's one of the most effective ways to boost mental clarity, lift your mood, and reduce symptoms of anxiety and depression (Centers for Disease Control and Prevention [CDC], 2023). Even something as simple as a walk outside or a few minutes of stretching can shift your mindset and improve focus.

Physically, exercise supports heart health, strengthens your lungs and muscles, improves energy levels, and helps regulate weight and sleep (CDC, 2023). The real key, though, is consistency and finding movement you actually enjoy. I'm a Pilates fan, my boyfriend is happiest hiking through the woods, one of my daughters is a runner, and the other lights up when she's spinning her flag. There's no "one right way" to move. The goal is to move more, in ways that fit your life and feel good.

Whether it's dancing, yoga, biking, or hiking, movement should feel like a gift, not a punishment. Try aiming for 150 minutes of moderate activity each week, or 75 minutes of more vigorous movement (CDC, 2023). And if you're someone who loves checking things off a list, a habit tracker can be a surprisingly motivating tool to keep you going.

Pause Here and Take a Moment to Reflect

> *Do you currently have an exercise routine? If so, what is it? If not, what would you like to try?*

Emotional Awareness

Being in tune with your emotions isn't about being overly emotional. It's about being honest with yourself. When we take the time to name what we're feeling, we often reduce the tension we're carrying and gain clarity on what we actually need. Emotions are messengers, not problems to fix. Learning to sit with them, understand them, and express them, without judgment, can lead to powerful self-awareness and healing. Emotionally healthy people tend to communicate more effectively and build stronger relationships because they're able to respond, not just react. Whether it's through journaling, using an emotion wheel, or having a heart-to-heart with a trusted friend, making space for your feelings is a crucial part of self-care. For more on emotional wellness, check out Chapter 2.

Joy

Joy is one of those feelings that doesn't just lighten your heart, but it can change your whole day. But let's pause for a moment and talk about something important: Joy is not the same as happiness. Happiness is often tied to external circumstances, such as getting good news, buying something you've wanted, or things going your way. Joy, on the other hand, is deeper. It's an internal state of well-being that can exist even in hard times (Brach, 2019). You don't need everything to be perfect to feel joy. It's found in connection, beauty, presence, and meaning. And while happiness may come and go, joy is something we can cultivate and return to again and again

Experiencing joy regularly has powerful effects on both emotional and physical health. Studies show that engaging in joyful or awe-filled activities can boost mood, reduce symptoms of depression, lower blood pressure, and even strengthen immune function (Fredrickson, 2013; Stellar et al., 2015). Joy isn't just about feeling good in the moment. It's about supporting long-term well-being.

You can also feel joy in your body. Beyond smiling or laughing, joy can bring sensations like a lightness in your chest, softer shoulders, or a deep, spontaneous breath. Sometimes it feels like warmth or tingling on your skin. In moments of deep joy, you might lose track of time, feel fully connected to others, or experience awe so strong it leaves you breathless (Stellar et al., 2015).

So, what brings you joy? Not the performative kind or the "supposed to make me happy" moments but real, soul-level joy. For many of us, it's the little things: the smell of fresh coffee, dancing in the kitchen, laughing with a friend, a walk in the sunshine, or a moment of unexpected beauty. These are your micro-joys, tiny, daily sparks that often go unnoticed if we're too busy or distracted. The good news? You can train yourself to notice them.

That's where mindfulness comes in. Mindfulness and joy go hand in hand. When we're fully present, we become more aware of the joyful moments that are already happening. We stop waiting for the weekend or the vacation to feel good, and we begin to notice the soft joy in everyday life. It allows us to let go of judgment, appreciate what is, and savor the softer joys of daily life (Kabat-Zinn, 2013).

Of course, it's not always easy. Stress, unrealistic expectations, and our brain's natural negativity bias can dim our joy (Hanson, 2016). But joy doesn't require perfection. It just asks for presence. And the more we practice noticing it, the more it grows.

So, make room for joy. Schedule it in, if you have to. Make it a ritual. Let it be small. Let it surprise you. Most importantly, let it count. Because joy isn't a luxury but a daily, necessary act of self-care.

Pause Here and Take a Moment to Reflect

> *What is something that brought you joy today? Can you anticipate what might bring you joy tomorrow?*

The "8 Breaths to Joy"

The "8 Breaths to Joy" is one of my favorite mindfulness practices because it's simple, grounding, and doesn't take more than a few minutes. Created by Tim Desmond (2017), this guided exercise helps you connect with the present moment while cultivating both joy and compassion, which are two things we could all use more of in our daily lives.

Each breath has a focus, gently guiding you into a deeper awareness of yourself and your surroundings:

1. **Breath:** Feel the rhythm of your inhale and exhale, letting each one fully complete.
2. **Body:** Notice all the sensations in your body, such as warmth, coolness, tension, ease, without judgment.
3. **Release:** With every exhale, imagine tension and discomfort leaving your body, softening what feels tight.
4. **Love:** Silently offer yourself kindness: "May I feel ease and lightness."
5. **Cravings:** Acknowledge any desires or aversions, allowing them to be there without trying to change them.
6. **Letting Go:** Recognize that some conditions for happiness are already here; shift your focus to the good in this moment.
7. **Alive:** Feel the miracle of simply being alive, noticing the energy of life in your body.

8. **Beauty:** Take in the beauty around you and within you, using all your senses to be fully present.

This practice is quick but powerful. It can leave you feeling calmer, more connected, and more resilient, even on hard days.

The Different Types of Tiredness and How to Rest

We all know the feeling of being tired, but not all tiredness is created equal. Sometimes it's your body that's worn out, while other times it's your mind, your emotions, or even your senses that need a break. Learning to identify *which* kind of tired you're feeling can change how you care for yourself. As Saundra Dalton-Smith (2019) explains in her research on rest, we often try to "fix" our exhaustion with the wrong type of break, for example, scrolling on our phones when we really need quiet or lying down when what we need is creative stimulation. Matching the type of rest to the type of fatigue helps you feel better not just in the moment but in a way that's sustainable.

Here's a breakdown of the most common types of tiredness and how to respond to each one with intentional, restorative practices:

Physical Tiredness
Signs: Feeling heavy or sluggish, fatigue in your body, little energy to move or perform tasks.

Rest Needed
- **Sleep:** Prioritize quality sleep with a consistent bedtime routine.
- **Relaxation:** Gentle stretching, yoga, or a warm bath to release tension.
- **Movement:** Paradoxically, light exercise like a walk can help restore energy over time (Dalton-Smith, 2019).

Mental Tiredness
Signs: Difficulty concentrating, mental "fog," or forgetfulness.

Rest Needed
- **Breaks:** Step away from work or screens regularly. Try structured breaks using the Pomodoro Technique (Cirillo, 1987).
- **Meditation:** Mindfulness or deep breathing can help reset focus.
- **Simplify:** Break tasks into smaller steps to reduce overwhelm.

Emotional Tiredness

Signs: Feeling overwhelmed, irritable, or emotionally drained; trouble managing stress or connecting with others.

Rest Needed
- **Emotional Expression:** Journal your feelings or talk with someone you trust.
- **Boundaries:** Limit exposure to emotionally taxing situations or people.
- **Comfort Activities:** Choose soothing activities like music, art, or reading to help your nervous system reset.

Social Tiredness

Signs: Feeling exhausted after social interactions, even with people you care about; craving solitude.

Rest Needed
- **Alone Time:** Spend time solo doing something restorative.
- **Selective Engagement:** Choose meaningful interactions over obligatory ones.
- **Quiet Connection:** Opt for low-energy ways to connect, like watching a movie together.

Creative Tiredness

Signs: Struggling to generate new ideas, feeling uninspired or "stuck."

Rest Needed
- **Switch Activities:** Do something unrelated, like cooking or gardening.
- **Consume Inspiration:** Read, listen, or watch something that sparks curiosity.
- **Play:** Make space for unpressured creativity like drawing, doodling, or experimenting just for fun (Dalton-Smith, 2019).

Sensory Tiredness

Signs: Feeling overstimulated by noise, light, screens, or crowds; sensitivity to your environment.

Rest Needed
- **Unplug:** Reduce screen time and disconnect from devices.
- **Quiet Time:** Spend time in a calm, low-stimulation space.

- **Nature:** Step outside to reset your senses with natural sounds and sights.

When you pause long enough to notice what kind of tired you're actually experiencing, your self-care shifts from being random to being restorative. It's about meeting your body, mind, and heart where they're at so your rest truly fills your tank.

Pause Here and Take a Moment to Reflect

> *Which type(s) of tiredness do you relate to the most? What specific steps can you take to address and rest in this area?*

Keeping Track of Eight Daily Factors of Self-Care

Remember, incorporating the eight daily factors of self-care—nutrition, hydration, sleep, mindfulness, time management, movement, emotional awareness, and joy—into your routine can significantly enhance overall well-being. This chart is designed to support your self-care journey, not to overwhelm you. There's no one "right" way to use it, so feel free to make it your own.

You might choose to focus on just one factor at a time. I suggest starting with sleep, as quality rest forms the foundation for all the other areas of well-being. Take time to review each of the eight factors and use the weekly tracker chart to guide your reflections.

Each day, you can check off what you completed, rate each factor, or jot down notes about how things went. At the end of the week, take a moment to reflect. What worked? What didn't? What might you adjust for the week ahead? Use the open space to write goals, celebrate wins, note challenges, or capture anything that feels important. This journal is here to support you, so use it in a way that feels helpful and empowering.

Self-Care Checklist

	M	T	W	T	F	S	S
Nutrition How were your eating habits today? Did you include nutrient-dense foods?							
Hydration Did you drink enough water today?							
Sleep How many hours of sleep did you get last night? Was it good quality sleep?							
Mindfulness Did you find moments of mindfulness during your day? Were you able to be present?							
Time Management Were you able to plan your day to create work/life balance?							
Exercise How many minutes of exercise did you get? Aim for 75–150 minutes/week.							
Connect With Your Emotions Did you stop to check-in with yourself?							
Joy Did something make you smile today?							
Other							

Self-Care Bingo

How to Play: Every time you complete a self-care activity, mark your bingo board. When you get 5 in a row, celebrate however you choose!

Self-Care Bingo Card

☐ Took a walk	☐ Meditated	☐ Read a book	☐ Called a friend	☐ Drank water
☐ Ate a healthy meal	☐ Listened to music	☐ Took a nap	☐ Practiced yoga	☐ Journaled
☐ Did a hobby	☐ Went to bed early	☐ Took a bath	☐ Watched a favorite show	☐ Spent time in nature
☐ Did a workout	☐ Practiced deep breathing	☐ Cooked a meal	☐ Played a game	☐ Spent time with family
☐ Drew or painted	☐ Did a puzzle	☐ Laughed out loud	☐ Practiced gratitude	☐ Stretched

Pause Here and Take a Moment to Reflect

How will you celebrate when you get BINGO?

Self-Care Swap

Instructions: Talk to your friends, family, and colleagues. Ask them some of the questions from the chart. Maybe you will get some new ideas to try!

How do you make time for exercise, and what kind of exercise do you like to do?	What do you do with your friends or family that re-energizes you?	How do you ensure you get enough sleep each night?
What do you do during the week to nurture your spiritual health?	Are there any devices, apps, or websites that you find helpful in your self-care practice?	How do you stay motivated to keep up with your self-care routine?
How do you carve out "me time" during the work day, and what do you do?	What morning routine helps you prepare emotionally for the day?	How do you manage your time effectively to reduce stress?
How do you unwind and recharge after work?	What activities or hobbies help you feel most relaxed?	What techniques do you use to stay positive and maintain a good mood?
How do you care for yourself when you have had an upsetting or stressful day?	How do you balance work and personal life to maintain your well-being?	How do you practice mindfulness or meditation, and how does it help you?
What strategies do you use to eat healthy?	What books or resources have you found helpful for self-care?	How do you celebrate small victories or achievements during the week?

150 Self-Care Ideas

- Read a book.
- Practice yoga.
- Meditate.
- Go for a walk in nature.
- Listen to music.
- Journal your thoughts.
- Cook a favorite meal.
- Practice deep breathing exercises.
- Paint or draw.
- Watch a favorite movie or TV show.
- Call a friend.
- Write a gratitude list.
- Try a new hobby.
- Get a massage.
- Light scented candles.
- Do a puzzle.
- Spend time with pets.
- Visit a museum.
- Go to the beach.
- Take a nap.
- Plan a fun outing.
- Exercise regularly.
- Practice positive affirmations.
- Declutter a space.
- Grow your own fruits and vegetables.
- Dance.
- Enjoy a cup of tea.
- Have a picnic.
- Visit a farmer's market.
- Volunteer.
- Practice mindfulness.
- Knit or crochet.
- Write letters to friends or family.
- Go for a bike ride.
- Explore a new place.
- Do a digital detox.
- Play a musical instrument.
- Watch the sunrise or sunset.
- Practice aromatherapy.
- Take a long drive.
- Spend time with loved ones.
- Visit a spa.
- Do some stretching exercises.
- Bake cookies or a cake.
- Listen to a podcast.
- Try a new recipe.
- Do a random act of kindness.
- Visit a library.
- Attend a workshop or class.
- Practice tai chi.
- Spend time in a park.
- Do some DIY crafts.
- Write a poem or short story.
- Watch a comedy show.
- Take a day trip.
- Practice grounding exercises.
- Visit a botanical or butterfly garden.
- Reflect on personal goals.
- Enjoy a healthy smoothie.
- Create a vision board.
- Attend a live performance.
- Make a scrapbook.
- Go bird watching.
- Plan a future vacation.
- Make a time capsule.
- Have a board game night
- Listen to live music.
- Create an indoor herb garden.
- Do a home workout.
- Try a new hairstyle.
- Try thrifting.
- Create a mission statement.
- Take a relaxing bath.
- Have a silent retreat.
- Make a bird feeder.
- Stargaze.
- Visit an art gallery.

- Try a new sport.
- Do a home spa day with friends.
- Attend a support group.
- Spend time by the water.
- Visit a zoo or aquarium.
- Go camping.
- Learn a new language.
- Explore local attractions.
- Have a tech-free day.
- Play with a pet.
- Take a mindfulness walk.
- Do a brainteaser.
- Create a personal mantra.
- Watch a documentary.
- Make a playlist of favorite songs.
- Write a letter to your future self.
- Practice self-compassion.
- Enjoy a favorite treat.
- Take a photography walk.
- Listen to an audiobook.
- Create a family tree.
- Take a scenic hike.
- Enjoy a cup of coffee at a café.
- Write down positive memories.
- Attend a fitness class.
- Have a gratitude jar.
- Paint rocks.
- Make homemade gifts.
- Write a bucket list.
- Go to a farmer's market.
- Organize a part of your home.
- Have a themed dinner night.
- Try guided imagery.
- Plant a tree.
- Do some charity work.
- Take a scenic route home.
- Listen to nature sounds.
- Try a new exercise routine.
- Visit a historical site.
- Spend time people-watching.
- Learn about a new culture.
- Watch a play.
- Make a photo album.
- Do a digital clean-up.
- Spend a day doing nothing.
- Read inspirational quotes.
- Try a new craft.
- Try a new type of cuisine.
- Visit a flea market.
- Go on a mini-adventure.
- Try a new fitness app.
- Spend time in silence.
- Write about your day.
- Have a laughter session.
- Do a social media cleanse.
- Learn about essential oils.
- Create a list of life goals.
- Go horseback riding.
- Try an escape room.
- Make homemade candles.
- Visit a new neighborhood.
- Take a scenic train ride.
- Try digital scrapbooking.
- Make a playlist of calm music.
- Reflect on achievements.
- Try a new meditation app.
- Write a letter to younger self.
- Spend time in a hammock.
- Attend a poetry reading.
- Make homemade soap.
- Try guided relaxation exercises.
- Do a detox diet.
- Take a pottery class.
- Attend a book club.
- Have a bonfire.
- Create a financial plan.
- Try calligraphy.
- Create a cozy reading nook.
- Plan a staycation.
- Visit a meditation center.

- Write in a travel journal.
- Go to a comedy club.
- Practice laughter yoga.
- Make a homemade face mask.
- Do a self-photo shoot.
- Create a list of favorite things.
- Visit a winery or brewery.
- Make homemade ice cream.
- Have a themed craft night.
- Do a walking tour of your city.
- Make a memory jar.
- Join a local sports team.
- Have a technology-free day.
- Visit a local farm.
- Try a new form of dance.
- Go fruit picking.

Pause Here and Take a Moment to Reflect

Which of these ideas would you like to try? Is there something not on the list?

Guided Meditation: Prioritizing Self-Care

Sit comfortably and close your eyes. Take a deep breath in, and exhale slowly. Let your body relax and your mind become calm.

Imagine a warm, golden light surrounding your body. This light represents self-care and well-being. As you breathe in, visualize the light filling your body, nurturing and healing every part of you.

Focus on any areas of tension or discomfort in your body. With each exhale, imagine the tension melting away, replaced by the warm, golden light.

Think about the self-care practices that nourish you. Visualize yourself engaging in these activities, feeling relaxed and rejuvenated. Whether it's taking a walk, reading a book, or spending time with loved ones, see yourself enjoying these moments of self-care.

> Silently affirm: *"I prioritize my well-being. I deserve to take care of myself."* When you're ready, open your eyes, feeling nurtured and committed to your self-care routine.

Key Takeaways

- Self-care is not selfish. It's strategic sustainability.
- True well-being includes body, mind, heart, and spirit.
- Your needs matter. Meeting them helps you meet the needs of others.
- Consistent micro-habits (like hydration, rest, joy, and boundaries) build long-term wellness.

Closing Message

Self-care is not a luxury. It's not a to-do list you have to "get right." It's not about having the perfect morning routine or checking off every box, every single day.

It's about knowing yourself well enough to say, *"I matter. My well-being matters. And I'm allowed to take care of me."*

Your self-care might look different from mine. And that's okay. The point isn't to copy someone else's list but to create your own.

So give yourself permission to start small, to check in, and to keep coming back to what you need.

You are allowed to feel your emotions and still have a good day. You are allowed to rest. You are allowed to take up space. And you are more than allowed. In fact, you are worthy.

Chapter 7 Notes

Engage and Reflect

What are some self-care practices you currently use to maintain your well-being?

How do you prioritize self-care amidst your busy teaching schedule?

Can you share a time when self-care positively impacted your professional life?

What challenges do you face in maintaining consistent self-care practices? How can you incorporate more self-care activities into your daily routine?

What role does physical health play in your overall well-being and resilience?

How can you create a self-care plan that addresses your specific needs and goals?

What are some ways to promote a culture of self-care and well-being among your colleagues and students?

References

Brach, T. (2019). *Radical compassion: Learning to love yourself and your world with the practice of RAIN*. Viking.

Centers for Disease Control and Prevention. (2023). *How much physical activity do adults need?* CDC. https://www.cdc.gov/physical-activity-basics/guidelines/adults.htm

Cirillo, F. (1987). *The Pomodoro Technique*. Crown Publishing.

Claessens, B. J. C., van Eerde, W., Rutte, C. G., & Roe, R. A. (2007). A review of the time management literature. *Personnel Review, 36*(2), 255–276. https://doi.org/10.1108/00483480710726136

Clear, J. (2014, July). *The Ivy Lee Method: The daily routine experts recommend for peak productivity*. James Clear. https://jamesclear.com/ivy-lee

Cleveland Clinic. (2025, March). *Dehydration and mental health: What's the connection?* https://health.clevelandclinic.org/dehydration-and-affect-on-mental-health

Covey, S. R. (1989). *The 7 habits of highly effective people*. Free Press.

Dalton-Smith, S. (2019). *Sacred rest: Recover your life, renew your energy, restore your sanity*. FaithWords.

Desmond, T. (2017). *The joy of half a cookie: Using mindfulness to lose weight and end the struggle with food*. HarperOne.

EatingWell. (2025, April). We asked 6 dietitians the healthiest habit to start before 9 a.m.—They all said the same thing. *EatingWell*. https://www.eatingwell.com/healthiest-habit-to-do-before-9-am-11719250

Fredrickson, B. L. (2013). *Love 2.0: How our supreme emotion affects everything we feel, think, do, and become*. Hudson Street Press.

Hanson, R. (2016). *Hardwiring happiness: The new brain science of contentment, calm, and confidence*. Harmony.

Health.com. (2023). Health benefits of drinking water. *Health.com*. https://www.health.com/benefits-of-drinking-water-7510285

Healthline. (2023). 7 science-based health benefits of drinking enough water. *Healthline*. https://www.healthline.com/nutrition/7-health-benefits-of-water

Kabat-Zinn, J. (2013). *Full catastrophe living: Using the wisdom of your body and mind to face stress, pain, and illness* (Revised ed.). Bantam.

McLean Hospital. (2024). The mental health benefits of better time management. *McLean Hospital*. https://www.mcleanhospital.org/essential/time-management

Mindful Health Solutions. (2024, March 15). Eat your way to happiness: The link between healthy eating and mental health. *Mindful Health Solutions*. https://mindfulhealthsolutions.com/eat-your-way-to-happiness-the-link-between-healthy-eating-and-mental-health/

New York Post. (2025, January 27). This easy habit first thing in the morning boosts your energy, mood, memory and metabolism. *New York Post.* https://nypost.com/2025/01/27/health/easy-habit-first-thing-in-the-morning-boosts-energy-mood-memory/

News Medical. (2020, September 16). Levels of hydration and cognitive function. *News Medical.* https://www.news-medical.net/health/Levels-of-Hydration-and-Cognitive-Function.aspx

North Bay Counselling Services. (2022). *Pomodoro Technique manual.* https://www.northbaycounselling.com/wp-content/uploads/2022/05/Cirillo-Pomodoro-Technique.pdf

PMC. (2019). Effects of dehydration and rehydration on cognitive performance. *Nutrition Reviews.* https://pmc.ncbi.nlm.nih.gov/articles/PMC6603652/

Real Simple. (2019). How much water should you drink a day? *Real Simple.* https://www.realsimple.com/health/how-much-water-to-drink-day

Stellar, J. E., Gordon, A. M., Piff, P. K., Cordaro, D., Anderson, C. L., Bai, Y., Sauter, K., Valdesolo, P., & Keltner, D. (2015). Self--transcendent emotions and their social functions: Compassion, gratitude, and awe bind us to others-. *Proceedings of the National Academy of Sciences, 112*(29), 8522–8527. https://doi.org/10.1073/pnas.1429012112

Times of India. (2025, July 27). 5 time management tips to boost productivity. *Times of India.* https://timesofindia.indiatimes.com/life-style/relationships/work/5-time-management-tips-to-boost-productivity/articleshow/122910482.cms

Tracy, B. (2001). *Eat that frog!: 21 great ways to stop procrastinating and get more done in less time.* Berrett-Koehler.

Walker, M. (2017). *Why we sleep: Unlocking the power of sleep and dreams.* Scribner.

8

Self-Compassion

> **Focus:** Cultivating self-compassion as a foundation for emotional resilience and well-being.
>
> **Content:** Exploring the three components of self-compassion (self-kindness, common humanity, and mindfulness), understanding how it differs from self-esteem and perfectionism, and practicing strategies to respond to oneself with care during difficult moments.
>
> Self-compassion isn't about letting yourself off the hook. Instead, it's about meeting yourself with the same kindness you'd offer a student or a friend. In a profession built on caring for others, it's easy to forget that you deserve care, too. This chapter helps educators shift from harsh self-criticism to gentle understanding, turning inward supportively instead of turning against themselves. Because being human isn't a flaw. It's the whole point.

Resolving to Embrace Enoughness

Every January, I used to dive into a fresh planner, convinced that *this* would be the year I'd finally get it all right: I'd lose ten pounds, learn Portuguese so I could eavesdrop on my boyfriend's conversations, and somehow juggle all the demands of work, motherhood, and life with a smile on my face. But as the days passed, the shiny newness faded, and that sneaky little voice of "not enoughness" crept in. *You didn't stick with your goals. You're falling short . . . again.*

That's how the cycle would go: I'd make a list of all the things I *needed to fix*, all the ways I believed I wasn't good enough yet. And every time I "failed" to meet those resolutions, I felt like I was failing at life. It was exhausting.

But then one January 1st, I stopped. I took a breath, put down the list of goals, and decided to try something different. Instead of asking myself, *What do I need to fix?*, I asked, *What have I already done? What have I done well, no matter how small?* I looked back at the year and celebrated the little wins: the time I went cross-country skiing in a snowstorm, the moments I laughed so hard I had to catch my breath, the way I showed up for my students, my family, my friends, even when it wasn't perfect.

And that's when it clicked: *Self-compassion isn't about striving for perfection or fixing what we think is broken.* It's about noticing what's already working. It's about extending kindness to yourself, recognizing your efforts, and remembering that you are enough, *exactly as you are*. It's about saying no without guilt, taking a deep breath when things feel overwhelming, and giving yourself grace, especially when you fall short of your own expectations.

For years, I thought self-esteem was the key to feeling better about myself. But here's the thing, self-esteem is often tied to our achievements, our successes, and how we measure up to others, and that can be a rollercoaster ride. When things go well, we feel great. But when we struggle or make mistakes, then self-esteem can take a nosedive.

Self-compassion is different. It's not based on winning or losing, succeeding or failing. It's about being kind to yourself no matter what. It's about saying, *"I'm human. I make mistakes. And I'm still worthy of love and care."* Self-compassion stays steady, even when everything else feels wobbly, and that's what I want for you, for me, for all of us.

So here's my invitation for this chapter: Let's stop making endless lists of things we think we need to fix. Let's stop chasing "perfection" as if we're a project to be completed. Instead of New Year's Resolutions, what if we called it a New Year's Reflection? What if we took time each year (or each season, or even each day) to notice and celebrate what we've already done, how we've grown, and the ways we've shown up with courage, kindness, and heart?

Let's practice seeing ourselves with softer eyes. Let's stop measuring our worth by our productivity or our ability to check all the boxes. Let's remember that every messy, human moment is part of our story, and it's worth celebrating.

You are enough. I am enough. *We are enough.*

Pause Here and Take a Moment to Reflect

> *What are some of your recent "small wins"?*
>
> *How can you celebrate your "small wins" this week?*
>
> *What does self-compassion look like for you in the middle of a tough day?*
>
> *What's one thing you could say "no" to, or let go of, to create space for rest and grace?*

Establishing Relevance

Teaching is one of the most rewarding and emotionally demanding professions. Educators are expected to lead with strength, show up with heart, and adapt with grace, often all at once. But behind the lesson plans and leadership lies a very human need: the need to be cared for, especially by ourselves.

Self-compassion is not self-indulgence or weakness. It's a resilience skill. It helps teachers bounce back from setbacks, manage stress more effectively, and stay connected to their purpose without burning out. Research shows that self-compassionate educators experience lower levels of anxiety and depression, along with higher levels of well-being, job satisfaction, and emotional intelligence (Barnard & Curry, 2011; Neff & Germer, 2013).

When we treat ourselves with kindness rather than criticism, we model emotional maturity, empathy, and authenticity for our students and colleagues. We also create space to thrive, not just survive, in our roles. Self-compassion doesn't make us less effective. It makes us sustainable.

What Is Self-Compassion, Really?

Let's clear something up, self-compassion isn't self-pity, and it's not giving yourself a free pass to avoid growth. (Though if you decide to eat three cupcakes, no shame. We've all been there.)

At its core, self-compassion means treating yourself with the same care and understanding you'd offer a good friend. According to Neff (2011), self-compassion has three core elements:

- **Self-Kindness:** Being gentle and supportive with yourself when you're struggling, instead of judgmental.
- **Common Humanity:** Remembering that everyone has hard days. You're not broken. You're human.
- **Mindfulness:** Being present with your emotions without ignoring them or letting them spiral.

How Is It Different From Self-Esteem?
- Self-esteem says: "I feel good about myself when I'm doing well." It depends on success, comparison, and external validation.
- Self-compassion says: "I care about myself even when I mess up." It sticks around when life feels messy because it isn't conditional (Neff, 2011).

Self-compassion is more sustainable than self-esteem because it's not about being perfect but about being human. And, as Neff explains in her TEDx talk, most of us are "average" in many areas, and that doesn't make us less lovable (Neff, 2015).

Common Barriers to Self-Compassion

Most of us don't lack compassion, but we just save it for others. Our inner voices can sound like:

- *If I go easy on myself, I'll get lazy.*
- *I don't deserve kindness because I should've known better.*
- *That tough voice in my head is just motivation . . . right?*

Here's the thing, if that voice wouldn't motivate a student, it probably won't work on you either. Self-compassion isn't laziness, It's fuel for resilience (Neff, 2011).

Practices for Moments of Struggle

Life (and the school day) has a way of throwing curveballs: Tech fails. Angry emails. You spill coffee on your only clean pair of pants. When those moments come, self-compassion tools can help you respond instead of react. They're research-backed strategies that help calm the nervous system, build resilience, and make hard days just a little more bearable (Neff & Germer, 2013).

Use Gentle Physical Gestures: Place a hand on your heart to remind your body you're safe (Neff, 2011).

Write Yourself a Letter: This strategy takes a little more time, but it can be deeply grounding. Sit down and write to yourself the way a supportive friend or mentor would as someone who believes in you, understands your struggles, and offers encouragement without judgment. Research shows that expressive writing like this can reduce stress, foster self-compassion, and even help process difficult emotions (Pennebaker & Chung, 2011). Keep the letter somewhere you can revisit on tough days, as a reminder of your own resilience and kindness.

Take a Self-Compassion Break

Take a Self-Compassion Break (Neff, 2011): This powerful mini-practice, created by Dr. Kristin Neff, is like a first-aid kit for your heart. It takes about 30 seconds, and you can do it anywhere, such as between classes, in your car, and while watching students play during your recess duty. It's made up of three steps, each reflecting one of the core components of self-compassion:

Step 1: "This Is a Moment of Suffering." (Mindfulness)
Say it silently or out loud. You're not dramatizing, you're *naming*. Naming what's hard helps your brain shift from fight-or-flight into *something resembling calm.*
No need to sugarcoat. You're just acknowledging: "Yep. This is tough."

Step 2: "Suffering Is Part of Life." (Common Humanity)
This is where you remember you're not weird, broken, or uniquely incapable.
Everyone struggles. Everyone messes up. Everyone has days where the lesson flops, the email stings, or the brain fog rolls in. You're not alone, and that matters.

Step 3: "May I Be Kind to Myself." (Self-Kindness)
Offer yourself a gentle wish or phrase like something you'd say to a friend.

- "May I give myself the compassion I need."
- "May I remember I'm doing the best I can."
- "May I treat myself with patience and love."

Bonus points if you pair it with a kind gesture: a hand over your heart, a deep breath, or even wrapping your arms around yourself like a cozy, invisible hug.

Why It Works

This short practice interrupts the inner critic and brings you back to your center. It gives your nervous system a chance to settle. And maybe most importantly, it reminds you: *You are not alone, and you are worthy of kindness, especially from yourself.* Try it the next time your lesson derails, your patience wears thin, or you just need a moment to regroup. This isn't just a suggestion. It's neuroscience-backed kindness, and it works.

Self-compassion isn't a luxury. It's a practice that helps you bounce back faster, stay connected to your purpose, and keep showing up in a sustainable way. It's what turns *I can't do this* into *This is hard, and I'm doing my best*. It's what makes space for rest, reflection, and the occasional cry in the supply closet (no judgment because we've all been there).

You are not a machine. You are a human being. And you're allowed to treat yourself like one.

Pause Here and Take a Moment to Reflect

Write yourself a letter from the voice of a supportive friend. What do you need to hear from a friend today?

It's Okay to Be Average

Most of us grow up thinking we need to stand out in order to matter and that being "average" isn't enough. But self-compassion teaches us a different truth: You don't have to be exceptional to be valuable.

In her 2015 TEDx talk, Dr. Kristin Neff explains that, statistically, most of us fall into the "average" category in many areas, and that's not just okay, it's normal (Neff, 2015). The constant pressure to be above average at everything doesn't make us better; instead, it fuels shame, burnout, and self-criticism.

When we stop chasing "extraordinary" in every area of life, we make space for something more meaningful: joy, connection, and self-acceptance. Our worth doesn't come from outperforming others; it comes from showing up with kindness, for ourselves and those around us.

> *To be human is to be average in many ways. It's not our achievements that make us worthy—it's our willingness to show up with compassion.*
> Dr. Kristin Neff (TEDx, 2015)

Normalize Average

List three things you're "average" at, and one way each of those things still adds value to your life or others.

Why is it so hard to accept "good enough"?

How can embracing average free up energy for joy, connection, and self-acceptance?

The High Five Habit: A Simple Practice to Reclaim Your Resilience

Here's something small but surprisingly powerful to start your day. Before the noise, the emails, and the chaos (including that student who inevitably shows up without their shoes), take just 10 seconds. Walk to the mirror, look yourself in the eyes, and give yourself a high five. Yes, really (Robbins, 2021).

Why It Works (And Why You Deserve It)
Your brain already knows what a high five means. Think about all the times you've given one, on the playground, in the hallway, after a win, or during a tough moment. A high five communicates encouragement, connection, and trust. By giving yourself one, you trigger the same neuro-association, signaling to your brain: *You're supported. Keep going* (Robbins, 2021).

It interrupts self-criticism. Teachers can be their own harshest critics, holding themselves to impossible standards. This simple ritual can help stop shame spirals, sending a message of compassion rather than criticism: *I see you trying, and that matters* (Robbins, 2021).

It builds trust and resilience. Every high five is a small act of self-affirmation: *I'm still here. I'm still showing up. I matter, too.* Over time, this consistency begins to rewire how you see yourself, reinforcing a supportive, resilient mindset (Robbins, 2021).

How to Practice the High Five Habit (adapted from Robbins, 2021)
1. Stand in front of the mirror, exactly as you are.
2. Take a breath and notice how you feel. There's no need to fake positivity.
3. Place your hand on the mirror and give yourself a high five.
4. Optionally, pair it with a quiet affirmation or word for the day, such as "Steady," "Capable," or "Enough."

This habit isn't about vanity or perfection. It's a micro-moment of mindfulness, a ritual of self-kindness, and a check-in with the version of you who keeps showing up, even on hard days. Tomorrow morning, give it a try. You've got nothing to lose and everything to gain.

> *When you high five your reflection, it's not about how you look—it's about what you've survived. And that changes everything.*
> (Robbins, 2021)

Draw yourself, giving yourself a high five. What do you want to tell yourself?

Guided Meditation: Self-Compassion Break

Take a moment to settle. Sit comfortably. Let your shoulders soften. You don't have to hold it all together right now. Let your breath find its own rhythm. Place one hand on your heart if that feels comforting. Or on your belly. Or wrapped around your arm. Anywhere that feels like support. Close your eyes if that feels okay or just soften your gaze.

Take a breath in . . . and exhale slowly. Now say to yourself: "This is a moment of struggle." Not to dramatize it. Not to dismiss it. Just to *name it*. Something feels hard right now. And that's real. Now say to yourself: "Struggle is part of being human." You're not broken. You're not alone. Every person walking this earth has felt overwhelmed, uncertain, not-enough. Let that reminder be a soft landing.

Now say to yourself: **"May I be kind to myself in this moment."** Say it slowly. Gently. You don't have to *believe* it yet. Just offer it.

You can also try: "I'm doing the best I can." "It's okay to rest." "I deserve compassion, too."

Breathe in kindness. Exhale the tightness, the self-judgment, the pressure to be perfect. Let yourself feel supported, by your own words. Now sit for a few more breaths. Let stillness wash over you. You don't have to fix anything. Just be here. Just breathe. When you're ready, slowly blink your eyes open. Notice the space around you. Notice how you feel. You gave yourself a moment of care.

And that matters.

Key Takeaways

- Self-compassion means treating yourself with the same care you offer your students and colleagues.
- You are allowed to be a work in progress and a work of art at the same time.
- Mistakes don't make you less worthy. They make you human.
- Being gentle with yourself is not weakness; it's one of the most powerful resilience tools you have.
- Talk to yourself the way you'd talk to a dear friend: with kindness, understanding, and encouragement.

Closing Message

You are not a project to fix. You are not a problem to solve. You are a whole, worthy, and imperfect human being, just like the rest of us.

Let's stop measuring our worth by how much we get done or how perfectly we perform. Instead, let's begin a new chapter where we replace criticism with compassion, comparison with gratitude, and striving with gentle presence.

Self-compassion isn't a one-time fix; it's a daily practice. It's the quiet voice that says, *You're doing your best, and that's enough.*

So take a deep breath, soften your expectations, and remind yourself: You are enough. Just as you are.

Chapter 8 Notes

Engage and Reflect

Where in your life are you holding yourself to an impossible standard?

What would change if you gave yourself permission to be "enough" instead of exceptional?

What does "You are a human being—not just a human doing" mean to you?

References

Barnard, L. K., & Curry, J. F. (2011). Self-compassion: Conceptualizations, correlates, and interventions. *Review of General Psychology, 15*(4), 289–303. https://doi.org/10.1037/a0025754

Neff, K. (2011). *Self-compassion: The proven power of being kind to yourself*. HarperCollins.

Neff, K. (2015, November). *The space between self-esteem and self-compassion* [Video]. TEDxUniversity of Texas. https://www.ted.com/talks/kristin_neff_the_space_between_self_esteem_and_self_compassion

Neff, K., & Germer, C. (2013). *The mindful self-compassion workbook*. Guilford Press.

Pennebaker, J. W., & Chung, C. K. (2011). Expressive writing: Connections to physical and mental health. In *Oxford handbook of health psychology* (pp. 417–437). Oxford University Press. https://doi.org/10.1093/oxfordhb/9780195342819.013.0018

Robbins, M. (2021). *The High 5 habit: Take control of your life with one simple habit*. Hay House.

9

Optimistic Outlook

> **Focus:** Cultivating optimism to enhance resilience and perseverance.
>
> **Content:** Strategies for maintaining a realistic yet hopeful perspective, identifying opportunities within challenges, and nurturing an optimistic mindset.
>
> Optimism isn't about ignoring challenges or pretending everything is perfect. Instead, it's about seeing possibilities even in the face of adversity. In this chapter, you'll explore practical ways to nurture an optimistic outlook, enabling you to remain hopeful, motivated, and resilient during difficult times. Cultivating optimism can strengthen your emotional stamina, enhance problem-solving abilities, and inspire those around you.

Trust the Evidence

Whenever I told my therapist that I was afraid I wouldn't finish something or wouldn't do it well, she'd say the same thing: "Trust the evidence."

At first, I'll be honest, I kind of brushed it off. It felt like a throwaway line, something you say to make someone feel better in the moment. It didn't seem like a real solution for my spiral of fear and doubt. But over time, those words started to sink in.

I remember one moment so clearly: I was preparing for a big presentation on mindfulness for educators. The stakes felt high, and the fear was loud in my head. *What if I don't know enough? What if I freeze up and forget everything? What if it's a total disaster?* That old, familiar spiral had me questioning whether I was even qualified to do this work. But then I stopped. I took a breath, and I heard her words in my mind: *Trust the evidence.*

So I started listing it out in my head: How many presentations had I done before? How many times had I prepared, practiced, and delivered something meaningful to an audience? Had I *ever* been completely unprepared, lost for words, or unable to connect with a group? No. Not once. The *evidence* told a very different story than my fear. The evidence said, *I've done this. I know how to show up, even when I'm nervous. I've figured things out before, and I can do it again.*

And it didn't stop at work. As a parent, I found myself questioning if I was raising my daughters the "right" way. Was I giving them enough attention? Was I teaching them the values they needed? Was I missing something crucial that would mess them up forever? But when I paused and *trusted the evidence*, I saw two strong, kind, resilient young women, who sometimes rolled their eyes at me, sure, but who were thoughtful, honest, and compassionate. The evidence said, *I'm doing okay.*

Even when my oldest daughter left for college and I worried about her health and safety, I reminded myself: *Trust the evidence.* She's always been smart, careful, and honest. That doesn't mean nothing bad will ever happen, but the evidence shows she's capable.

I've come to realize that optimism isn't about pretending everything is fine or hoping life will magically work out perfectly. It's about *choosing* to focus on what's already true, on what you've already proven to yourself. It's about reminding yourself that the path ahead is built on the foundation you've been creating all along.

Now, when fear shows up, because it *still* does, I pause, take a deep breath, and say to myself, *Trust the evidence.* Because the evidence? It's right there in front of me. And it tells a story of resilience, growth, and the ability to figure it out, one step at a time.

Pause Here and Take a Moment to Reflect

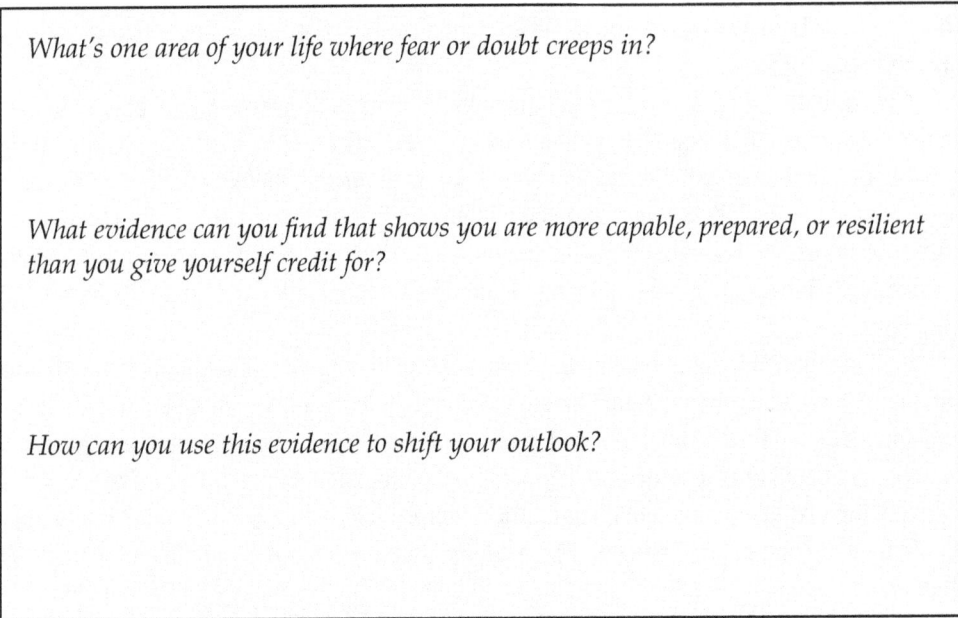

What's one area of your life where fear or doubt creeps in?

What evidence can you find that shows you are more capable, prepared, or resilient than you give yourself credit for?

How can you use this evidence to shift your outlook?

Establishing Relevance

Some days in education feel like an uphill climb in flip-flops. Between shifting expectations, emotional labor, and that one student who seems to test every ounce of your patience, it's easy to get stuck in survival mode. But what if there were a mindset shift that could actually *strengthen* your resilience and help you ride out the storms with more clarity, creativity, and steadiness?

That's where optimism comes in. And, no, it's not about ignoring the hard stuff or putting on a fake smile. Optimism is about *how* you choose to interpret what's happening around you, especially when things get tough. It's a quiet but powerful belief that positive outcomes are possible, even when you're knee-deep in challenges.

The Science of Optimism (Yes, It's Real!)

Psychologist Martin Seligman, the founder of positive psychology, describes optimism as a learned habit, as something you can practice and grow, just like any other skill (Seligman, 1991). It's less about being born a "glass-half-full" person and more about training your brain to reframe how you see obstacles.

Optimistic people don't pretend life is perfect. They just tend to see setbacks as *temporary* and *situational*, not personal or permanent (Carver & Scheier, 2014). This subtle shift creates space for problem-solving, hope, and emotional recovery. In fact, research shows that people who lean into optimism are more resilient, less prone to rumination, and better equipped to navigate stress (Peterson, 2000).

And here's the kicker: It's not just a mindset thing. Optimism impacts your *body*, too. Studies show that optimistic people have lower blood pressure, stronger immune systems, and even live longer (Boehm & Kubzansky, 2012). The way we think actually influences how we *feel*, physically and emotionally.

Optimism also fuels perseverance. It helps you stay committed to your goals even when progress feels slow. Optimists view failure as feedback, not a final verdict, which makes them more likely to try again, adapt, and grow.

So, no, this isn't toxic positivity. It's real, grounded, evidence-backed belief in your capacity to move forward, even when things are hard.

But What If Your Brain Is Velcro for the Bad Stuff?

You're not imagining it: Negative thoughts *do* stick more easily than positive ones. It's called the negativity bias, and it's an evolutionary survival tool. As Dr. Rick Hanson explains, "The brain is like Velcro for the bad and Teflon for the good" (Hanson, 2013). Great if you're running from a saber-toothed tiger, not so great when you're trying to get through Tuesday with 90 minutes of sleep and a mountain of grading.

The good news? You can rewire your brain. Thanks to neuroplasticity, we know that consistent, intentional practice can literally strengthen the brain's capacity for hope and positivity. One tool Dr. Hanson offers is "taking in the good." When something good happens, such as a compliment, a laugh, a breath of quiet, pause for 10–20 seconds and *feel it*. Let it land. This simple habit helps lodge that positive moment into long-term memory, creating new neural pathways for resilience.

Like going to the gym, rewiring for optimism takes repetition and intention. It means noticing the good, reframing the hard, and building small but mighty habits, like gratitude, mindfulness, and self-compassion, into your daily life. Over time, these practices create a sturdy internal foundation that supports you even when your external environment feels shaky.

Reframing in Action

Try swapping out these thoughts the next time things get heavy.

Instead of:	Try This:
"I can't get through to my students."	"I will find another way to reach them."
"Managing this classroom is impossible."	"I can handle this with patience and consistency."
"Everything I'm doing is wrong."	"I did a few things really well today."
"These students don't care about learning."	"Some are starting to engage and show interest."

Shift Happens: Reframe the Story

When I transitioned from elementary to high school, I expected a learning curve, but nothing prepared me for what that first year would bring. I was assigned to teach ninth-graders health, which quickly became my biggest challenge in all my years of teaching. Many in my class refused to engage with the work or with me. It felt like chaos. Out of two full classes, I only built relationships with two or three students. There were days I walked out of the building completely drained and teary eyed. I questioned my decision to leave public education. I even drafted a resignation email mid-year. The story I was telling myself was: You don't belong here. You're not cut out for this. Maybe your best teaching years are behind you.

But slowly, I began to reframe the experience. Instead of seeing it as failure, I started viewing it as a calling to grow in new ways. If I were my own coach, I'd say: "This is hard because it matters. You're being stretched, not broken. These kids don't know how to connect yet, but you're showing up for them anyway."

I practiced what I teach. I held space for myself when I was upset, without shame. I took a mental health day when I needed it and didn't feel guilty for prioritizing my well-being. I celebrated even the smallest victories: a hallway wave from a previously defiant student, a completed assignment that had been weeks in the making. I gave myself credit for continuing to show up with compassion despite how much I was struggling.

And outside of school, I made a conscious decision to add more adventure to my personal life like weekend trips, hikes, spontaneous outings, anything that reminded me of who I was *beyond* my job. That helped me regain balance and perspective.

Looking back, I'm genuinely grateful for that year. It taught me how to build emotional stamina, how to set boundaries without losing empathy, and how to honor my own humanity. Optimism didn't mean pretending everything was fine. After all, it wasn't fine. It meant believing I could make it through, grow from it, and still find joy along the way. Are you ready to reframe your story?

Shift Happens: Your Turn to Reframe the Story

This activity will help you reflect on a challenging situation and shift your mindset using realistic optimism and gratitude. You'll explore your emotional response, reframe the experience, and uncover silver linings.

Step 1: The Storm

> *Think of a recent professional or personal challenge you faced. Describe it briefly.*
>
> *What happened? (Just the facts.)*
>
> *How did you feel at the time?*
>
> *What story were you telling yourself about this situation?*

Step 2: The Reframe

> *Now, step into an optimistic but realistic mindset. What might this situation have taught you? How could it be a catalyst for growth or connection?*
>
> *If you were your own wise coach, what advice would you give yourself about this?*

> *What silver linings or opportunities came from this experience?*
>
> *What strengths did you demonstrate (or could you develop) in this situation?*

Step 3: The Gratitude Lens

> *Gratitude fuels optimism. Look back at the same situation: What is something, even a small thing, you can genuinely feel grateful for? I am grateful that . . .*
>
> *This gratitude reminds me that . . .*

Step 4: Closure and Takeaway

> *Write one optimistic affirmation or mantra inspired by your reflection and keep it somewhere visible.*
>
> *Examples:*
> - *I can handle hard things with a hopeful heart.*
> - *Setbacks are setups for comebacks.*
> - *Even the mess can become part of the message.*

Guided Meditation: Cultivating Optimism

Find a comfortable position, either seated with your feet grounded or lying down with your hands resting gently by your sides. Close your eyes if that feels right for you, and take a slow, deep breath in through your nose. Hold it gently at the top . . . and then exhale slowly through your mouth, releasing any tension you may be holding. Let your breathing find a natural rhythm, steady, easy, and calm.

Now, imagine yourself in a tranquil place. This could be a peaceful beach at sunrise, a quiet meadow with wildflowers swaying in the breeze, or a cozy spot by a crackling fire. Let the details of this place come into focus. Notice the colors, the sounds, the scents, the textures. Feel the sense of *safety*, *contentment*, and *ease* that this place brings.

With each inhale, visualize yourself drawing in positivity, hope, and strength. Picture these qualities as a soft, golden light that fills your chest, radiating warmth and possibility. As you exhale, imagine releasing any negativity, fear, or doubt. Picture it leaving your body like a dark mist, dissolving into the air around you. Let it go.

Now, bring to mind a current challenge you are facing. It could be something big or small, just something weighing on your heart. Without judgment, simply notice it.

Picture yourself facing this challenge with confidence, creativity, and resilience. See yourself navigating the situation with grace while thinking clearly, acting with kindness, and staying true to yourself. Feel a sense of ease and flow, like you have everything you need within you. Let a gentle wave of gratitude wash over you. Be thankful for the times you've faced difficulties in the past and found a way through. Be thankful for the strength you've built, for the optimism you're cultivating, and for the hope you hold, even in uncertain times.

Breathe in possibility. Breathe out self-doubt.

When you're ready, slowly bring your awareness back to the present moment. Wiggle your fingers and toes, feel the ground beneath you, and gently open your eyes. Carry this sense of optimism and gratitude with you as you move forward.

Key Takeaways

- Optimism is not blind positivity. It's the belief that *better is possible*, even when the path forward isn't clear. Hope fuels action. It helps you show up, speak up, and stand tall, even when the future feels uncertain.
- Optimistic thinking can be cultivated through practice, language, and intention. It's a mindset you build, not something you're born with.
- A brighter outlook doesn't ignore struggle but helps you navigate it with courage, perspective, and heart.
- When fear or doubt creeps in, trust the evidence of your past resilience. You've faced challenges before, and you have the strength and resourcefulness to do it again.

Closing Message

Optimism isn't about pretending that everything will be perfect. It's about shifting your mindset from fear to hope, from doubt to possibility. It's about choosing to believe in the good, even when the road ahead feels uncertain.

You can train your mind to look for what's working instead of what's missing. To trust the evidence of your past resilience. To remind yourself that setbacks are temporary and challenges are opportunities to grow.

You don't have to be "naturally positive" to cultivate an optimistic outlook. It's not about denying hard things. Rather, it's about learning to see beyond them. It's about taking a breath, pausing, and gently telling yourself: *I have done hard things before, and I can do this, too.*

When fear shows up, ask: *What's the evidence that I can do this?* When doubt whispers, remember: *There is always another way.* Your mindset is a powerful tool. Use it with kindness, curiosity, and courage.

Chapter 9 Notes

Engage and Reflect

Reflect on a situation where optimism significantly changed your approach or outcome. What specific mindset shifts occurred?

How does your current outlook influence your interactions with students and colleagues?

What daily practices can you implement to foster a consistently optimistic outlook?

Identify barriers that challenge your optimism. How might you overcome or mitigate these barriers in the future?

Trust the Evidence

References

Boehm, J. K., & Kubzansky, L. D. (2012). The heart's content: The association between positive psychological well-being and cardiovascular health. *Psychological Bulletin, 138*(4), 655–691. https://doi.org/10.1037/a0027448

Carver, C. S., & Scheier, M. F. (2014). *Perspectives on personality* (7th ed.). Pearson Higher Ed.

Hanson, R. (2013). *Hardwiring happiness: The new brain science of contentment, calm, and confidence.* Harmony Books.

Peterson, C. (2000). The future of optimism. *American Psychologist, 55*(1), 44–55. https://doi.org/10.1037/0003-066X.55.1.44

Seligman, M. E. P. (1991). *Learned optimism.* Knopf.

10

Building Resilience Through Play

> **Focus:** Embracing play as a tool for joy, creativity, and resilience.
>
> **Content:** Understanding the importance of play for adults, identifying personal barriers to play, exploring ways to incorporate play into everyday life, and developing a playful mindset that fosters well-being and connection.
>
> Play isn't just for kids. It's a powerful way to spark joy, build resilience, and keep life from feeling too heavy. This chapter invites educators to let go of perfection, embrace curiosity, and rediscover the small, everyday moments of fun that bring energy and creativity back into their lives.

From Panic to Play: Finding Fun in the Unexpected

I had pictured a weekend of perfect family bonding with cozy nights in the bunkhouse, scenic trails bathed in sunlight, and plenty of laughs along the way. Instead, it was a total mess . . . and exactly what we needed.

I'm not exactly what you'd call an outdoorsy person, but when my partner suggested a weekend of skiing and camping with his daughters, I said yes. I'll admit, I was nervous. My idea of a winter getaway usually involves a cozy blanket and a hot cup of cocoa, not braving the cold in the middle of the woods. But I wanted to try something new. I'm always looking for ways to bring more play into my life.

The first day, I tried my hand at alpine skiing, and let's just say, it wasn't pretty. One blue trail, a few tears, and a minor panic attack later, I ditched the skis and made my way down the hill on my backside. Not my proudest moment, but hey, I survived. His 10-year-old may or may not have considered launching a mini-rescue mission for me, while his 13-year-old graciously guided me back to the lodge. I'll never forget the mix of concern, humor, and teamwork in that moment.

The next day, we packed up the car and headed further north for a Nordic skiing adventure. We were all excited for the next part, but the trip quickly became more complicated thanks to a Nor'easter that decided to join us. Those hours traveling were filled with unexpected detours and a battle with car sickness in the backseat. By the time we reached the trailhead, we were soaked through, hungry, and tired before we even started. But something shifted once we hit the trail.

We skied through the storm, laughing at the chaos, wiping snow off our faces, and helping each other up when we fell. At one point, I took a few spills, but at least they were on level ground this time. We were a mess, but we were together, and that made all the difference.

When we finally reached the bunkhouse, tired, cold, and drenched, I discovered that my partner had packed a sleeping bag for me . . . that didn't actually fit. It was a toddler-sized mummy bag. There I was, half-zipped in, shivering, and all I could do was laugh at the absurdity of it all.

Looking back, it wasn't a perfect trip. It was messy, unexpected, and full of little hiccups. But it was also playful. We let go of the pressure to "get it right" and found joy in simply being together, imperfectly, hilariously, and fully alive in the moment.

That's the heart of play. It's not about being good at something. It's about trying, laughing, and being willing to look a little silly. It's about stepping out of your comfort zone, letting go of control, and remembering that sometimes the best memories are the ones that don't go as planned.

Pause Here and Take a Moment to Reflect

> *How can you bring a playful spirit into your daily life, even when things feel imperfect or challenging?*

Establishing Relevance

What Is Play and Why It Matters for Adults

Dr. Stuart Brown defines play as "a state of being that is purposeless, voluntary, and pleasurable. The activity is done for its own sake." It's not about being productive, checking a box, or doing something because you *have* to. It's about doing something simply because it's fun and it makes you feel good. For adults, we don't always think of play as essential, but Brown makes it clear: Play helps us connect, stay creative, and feel free. It's not just for kids. *We* need it, too. In fact, Brown, founder of the National Institute for Play, emphasizes that play is essential to human functioning and as vital as sleep, nutrition, and connection. It helps adults access joy, process emotions, recover from stress, and more!

1. **Play Activates the Brain's Reward System:** Engaging in play through games, laughter, movement, or creativity releases dopamine and oxytocin, chemicals that boost motivation, mood, and connection. It disrupts cortisol cycles and supports emotional regulation.
2. **Play Boosts Creativity and Problem-Solving:** Play supports cognitive flexibility, divergent thinking, and low-risk experimentation, which are all crucial for innovation and adaptability in complex environments like schools.
3. **Play Strengthens Connection and Belonging:** Group play builds trust, empathy, and psychological safety, whether in classrooms or teams. Laughter and play reduce hierarchy, encourage vulnerability, and promote community.
4. **Play Prevents Burnout:** Play acts as a pressure valve for stress and reintroduces lightness into the workweek. It boosts positive affect, buffers against exhaustion, and restores joy and energy.
5. **Play Reconnects Us to Ourselves:** Play helps adults rediscover their authentic self, or the part of us that is spontaneous, imaginative, and intrinsically motivated. For educators, play can be deeply healing and sustaining.

The Science Behind Play

Research Area	Why It Matters	Suggested Activity
Brain Health	Enhances memory, attention, and neuroplasticity. Supports executive function through playful problem-solving.	Try a collaborative logic game, improv, or escape room–style challenge.
Resilience	Helps adults "reset," experiment safely, and bounce back from stress.	Build a "Resilience Fortress" using LEGOs or recycled materials.
Connection	Boosts oxytocin, empathy, and psychological safety through shared fun.	Facilitate a group doodling challenge or "Yes, and . . ." circle.
Burnout Prevention	Reintroduces joy, autonomy, and recovery into the workweek.	Lead a laughter yoga session or silly movement-based game.

Dr. Stuart Brown's Eight Play Personalities
- The Joker
- The Kinesthete
- The Explorer
- The Competitor
- The Director
- The Collector
- The Artist/Creator
- The Storyteller

Play isn't just a bonus. It's a vital part of building joy, connection, and resilience (Brown, 2009). Understanding your unique play style helps you sustain these habits and find fun that truly fuels you.

We all play differently. Most of us identify with more than one style, and our preferences can shift depending on our stress level, energy, or the season of life we're in. Brown's research (2009) on the eight play personalities helps us see how we naturally bring joy into our lives and how we can tap into play to fuel our energy and well-being.

The Joker

"*Sometimes silliness is the most serious self-care.*"
Core Joy: Laughter and playful absurdity.
Loves: Jokes, goofy videos, puns, improv, being silly with friends.
Why It Works: Humor lowers stress, builds connection, and creates quick bursts of joy (Brown, 2009).
Try This: Start class with a meme, a funny icebreaker, or a two-minute joke exchange.
Great For: Breaking tension, lightening heavy days, and building community.

The Kinesthete

"*When I move, my mind clears.*"
Core Joy: Movement and physical expression.
Loves: Yoga, dancing, hiking, stretching, fidgeting while thinking.
Why It Works: Movement stimulates the brain, boosts mood, and helps you reach flow (Ratey, 2008).
Try This: Add a walk between classes, a quick dance break, or chair yoga to reset your energy.
Great For: Stress relief, mindfulness, and recharging during the day.

The Explorer

"*I feel alive when I'm discovering something new.*"
Core Joy: Discovery and novelty.
Loves: Trying new places, recipes, workshops, ideas, or hobbies.

Why It Works: Novelty activates dopamine, keeping your brain engaged and curious (Kashdan & Silvia, 2009).
Try This: Take a new route to work, test a different teaching method, or explore a hobby you've put off.
Great For: Reigniting motivation and avoiding burnout through variety.

The Competitor

"I bring out my best when I'm playing to win—with kindness."
Core Joy: Structured challenges and winning.
Loves: Board games, trivia nights, sports, escape rooms, playful contests.
Why It Works: Friendly competition boosts motivation, engagement, and morale (Brown, 2009).
Try This: Organize a classroom challenge, trivia session, or a lighthearted staff competition.
Great For: Building energy, teamwork, and shared goals.

The Director

"Play feels better when I've set the stage."
Core Joy: Planning, organizing, and orchestrating experiences.
Loves: Hosting events, arranging schedules, creating group games or skits.
Why It Works: Directing gives purpose, structure, and creative control (Brown, 2009).
Try This: Plan a themed class day, facilitate a group activity, or lead a team-building exercise.
Great For: Leading with vision while sparking group joy.

The Collector

"Every item tells a story—and stories bring me joy."
Core Joy: Gathering and curating items or experiences.
Loves: Collecting books, plants, quotes, art, or memories.
Why It Works: Collecting offers grounding, meaning, and a sense of accomplishment (Brown, 2009).
Try This: Create a gratitude jar, a classroom "joy wall," or curate a small personal collection to brighten your space.
Great For: Staying anchored in what matters most.

The Artist/Creator

"Making things helps me make sense of things."
Core Joy: Making and building, whether tangible or digital.
Loves: Drawing, writing, gardening, cooking, crafting, and designing.
Why It Works: Creative acts bring flow and regulate emotions (Csikszentmihalyi, 1990).

> **Try This:** Journal, make a vision board, or set aside time to create purely for yourself.
> **Great For:** Stress relief, reflection, and deep creative satisfaction.

The Storyteller
> *"Stories help me connect—with others and myself."*
> **Core Joy:** Imagination, drama, and narrative.
> **Loves:** Reading, writing, acting, podcasting, role-play, daydreaming.
> **Why It Works:** Stories help us process emotions, rehearse empathy, and make meaning (Brown, 2009).
> **Try This:** Write a fictional journal entry, try a storytelling warm-up, or play a role-based game with friends or colleagues.
> **Great For:** Processing experience and building emotional intelligence.

Why Play Matters in REST

If you've been following along, you've probably noticed: I take resilience seriously, but I don't take myself too seriously. That's intentional. Play isn't just a break but, actually, a resilience strategy.

Brown's research (2009) shows that play is hardwired into us as a biological need, essential for emotional health and learning. One of the things that sets REST apart from traditional professional development is the way it weaves play into meaningful work, without losing depth. Play isn't an add-on or a distraction from the "real" work; it *is* part of the work. It helps us process emotions, manage stress, build connection, and stay grounded in what truly matters.

Using Brown's eight play personalities as a lens, REST integrates a variety of play styles, such as storytelling, exploration, artistic expression, movement, humor, and collaboration, throughout each resilience-building chapter. You'll find playful moments in journal prompts, visual goal-setting tools, and activities designed to spark laughter, curiosity, or connection. These elements aren't filler; they're intentional tools to help you engage deeply, recharge, and grow.

Play fuels curiosity, strengthens relationships, and helps us navigate challenges with creativity and compassion, even on the hardest days. When you honor your play personality and intentionally weave small moments of joy, movement, or imagination into your day, you're not just lifting your own mood but modeling what sustainable resilience looks like.

Keep it light. Keep it human. Keep it going.

What's Your Play Personality?

Instructions: For each question, choose the activity that sounds more fun or energizing to you. Don't overthink, but go with your gut!

1. A. Hosting a themed dinner or event (Director)
   B. Exploring a new trail or city (Explorer)
2. A. Playing a competitive board game (Competitor)
   B. Dancing or doing yoga to de-stress (Kinesthete)
3. A. Making people laugh with impressions or jokes (Joker)
   B. Curating a Pinterest board or vision journal (Collector)
4. A. Crafting something with your hands (Artist/Creator)
   B. Telling a dramatic or funny story to a group (Storyteller)
5. A. Brainstorming a plan and assigning roles (Director)
   B. Jumping into a spontaneous adventure (Explorer)
6. A. Trying to beat your personal best at something (Competitor)
   B. Creating music, poetry, or visual art (Artist/Creator)
7. A. Cracking jokes during awkward moments (Joker)
   B. Leading a team project with clear goals (Director)
8. A. Organizing collectibles, cards, or playlists (Collector)
   B. Joining a dance, fitness, or martial arts class (Kinesthete)
9. A. Rewatching your favorite comedy scenes (Joker)
   B. Starting a new DIY project just for fun (Artist/Creator)
10. A. Exploring a local market or new café (Explorer)
    B. Writing or narrating personal experiences (Storyteller)
11. A. Collecting meaningful or rare items (Collector)
    B. Jumping in a game and keeping score (Competitor)
12. A. Designing an experience or event from scratch (Director)
    B. Moving your body to recharge or reset (Kinesthete)
13. A. Being the class clown or comic relief (Joker)
    B. Trying something you've never done before (Explorer)
14. A. Writing a blog, journal, or fictional tale (Storyteller)
    B. Creating a sculpture, painting, or handmade item (Artist/Creator)
15. A. Planning and leading a team scavenger hunt (Director)
    B. Making a themed scrapbook or curated gallery (Collector)
16. A. Practicing to win at a sport, game, or competition (Competitor)
    B. Walking, swimming, or moving just because it feels good (Kinesthete)
17. A. Spinning a funny or dramatic version of your weekend (Storyteller)
    B. Hosting a comedy night or joke contest (Joker)
18. A. Exploring new genres of books, movies, or podcasts (Explorer)
    B. Building or decorating something from scratch (Artist)

19. ◉ A. Competing in a timed challenge (Competitor)
    ◉ B. Collecting things that tell a story (Collector)
20. ◉ A. Facilitating a collaborative group effort (Director)
    ◉ B. Telling or listening to a heartfelt personal story (Storyteller)

Your Results: Count how many times you chose each type and record your results. The one you picked most often is likely your primary play personality. If two or more tie, you have a blended style!

Joker	Director
Kinesthete	Collector
Explorer	Artist/Creator
Competitor	Storyteller

Pause Here and Take a Moment to Reflect

Did your results surprise you? Why or why not?

What types of activities do you enjoy doing? List them here. Looking to try something new? Add that to your list, too!

Explorer Activity: "How Else Could You Use This?"
This activity is inspired by the Alternative Uses Task (AUT), a creativity exercise developed by psychologist J.P. Guilford in 1967. The task challenges individuals to think of as many uses as possible for a common object, like a paperclip or a trash can, beyond its typical function. Guilford introduced this activity as a way to assess divergent thinking, which is the ability to generate multiple, creative solutions to open-ended problems (Guilford, 1967).

At its core, divergent thinking helps people break out of rigid thinking patterns and approach challenges with curiosity, flexibility, and innovation. Practicing this kind of thinking strengthens mental agility, supports problem-solving, and encourages playfulness, especially in environments where stress or routine can dull creativity.

How to Play
1. **Set the Scene:** Assign an object to the participants. You can use ANY everyday object, like an umbrella, shoe, binder clip, etc. Challenge your brains to think beyond the obvious and tap into the power of possibility. Example: "Imagine you have a _____. Now forget everything you *think* it's used for."
2. **Group Challenge:**
    - Break into small groups (2–5 people).
    - Ask: "How many creative uses can you think of for a _____?"
    - Give a time limit (3–5 minutes).
    - Encourage *wild, impractical, funny, and genius* ideas.
    - Have someone jot them down or use sticky notes.

For example: "How many creative uses can you think of for a trash can?" Here is my list of ideas.

Laundry hamper
Ice bucket for drinks at a party
Storage bin for sports equipment
Planter for a tree or large plant
Umbrella holder near a door
DIY compost bin
Toy chest
Makeshift cooler for tailgating
Pet bath (small dog edition!)
Rainwater collector

Robot costume
Giant drum
Sled for a snowy hill
Time capsule
Hat for a giant
A seat (flip it over!)
Popcorn bowl for a movie night with 10 friends
Side table

Group Share and Discussion

Each group picks their top 2–3 most creative or ridiculous ideas and shares aloud. Celebrate with laughter, applause, or a "wildest idea" shout-out.

Reflection Questions:
- What made this fun or challenging?
- Did anyone surprise themselves with an idea?
- How can thinking like this help us at work/in life?
- What happens when we let go of "the right answer"?

Practicing divergent thinking boosts creativity, improves problem-solving, and helps you see situations from new angles. It strengthens your mental flexibility and helps you become more comfortable thinking outside the box. These are the kinds of skills that support innovation, adaptability, and even confidence in uncertain situations. A reproducible version of this activity is included, so you can try it yourself or use it with a group.

"How Else Could You Use This?"

Purpose: Practice thinking beyond the obvious by finding new possibilities for everyday items. This builds creativity, curiosity, and flexible thinking!

Today's Object: _____

(Choose any common item, e.g., a spoon, binder clip, yoga block, shoelace, pillowcase)

Challenge Instructions: In your group, brainstorm as many alternative uses for the object as possible.

- Don't worry if they're silly, strange, or impractical. The goal is quantity, not perfection!
- Set a timer for 5 minutes
- Write down every idea, no matter how wild.

Brainstorm List:

(Use the space below to list your group's ideas. Aim for 10+!)

1. _____
2. _____
3. _____
4. _____
5. _____
6. _____
7. _____
8. _____
9. _____
10. _____

After time is up, circle your TOP 3 most creative ideas. Be ready to share!

Group Reflection (optional): What made this fun or challenging? Which idea surprised you the most? How does this type of thinking help in real life?

Storyteller Activity: "Silly Scripts for Serious People"

For those of you who enjoy reading and writing, this story activity is for you!

REST in Progress: A True Story

Fill in the blanks provided. Then, place them in the corresponding spaces in the story that follows. Read your silly story!

Word List

1. Name of person: _____
2. Adjective: _____
3. Adjective: _____
4. Noun: _____
5. Noun: _____
6. Beverage: _____
7. School-related mishap: _____
8. Positive adjective: _____
9. Emotion: _____
10. Sound effect: _____
11. Another emotion: _____
12. School supply: _____
13. Plural noun: _____
14. Liquid: _____
15. Reality TV show: _____
16. Song title: _____
17. Strange object: _____
18. Verb: _____
19. Self-care action: _____

REST in Progress: A True Story

This week, (1) _____ led the most (2) _____ professional development ever created. It was called the (3) _____ (4) _____. With their trusty (5) _____ in hand and a full cup of (6) _____, they were ready to take on burnout, stress, and the occasional (7) _____. Each session began with a calming breath and a dramatic reading of their favorite affirmation: "I am (8) _____ and (9) _____." Participants responded with (10) _____ and at least one person shouted, "I feel (11) _____ already!" In Session 3, while guiding a mindfulness exercise, _____ (same person as 1) accidentally knocked over a (12) _____ and nearly landed in a pile of (13) _____. But they handled it with grace and a quick chair pose, followed by yelling, "Everything is fine!" By Session 6, educators were sipping (14) _____ with intention and throwing around words like "boundaries" and "stretch" like they were on a (15) _____. The final session featured a celebratory dance to (16) _____, lots of laughter, and a heartfelt affirmation circle that made everyone (17) _____ and (18) _____ spontaneously. _____ (Same person as 1) looked around the room and said, "We did it, friends. Now go forth, hydrate, and don't forget to (19) _____."

Guided Meditation: Rediscovering Play

Find a comfortable position, either seated or lying down, and gently close your eyes. Take a deep breath in through your nose . . . and a slow, steady breath out through your mouth. Let your shoulders soften. Let your jaw unclench. Feel the ground supporting you.

Now, bring to mind a moment in your life when you were completely immersed in play, when time seemed to melt away and joy felt effortless. Where were you? What were you doing? Who was with you? Or were you happily alone, lost in your own world?

Let the scene come alive. Feel the air on your skin. Notice the colors, the sounds, the smells. Maybe you were laughing, running, splashing, or dancing. Maybe you were drawing, exploring, or building. What did your body feel like in that moment? Was it light? Energized? Calm? Let yourself remember the *feeling* of play, the ease, the excitement, the freedom.

Let your breath soften as you remember. Let the smile rise on your face, the joy stir in your chest.

That version of you. the curious, creative, playful one, is *still here*. It's not a thing of the past or something you have to "earn" after your work is done. It's part of you, waiting for an invitation.

This meditation is a gentle reminder to reconnect with your natural play style. To let your nervous system remember what lightness feels like. To soften the edges of your day and make room for curiosity, joy, and ease.

Take one more deep breath in . . . and let it go with a sigh.

When you're ready, gently wiggle your fingers and toes. Open your eyes, and carry that playful energy with you into the rest of your day.

Key Takeaways

- Play isn't just for kids. It's a powerful way to recharge, reconnect, and restore.
- When we play, we activate creativity, reduce stress, and strengthen joy.
- Your "play personality" is unique, so find what lights you up and make space for it.
- Play builds community, strengthens relationships, and brings levity to heavy moments.
- Laughter, lightness, and fun are essential ingredients for long-term resilience.

Closing Message

Play is where we remember how to be fully human. It's where we let go of perfection, embrace the unexpected, and give ourselves permission to be a little silly. It's not about being good at something or having all the pieces in place but about showing up, trying, and finding joy in the moment.

Life is messy. Plans go sideways. And that's exactly where play can shine the brightest, when we release control, laugh through the hiccups, and reconnect with what matters most.

So, as you move forward, ask yourself: Where can I make room for play? How can I bring a sense of lightness, curiosity, and fun into my day, even in small ways?

Remember, the goal isn't to be perfect. The goal is to play.

Chapter 10 Notes

Engage and Reflect

What is your primary Play Personality? (Use the quiz or reflect on activities that energize you.)

When was the last time you felt playful, light, or silly? What were the conditions that allowed that?

What types of play feel restorative, and not performative, to you?

How can you integrate small moments of play into your workweek?

Be Playful

References

Brown, S. (2009). *Play: How it shapes the brain, opens the imagination, and invigorates the soul*. Avery.

Csikszentmihalyi, M. (1990). *Flow: The psychology of optimal experience*. Harper & Row.

Guilford, J. P. (1967). *The nature of human intelligence*. McGraw-Hill.

Kashdan, T. B., & Silvia, P. J. (2009). Curiosity and interest: The benefits of thriving on novelty and challenge. In C. R. Snyder & S. J. Lopez (Eds.), *Oxford handbook of positive psychology* (pp. 367–374). Oxford University Press.

Ratey, J. J. (2008). *Spark: The revolutionary new science of exercise and the brain*. Little, Brown and Company.

11

Celebrating Educators

Focus: Recognizing and appreciating the hard work and dedication of educators while reinforcing resilience-building strategies.

Content: Celebrate educators' achievements, share success stories, and discuss ways to maintain resilience and motivation. Includes activities that foster appreciation and self-reflection.

Let's wrap things up by celebrating our journey. This chapter is all about recognizing hard work and appreciating each other. It's like a big group hug for the soul. Celebrating achievements boosts morale and reminds educators why they do what they do.

We Show Up

I'll never forget the day a student left a small note on my desk at the end of class. It was written in pencil, on the corner of a torn-out notebook page. The handwriting was a little messy, the words simple:

Thank you for being the kind of teacher who cares.

I'll be honest. On that day, I wasn't feeling particularly like the "kind of teacher who cares." I was tired. I had a headache. I had a to-do list a mile long and a pile of ungraded papers waiting for me. But that note? It reminded me of something I had lost sight of in the daily grind: *the impact we have, even when we don't feel like we're at our best.*

Teachers show up. Day after day, we open our doors, our hearts, and our energy to students. We juggle the expectations, the ever-changing demands, and the invisible emotional labor that comes with being an educator. And even on the days when we feel like we're barely holding it together, we're still making a difference.

That's why it's so important to celebrate educators, not just for their achievements or the perfect lessons but for the *showing up*. For the hallway smiles, the quiet encouragement, the extra snacks handed out, the compassion in the face of a child's tears. For the way they hold space for learning, growth, and belonging, especially when the world feels heavy.

We often wait for Teacher Appreciation Week, end-of-year celebrations, or retirement parties to say "thank you." But let's not wait. Let's celebrate each other every day, in small ways and big. Let's remind one another that we are enough, that we matter, and that what we do every single day is extraordinary. Gratitude practices like these are shown to improve emotional well-being and strengthen relationships (American Psychological Association, n.d.).

Pause Here and Take a Moment to Reflect

> *First, think of a colleague, such as a fellow educator, support staff, or administrator. Write a note to them in the space provided, telling them how great they are doing. Be specific. What is one thing you want to acknowledge and celebrate about their work?*
>
>
> *Now, turn that same kindness toward yourself. What is one thing you want to celebrate about your own work?*

Establishing Relevance

Importance of Teacher Appreciation
1. **Emotional Support:** Recognizing and appreciating educators fosters a sense of belonging and emotional well-being.
2. **Motivation and Morale:** Celebrating achievements boosts motivation and morale, helping teachers stay passionate about their work (Aguilar, 2013).
3. **Community-Building:** Appreciation activities strengthen the sense of community and support among educators.
4. **Sustaining Resilience:** Acknowledging hard work and successes reinforces the resilience strategies discussed throughout this guide.

Ways to Celebrate Your School-Year Achievements

With Colleagues
- **Gratitude Circle:** Gather a small group and share one highlight and one appreciation for someone in the room.
- **"Cheers to Us" Lunch or Potluck:** Host a low-key get-together where each person toasts their favorite success or funny memory.
- **Teacher Awards Ceremony:** Make silly, heartfelt or creative awards (e.g., "Queen of Calm," "Spreadsheet Sorcerer," "Most Likely to Say 'Check Google Classroom'").
- **Year-End Reflection Wall:** Create a bulletin board or digital slide deck where everyone adds a "This year, I'm proud that I . . ." statement.
- **Memory Jar:** Pass around a jar at a staff meeting for people to drop in favorite quotes or funny moments from the year, then read them aloud or share as a keepsake.

With Friends or Family
- **"Let Me Brag" Dinner:** Ask your partner, roommate, or friend to sit down and let you share everything you're proud of, from student wins to surviving tough days.
- **Reverse Report Card:** Have your kids, spouse, or best friend give *you* a report card with grades like "compassion," "problem-solving," and "making it through Mondays."
- **Vision and Victory Night:** Share your goals from earlier in the year (if you had them!) and talk about how far you've come, then dream up a summer goal or intention.

- **Celebrate Small Wins Night:** Watch your favorite show, make your favorite meal, and toast the little victories (like finally getting your inbox to zero . . . even for an hour).
- **Write Yourself a Letter:** Reflect on your resilience, humor, creativity, and care this year, and seal it to open next June.

On Your Own
- **Create a Highlight Reel:** Journal or make a visual list of moments that made you proud, laugh, or grow. Bonus: include a photo collage or playlist.
- **Buy Yourself a "Survival Trophy":** Get yourself something fun or meaningful, such as a plant, mug, piece of jewelry, or even a crown from the dollar store. I once bought myself a small trophy that says "World's Best Teacher"!
- **Take a Solo Celebration Day:** Go for a walk, a coffee shop break, or a bookstore visit, just to acknowledge how far you've come.
- **Burnout Bonfire (literal or symbolic):** Write down things you want to leave behind like stress, perfectionism, overworking and release them.
- **Make a "Done List":** Not a to-do list but a **done** list. Everything you accomplished deserves recognition.

Pause Here and Take a Moment to Reflect

What is on your "Done List"?

Directions: Use the space provided (Figure 11.1) to highlight your personal or professional wins this year! In each box, write one thing you're proud of, big or small. Think of this as your own **"Highlight Reel"** of accomplishments.

Figure 11.1 Highlight Reel

Directions: You deserve a trophy. What would you like to celebrate? Give yourself an award!

Guided Meditation: Appreciating Your Journey

Find a comfortable seat or position. Gently close your eyes and take a slow, deep breath in through your nose . . . and a long, steady exhale out through your mouth. Feel the air filling your lungs. Feel your body soften and settle. Let your shoulders drop away from your ears, your hands rest gently, and your breath become smooth and natural. Allow your mind to quiet as you focus on the present moment.

Now, bring to mind your journey as an educator. Think back to where it all began, whether it was years ago or just last year. Picture the faces of the students you've taught, the moments when you felt unsure, and the times you pushed through challenges, even when it felt impossible. See the growth in your classroom, the sparks of understanding, the small victories, and the meaningful connections you've made along the way.

Imagine yourself standing in a beautiful garden, bathed in warm, golden sunlight. Around you, flowers bloom, and each one represents a moment of care, a lesson taught, a breakthrough achieved, a challenge overcome. Notice the colors, the scents, the beauty of this space you've cultivated through your work, your dedication, and your love.

As you walk slowly through the garden, pause at each flower. Let yourself feel a sense of pride, knowing that each bloom exists because of your care and effort. Reflect on a moment when you lifted a student's spirits, a time you showed patience and compassion, a lesson that sparked curiosity, a quiet act of kindness you shared with a colleague. With each breath, silently affirm: *I am proud of my journey. I honor my hard work, my dedication, and my growth. I am grateful for the impact I have made.*

Take a moment to extend that appreciation outward, to your fellow educators, colleagues, and mentors. Picture them standing in their own gardens, each one unique, each one beautiful. Together, you form a community of care, strength, and resilience.

Feel this sense of gratitude and connection fill your heart. Breathe it in deeply. When you're ready, take one more deep breath in . . . and gently open your eyes, carrying this feeling of appreciation, pride, and gratitude with you into the rest of your day. You are enough. You are appreciated. And you are making a difference, every single day.

Key Takeaways

- Celebration matters because it validates effort, sparks joy, and builds connection (Fredrickson, 2009).
- Reflecting on how far you've come reinforces what's possible ahead.
- When we lift each other up, we all rise.
- You are part of a resilient, radiant, real community. And that is worth celebrating.

Closing Message

Educators are the heartbeat of every school community. They are the steady presence, the quiet encouragers, the problem-solvers, and the champions of growth. They show up day after day, sometimes exhausted, sometimes unsure, but always with a heart ready to serve.

Whether you're handing out snacks, crafting lessons, or just making it through a hard day, what you do is extraordinary.

This is your reminder that your work matters, whether it's seen or unseen, celebrated by others or simply felt by the students and colleagues you support. You are enough, exactly as you are.

Take a moment to pause and celebrate *you*, that is, your dedication, your creativity, your care, and your unwavering commitment to making a difference. Celebrate. Not just because you made it to the end but because you showed up with heart.

And just as you celebrate yourself, remember to lift up the educators around you. A kind word, a small gesture of gratitude, or a simple "thank you" can be the spark that keeps someone going.

Together, we create a community where every educator feels valued, seen, and appreciated (Hanh & Weare, 2017). Thank you for all you do.

Chapter 11 Notes

Engage and Reflect

How do you recognize and appreciate your own achievements as an educator?

What are some ways to celebrate the successes of your colleagues and students?

Can you share a moment when you felt truly appreciated and valued in your teaching career?

How can you create a culture of appreciation and recognition in your school or community?

Celebrate

References

Aguilar, E. (2013). *The art of coaching: Effective strategies for school transformation*. Jossey-Bass.

American Psychological Association. (n.d.). *Gratitude*. https://www.apa.org/news/press/releases/2019/04/gratitude-mental-health

Fredrickson, B. L. (2009). *Positivity*. Crown Publishing.

Hanh, T. N., & Weare, K. (2017). *Happy teachers change the world: A guide for cultivating mindfulness in education*. Parallax Press.

12

Sustaining Resilience and Moving Forward

> **Focus:** Strategies for sustaining resilience over the long term.
>
> **Content:** Review key concepts, create a personalized resilience action plan, and discuss ways to continue building and sustaining resilience beyond this book.
>
> Resilience is like a muscle, and the more we use it, the stronger it gets. This chapter focuses on maintaining and growing resilience over time. It's like resilience boot camp, but with more laughter and less yelling. Sustaining resilience ensures that educators can continue to thrive even when the going gets tough.

Clearing Out My Closet

A while back, I found myself standing in front of my closet completely overwhelmed. It wasn't just a little messy; it was *chaotic*. Clothes I hadn't worn in years were shoved in alongside bags stuffed into other bags, old yoga mats rolled up with wrapping paper, ski boots mixed in with dress shoes. It was a tangled mess of good intentions and unfinished plans.

As I stood there, staring at the mess, I realized this closet wasn't just about clothes. It was a mirror for my life. I had been holding on to so much, including old habits, outdated beliefs, the need to say "yes" to everything, and the fear that if I let go, I might miss something important. I had been carrying it all, feeling heavier and more exhausted by the day.

So, I grabbed some trash bags and started clearing it out. Not just the clothes, but the mindset, too. I asked myself: *What do I really need to hold onto? What's just taking up space? What am I afraid to release?*

Resilience, I realized, isn't about holding on to everything. It's about knowing what to release so you have room to grow.

That's what this chapter is all about: sustaining resilience by letting go of what no longer serves you, carrying forward the lessons you've learned, and making space for what truly matters.

Letting go wasn't easy. Some things had sentimental value. Others felt like safety nets. But I knew I couldn't keep everything if I wanted to move forward with more clarity, energy, and joy. That day, as I cleared out the physical clutter, I also cleared out a bit of my mental clutter like the self-doubt, the guilt, the "shoulds" that weighed me down. And in doing so, I created space for what really matters, the relationships, the passions, and the moments of joy that make life meaningful.

Pause Here and Take a Moment to Reflect

> *What are some things that you would like to let go of?*

Establishing Relevance

As educators, we're no strangers to change, pressure, and the feeling of constantly being "on." It's easy to pour everything into our students, our lessons, and our school communities and still feel like it's not enough. That's why this chapter matters.

We've spent time building resilience skills to help us manage the day-to-day, but this chapter is about something bigger: sustaining that resilience long-term. Because resilience isn't a one-time fix but a lifestyle, a mindset, and a professional commitment.

- ♦ **Teaching is a marathon, not a sprint.** Educators face ongoing stressors year after year, and this chapter provides strategies to build endurance and avoid burnout.

- **Sustainability is key.** Even the most resilient educators need tools to maintain well-being over time. This chapter helps them future-proof their resilience.
- **Reflection deepens impact.** Taking time to reflect on what worked (and what didn't) throughout this guide turns experience into insight.
- **Resilience is personal and professional.** The tools provided (like the Self-Evaluation and Resilience Wheel) help educators develop resilience across multiple domains, emotional, physical, cognitive, and more.
- **Customization matters.** The action plan allows you to create *personalized* goals that fit your lifestyle, challenges, and values.
- **We grow what we measure.** Revisiting and rating your resilience helps you track real growth, which is something educators rarely get to do for themselves.
- **Commitment to self-care is a radical act in education.** By planning how to *sustain* your well-being, you model and practice what you often encourage in others.

Creating a Resilience Action Plan for Sustaining Resilience and Moving Forward

Let's revisit the Self-Evaluation Tools from Chapter 1. Then, you'll identify target areas and create a personalized Resilience Action Plan to continue building and sustaining resilience beyond this guide.

Review and Reflect
   Activity: Reflection on Learning If applicable, reflect on the previous chapters. What were your key takeaways? Which strategies resonated most with you? What changes have you noticed in yourself over the course of reading this guide?

Pause Here and Take a Moment to Reflect

Educator Resilience Self-Evaluation

How to Use This Tool
1. Just as in Chapter 1, read each statement and think of related specific situations.
2. Rate yourself on the statement by marking the appropriate box (very difficult, difficult, easy, or very easy for you to do).
3. When you finish, search for patterns of strengths and challenges. This information is for you, so answer accurately without judging responses as "good" or "not as good."
4. Compare these responses to those on your first self-evaluation. Review your responses and take action in light of what you learn.

Introduction to Resilience

Statement	Very Difficult 1	Difficult 2	Easy 3	Very Easy 4
I understand what resilience means in the context of education.				
I can identify factors that contribute to my resilience.				
I recognize the signs of resilience in myself and others.				
I see the importance of community in fostering resilience.				
Total (_____ / 16) Notes:				

Self-Awareness and Emotional Intelligence

Statement	Very Difficult 1	Difficult 2	Easy 3	Very Easy 4
I can identify and name my emotions in the moment.				
I use self-reflection to understand the factors that contribute to my emotions.				
I recognize when my emotions influence my behavior and reactions.				
I understand my emotional triggers and have strategies for managing them.				
Total (_____/ 16) Notes:				

Mindfulness and Stress Management

Statement	Very Difficult 1	Difficult 2	Easy 3	Very Easy 4
I incorporate mindfulness practices into my daily routine.				
I use mindfulness to manage stress and maintain my well-being.				
I practice breathing exercises to reduce stress.				
I can stay present and focused in stressful situations.				
Total (_____/ 16) Notes:				

Building Strong Relationships

Statement	Very Difficult 1	Difficult 2	Easy 3	Very Easy 4
I connect meaningfully with colleagues and students.				
I listen actively and empathetically to others.				
I can navigate conflicts and maintain positive relationships.				
I build and maintain a supportive community.				
Total (_____/ 16) Notes:				

Professional Purpose and Passion

Statement	Very Difficult 1	Difficult 2	Easy 3	Very Easy 4
I feel connected to my professional purpose.				
I am passionate about my work as an educator.				
I set professional goals and work toward them.				
I reflect on my core values and align my work with them.				
Total (_____/ 16) Notes:				

Adaptive Thinking and Problem-Solving

Statement	Very Difficult 1	Difficult 2	Easy 3	Very Easy 4
I view challenges as opportunities for growth.				
I use creative problem-solving strategies.				
I stay flexible and resilient in the face of challenges.				
I encourage a growth mindset in myself and others.				
Total (_____/ 16) Notes:				

Self-Care and Well-Being

Statement	Very Difficult 1	Difficult 2	Easy 3	Very Easy 4
I prioritize self-care and maintain my well-being.				
I have a personal self-care plan with specific actions.				
I practice gratitude regularly.				
I engage in activities that promote my physical, emotional, and mental well-being.				
Total (_____/ 16) Notes:				

Self-Compassion

Statement	Very Difficult 1	Difficult 2	Easy 3	Very Easy 4
I speak to myself with kindness during hard moments.				
I understand the difference between self-esteem and self-compassion.				
I notice when I'm being self-critical and can pause to shift my tone.				
I practice self-compassion regularly.				
Total (_____ / 16) Notes:				

Optimistic Outlook

Statement	Very Difficult 1	Difficult 2	Easy 3	Very Easy 4
I can find positives even during challenging times.				
I maintain hope and motivation for the future, even when facing obstacles.				
I encourage a positive outlook in myself and others.				
I balance optimism with realistic action steps toward my goals.				
Total (_____ / 16) Notes:				

Building Resilience Through Play

Statement	Very Difficult 1	Difficult 2	Easy 3	Very Easy 4
I incorporate play, creativity, or humor into my routine.				
I recognize the value of play in adult learning and well-being.				
I feel re-energized by creative or joyful activities.				
I help create space for lightness and joy in my work community.				
Total (_____/ 16) Notes:				

Celebrating Educators

Statement	Very Difficult 1	Difficult 2	Easy 3	Very Easy 4
I recognize and appreciate my achievements as an educator.				
I celebrate the successes of my colleagues.				
I feel seen and valued in my professional community.				
I participate in or initiate appreciation activities that uplift others.				
Total (_____/ 16) Notes:				

Sustaining Resilience and Moving Forward

Statement	Very Difficult 1	Difficult 2	Easy 3	Very Easy 4
I have strategies in place to sustain my resilience over time.				
I regularly review and adjust my resilience action plan.				
I feel supported by my professional community.				
I am committed to continuous growth and resilience.				
Total (_____/ 16) Notes:				

Identifying Areas for Improvement in Resilience

Review Your Ratings

1. Go through each section (Introduction to Resilience, Self-Awareness and Emotional Intelligence, Mindfulness and Stress Management, Building Strong Relationships, Professional Purpose and Passion, Adaptive Thinking and Problem-Solving, Self-Care and Well-Being, Self-Compassion, Optimistic Outlook, Building Resilience Through Play, Sustaining Resilience and Moving Forward, Celebrating Educators) and look at your ratings for each statement.
2. Highlight or note down the statements where you rated yourself as "Easy" or "Very Easy."
3. Highlight or note down the statements where you rated yourself as "Difficult" or "Very Difficult."
4. How do these results compare to your initial self-evaluation?

Notes

Look for Patterns
1. Identify common themes or recurring areas of difficulty across different sections. These may or may not be different from your initial self-evaluation.
2. For example, if multiple statements about managing stress are marked as difficult, it suggests a need to focus on stress management.

Notes

Reflect on Impact
1. Consider how the areas marked as difficult impact your interactions with students, peers, and your overall effectiveness as an educator.
2. Ask yourself questions like: *How do these challenges affect my daily work? How would improving in these areas enhance my professional and personal life?*

Notes

Monitor and Reflect
Regularly revisit your self-evaluation and action plan to track progress and/or your smart goal. Reflect on any changes in your ratings over time and adjust your strategies as needed.

Using the Resilience Wheel
Activity: Wheel of Resilience Update
Using the Resilience Wheel
The Resilience Wheel is a visual tool designed to help you assess and reflect on various aspects of your resilience. For each category, rate your resilience on a scale of 1 to 10 (1 being the lowest and 10 the highest). Use the guiding questions provided to assist in your reflections. Shade in portions of the wheel corresponding to your ratings to create a visual representation of your resilience. Take a few minutes to reflect, considering your strengths and identifying areas where additional support may be beneficial.

- Revisit the Resilience Wheel from Chapter 1.
- Reflect on changes and progress in each area as you complete another Resilience Wheel. Consider in what areas you feel you've become stronger.
- Identify areas where there is room to improve or focus more attention.

Complete Another Resilience Wheel in Order to Move Forward With Creating a SMART Goal
1. Read the definitions and questions pertaining to each component of the wheel.
2. Rate your resilience level from 1–10 for each component.
3. Color in the corresponding amount in that section of the wheel.

Guiding Questions

Emotional: *How do I manage stress and emotions? What strategies do I use to stay emotionally balanced?*

Physical: *How do I take care of my physical health? What activities or routines help me stay physically resilient?*

Social: *Who are my key support people? How do I maintain and strengthen these relationships?*

Professional: *How do I stay motivated and passionate about my work? What professional goals am I working toward?*

Cognitive: *How do I keep my mind sharp and engaged? What learning activities do I enjoy?*

Community: *How am I involved in my community? How does my community support my resilience?*

Spiritual: *What practices help me find meaning and purpose? How do I nurture my spiritual well-being?*

Other: *Are there any other aspects of my life that contribute to my resilience? Cultural? Financial? Something else?*

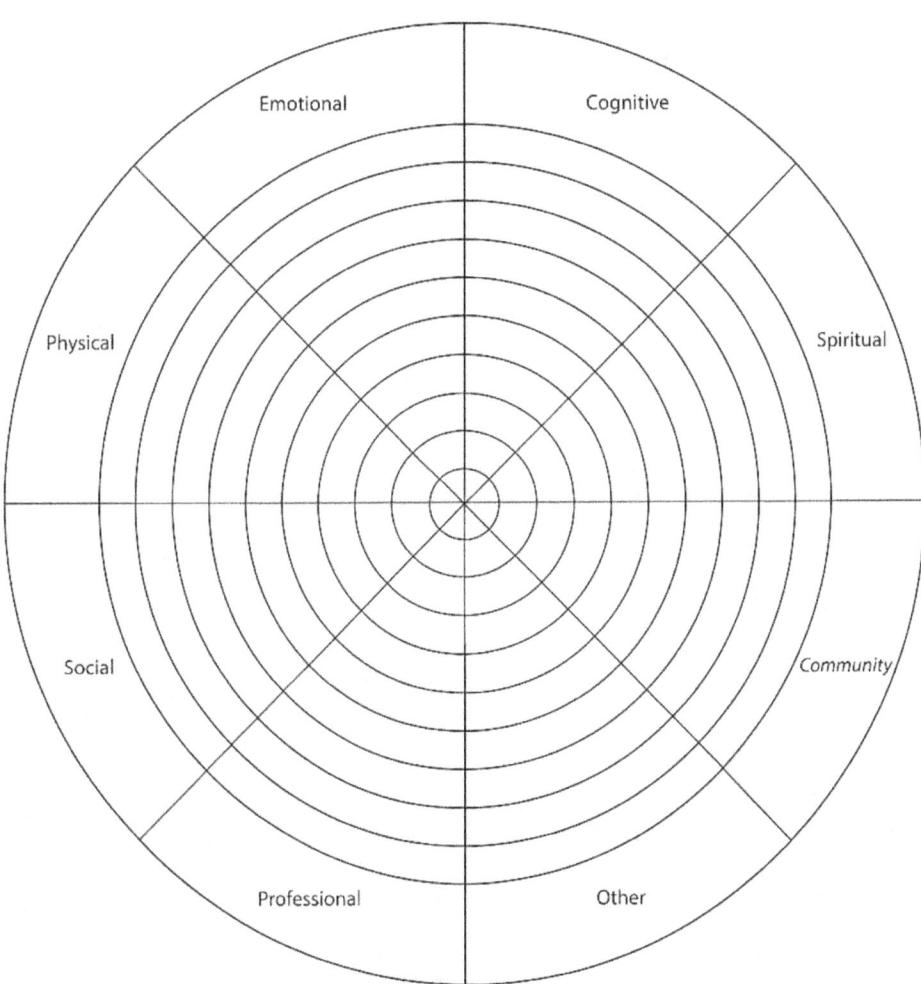

Figure 12.1 Resilience Wheel

Use your wheel as a living, breathing document. Revisit it, revise it, and remember: You're not behind. You're just building. One reflection at a time.

Pause Here and Take a Moment to Reflect

Notes

Updated Resilience Wheel
- Areas of Strength:
  - _____
  - _____
- Areas for Growth:
  - _____
  - _____

Set Specific, Measurable Goals
Activity: SMART Goals
- Set SMART (specific, measurable, achievable, relevant, time-bound) goals.
- Set at least one goal for an area of growth on the resilience wheel and/or self-evaluation.
- Specific: What exactly do you want to achieve?
- Measurable: How will you know when you've achieved it?
- Achievable: Is this goal realistic and attainable?
- Relevant: How does this goal relate to your overall resilience?
- Time-Bound: What is your deadline for achieving this goal?

Goal 1: _____
- Specific: _____
- Measurable: _____
- Achievable: _____
- Relevant: _____
- Time-Bound: _____

Goal 2: _____
- Specific: _____
- Measurable: _____
- Achievable: _____

- Relevant: _____
- Time-Bound: _____

Plan for Action
Activity: Action Steps and Resources
- ◆ For each SMART goal, identify the specific steps needed to achieve it.
- ◆ List any resources or support needed (e.g., books, online resources, support from peers).
- ◆ Example prompts:
  - What steps do I need to take to achieve this goal?
  - What resources or support will help me succeed?
  - What obstacles might I face, and how can I overcome them?

Action Steps and Resources
Action Steps for Goal 1
- ◆ _____
- ◆ _____
- ◆ _____
- ◆ _____

Resources Needed
- ◆ _____
- ◆ _____
- ◆ _____

Action Steps for Goal 2
- ◆ _____
- ◆ _____
- ◆ _____
- ◆ _____

Resources Needed
- ◆ _____
- ◆ _____
- ◆ _____

Accountability and Support
Activity: Peer Accountability Partners
- ◆ Identify an accountability partner.
- ◆ Share goals and action plans with each other.
- ◆ Encourage regular check-ins (e.g., bi-weekly or monthly) to discuss progress and challenges.

- Example prompts:
  - How can your partner support you in achieving your goals?
  - When will you check in with each other to discuss progress?

Name: _____ Check-in Schedule: _____

Review and Adjust

Activity: Regular Reflection and Adjustment
- Schedule regular times (e.g., monthly) to review action plans. Consider putting reminders on your phone.
- Reflect on progress, celebrate successes, and adjust goals as needed.
- Example prompts:
  - What progress have I made toward my goals?
  - What have I learned from any setbacks or challenges?
  - Do I need to adjust my goals or action steps?

Regular Reflection and Adjustment
- **Next Review Date:** _____
- **Reflection Prompts:**
  - *Progress Made:* _____
  - *Learnings:* _____
  - *Adjustments Needed:* _____

Regular Reflection and Adjustment
- **Next Review Date:** _____
- **Reflection Prompts:**
  - *Progress Made:* _____
  - *Learnings:* _____
  - *Adjustments Needed:* _____

Celebrate Achievements

Date of Completion: _____
- **Achievements Since the Workshop:**
  - _____
  - _____
- **How will I celebrate?**
  - _____
  - _____
- **Next Steps:**
  - _____
  - _____

Example Resilience Action Plan for Jane Doe

1. Reflection on Learning
- Key Takeaways From the Guide:
  - Building resilience involves emotional, physical, and social aspects.
  - Mindfulness practices can significantly reduce stress.
  - Having a supportive community is crucial for maintaining resilience.

2. Updated Self-Evaluation and Resilience Wheel
- Areas of Strength:
  - Social: Strong relationships with colleagues and friends.
  - Emotional: Good at managing stress through mindfulness practices.
- Areas for Growth:
  - Physical: Need to incorporate regular exercise.
  - Professional: Want to reconnect with my passion for teaching.

3. SMART Goals
- Goal 1 (Physical): Incorporate regular exercise into my routine.
  - Specific: Walk for 30 minutes every day.
  - Measurable: Track the walks using a fitness app.
  - Achievable: Start with walking and gradually include other exercises.
  - Relevant: Improve physical health and reduce stress.
  - Time-Bound: Achieve this goal within three months.
- Goal 2 (Professional): Reconnect with my passion for teaching.
  - Specific: Participate in one professional development workshop per month.
  - Measurable: Attend and complete at least three workshops in the next three months.
  - Achievable: Choose workshops that are of personal interest and relevance to my teaching.
  - Relevant: Enhance teaching skills and rekindle enthusiasm.
  - Time-Bound: Achieve this goal within three months.

4. Action Steps and Resources
- Action Steps for Goal 1:
  - Schedule daily walks in the morning or evening.
  - Use a fitness app to track progress.
  - Gradually include other exercises like yoga or cycling.

- ◆ Resources Needed:
  - – Fitness app (e.g., Strava or Fitbit)
  - – Comfortable walking shoes
  - – Yoga mat
- ◆ Action Steps for Goal 2:
  - – Research and sign up for professional development workshops.
  - – Allocate time in my schedule for attending workshops.
  - – Reflect on and implement new strategies learned from workshops.
- ◆ Resources Needed:
  - – List of available workshops (school, online platforms like Coursera)
  - – Journal for reflections and notes

5. *Accountability Partner*
- ◆ Name: John Smith
- ◆ Check-in Schedule: Bi-weekly on Fridays

6. *Regular Reflection and Adjustment*
- ◆ Next Review Date: August 30, 2026
- ◆ Reflection Prompts:
  - – Progress Made: Completed daily walks for the past month and attended one workshop.
  - – Learnings: Walking helps reduce stress and attending the workshop renewed my enthusiasm.
  - – Adjustments Needed: Increase the duration of walks to 45 minutes and explore more interactive workshops.

7. *Celebrate Achievements*
- ◆ Achievements Since the Workshop:
  - – Consistently walking every day for 30 minutes.
  - – Successfully attended and enjoyed a professional development workshop.
- ◆ Next Steps:
  - – Continue with the current exercise routine and gradually add more activities.
  - – Research and sign up for the next professional development workshop.

Dream Big: A Vision-Based Approach to Goal-Setting

Not everyone vibes with rigid SMART goals. Maybe they feel too structured, too impersonal, or, let's be honest, too much like homework. If that sounds like you, here's a more soulful spin on goal-setting inspired by Steve Harvey's *Jump* (2016). His approach is rooted in dreaming big, trusting the process, and celebrating each small step along the way. It's less about checking boxes and more about building a life that lights you up.

This method can help you reframe goal-setting as a joyful, purpose-driven, and flexible journey, one that nurtures both resilience and hope.

1. Write It All Down: Your Vision List
Writing your dreams down gives them a place to live outside your head, and that's where the magic begins. Putting pen to paper transforms your intentions into something you can see, revisit, and act on.
- **Create a Vision List:** Try this bold exercise. Write down *300 things* you want to do, see, experience, or become in your lifetime. At first, it might feel overwhelming. That's okay. Keep going. You'll stretch beyond surface goals and reach into the deeper corners of your heart.
   Examples: "Write a book," "Travel to Italy," "Build a treehouse," "Learn to salsa dance," "Teach a wellness course," "Take a silent retreat."
- **Keep It Close:** Tuck this list somewhere easy to access. Revisit it often. Add new dreams, check off accomplishments, and let it evolve with you. Watching your own dreams come true, one by one, is powerful proof that you're capable of more than you imagined.

2. Dream Big, Bold, and Fearless
   SMART goals ask, *Is this realistic?*
   This method asks, *Does this light me up?*

- **Think Beyond the Limits:** Don't shrink your dreams to fit your fear. Expand your vision to meet your potential. Dream the dream that makes your heart beat faster.
   Example: Instead of "Get a promotion in two years," try "Become a compassionate leader who mentors others."
- **Root Goals in Your Values:** Let your dreams reflect what matters most to you, whether that's family, freedom, creativity, service, or joy. This ensures your goals aren't just impressive but also meaningful.

3. Visualize It: Mental Movies and Vision Boards

As we explored in Chapter 5, visualization is like setting a GPS for your life. You don't need to know every turn. You just need to see the destination.
- **Mental Movies:** Close your eyes and imagine it. The colors, the sounds, the emotion. Feel it in your body. If your goal is to buy a home, picture yourself opening the front door, sunlight pouring in, laughter echoing in the kitchen.
- **Create a Vision Board:** Clip photos, quotes, or symbols that represent your dreams and make a physical or digital collage. Hang it somewhere you'll see often as a daily visual nudge that says, *Keep going.*

4. Take Aligned Action

Dreaming is the beginning, but action is where the dream learns to walk.
- **Start Small, Start Now:** Don't wait for the perfect moment or perfect conditions. Begin with what you have.
  Example: Want to launch a business? Start with a single conversation. Want to get healthier? Take a walk today.
- **Act With Faith:** Harvey emphasizes belief as a guiding force and as faith that your steps will lead somewhere beautiful, even when the path isn't clear. Trust your gut. Trust your grit.

5. Reflect, Adjust, Repeat

Growth isn't linear, and neither is your path. Real resilience comes from adapting along the way.
- **Learn From Setbacks:** Every misstep teaches something. A detour might give you more time to prepare or a whole new perspective. Reflect, recalibrate, keep moving.
  Example: Didn't land the job? Use the feedback to improve and try again. Better equipped, bolder than before.
- **Revisit Your List:** You're allowed to grow out of your goals, just like you outgrow shoes. Maybe a dream no longer fits. That's not failure but evolution.

6. Celebrate the Journey and Practice Gratitude

One of the most joyful parts of this method? Celebrating *along the way.* Not just when you "arrive."
- **Celebrate Progress:** Whether it's a 5K on the way to a marathon or writing the first page of your book, every win counts. Acknowledge it. Honor it.

- **Practice Gratitude Daily:** Jot down one thing you're grateful for, big or small. The warmth of coffee. A kind word from a student. A good night's sleep. Gratitude shifts your focus from what's missing to what's blooming.

Why This Method Works

This approach makes goal-setting feel more human. It honors your passions. It leaves space for grace. It's not about having a perfectly measured plan but about believing in yourself enough to take the first step and enjoy the view along the way.

So write your list. Dream big. Take action. Celebrate wildly.

Your journey is allowed to be as bold, beautiful, and unique as you are.

Guided Meditation: Committing to Long-Term Resilience

Find a comfortable position, either seated or lying down, and gently close your eyes. Let your hands rest softly in your lap or by your sides. Take a slow, deep breath in . . . and a long, steady exhale out. Feel your shoulders drop away from your ears, your jaw unclench, your body begin to soften.

Let your breath settle into a smooth, natural rhythm. Now, reflect on the journey you've taken throughout this process. Think back to the moments of insight, the small shifts, the new tools you've gathered, and the growth you've experienced. Remember a time when you faced a challenge and found the strength to keep going, surprising yourself with your own resilience.

Visualize your personal Resilience Wheel, glowing softly in front of you. Each spoke of the wheel represents a strength you've cultivated: self-awareness, self-care, emotional intelligence, relationships, optimism, purpose, play, and more. See how each part of the wheel shines in its own way, forming a complete and balanced whole.

Now, imagine a path stretching out ahead of you. This path represents your journey moving forward, the path of your life, your career, your well-being. Along the edges of the path, the spokes of your resilience wheel light the way like lanterns, reminding you of the tools you can return to when challenges arise.

With each step you take on this path, feel a sense of *commitment* to yourself, your growth, your health, your happiness. Feel the ground steady beneath you, the air around you light and expansive.

>Silently affirm: *I am committed to my resilience. I am stronger than I know. I will continue to grow, to learn, and to thrive*. Pause here for a moment. Let this sense of strength and determination fill your heart. Know that you carry everything you need within you, including the tools, the wisdom, the capacity to care for yourself and for others.

When you're ready, gently bring your awareness back to the present. Wiggle your fingers and toes. Take a deep breath in . . . and exhale slowly. Open your eyes, carrying this commitment to long-term resilience with you, ready to continue your journey with courage, compassion, and purpose.

Key Takeaways

- Resilience is a lifelong practice. There is no final destination, only evolution.
- A personalized action plan keeps your well-being goals realistic and rooted.
- Sustaining growth requires reflection, recommitment, and community support.
- Celebrate your progress. Every small shift counts.

Closing Message

Resilience is not a destination but a lifelong journey. The work you've done through this guide has planted seeds of strength, self-awareness, and self-compassion. It's a reminder that you don't have to do everything perfectly or have all the answers. What matters is that you keep showing up, choosing to care for yourself, seeking support, and staying open to growth.

The path ahead may have challenges, but you've built a foundation. You have tools, strategies, and a community that believes in you. So as you move forward, remember: Resilience is not just about bouncing back but about moving forward with courage, with care, and with a deep knowing that you are enough. Thank you for all you do. Keep going. Keep growing. You've got this.

Chapter 12 Notes

Engage and Reflect

How do you sustain resilience over the long term in your teaching career?

What are some strategies you use to stay motivated and focused on your goals?

Can you share an example of when you successfully sustained resilience through a challenging period?

How do you regularly review and adjust your resilience action plan?

What role does continuous learning and professional development play in sustaining resilience?

How can you create a support network that helps you maintain your resilience?

What are some ways to celebrate your achievements and progress in building resilience?

How can you apply the lessons learned from this guide to your future teaching practice?

Continuing the Journey

Resilience is not a destination. It's not a box you check off or a goal you reach and then coast through the rest of your life. It's something messier, more beautiful, and more human than that.

Resilience is about creating a life you want to wake up for, even on the mornings when you'd rather pull the covers over your head and hide. It's choosing to keep showing up, to keep breathing, to keep trying, even when your heart feels heavy or the path ahead is unclear.

I learned that the day I moved my eldest daughter, Ana, into her dorm for her freshman year of college.

It was August and hot, humid, and sticky in the way only Massachusetts can be. We were opening and emptying bin after bin, and I tried so hard to be light, to be funny.

"Did you bring your wallet?" I asked for the third time, the words tripping out of my mouth like a broken record.

"Yes, Mom," she groaned, rolling her eyes. "You asked me that already. Twice."

I laughed, but it caught in my throat.

"Okay, okay . . . just making sure."

We put her photos on her desk, new pens in her drawer, plugged in her fridge, and lined up her stuffies on her bed.

The stuffies. She brought her stuffies.

These stuffed animals have been a part of her life forever. I thought back to all the times I tried to get my girls to reduce their collection.

"No, Mom, we can't get rid of Mrs. Bunny! That was a gift from Grammy!"

Figure 12.2 Stuffed Animals

"The puppy? No way! That was from Uncle Jesse!"

My daughters had a name for every animal and a story for each one. I remember having them take a picture once, all piled high on the sofa (Figure 12.2). Each one representing special moments, special people in their lives. How lucky are we to have so many memories, so much love.

I took a picture of the girls sitting on the hard dorm mattress (Figure 12.3) (the egg crate was still out for delivery). I felt so many emotions but mostly excitement.

Allie and I loaded the empty bins into the car to bring home. Ana knew we were leaving. Her eyes got wide.

"One last picture, girls!"

She hugged her sister, squeezing her tight (Figure 12.4). Allie tried to look cool, but I saw her blink hard, willing the tears not to fall.

"Don't forget to check your email and look at your schedule," I called as I climbed into the driver's seat.

"I won't," she promised, her voice softening for just a moment.

Allie and I left with an empty car, no pillows, no plastic bins, no Ana.

Allie sat next to me, quiet.

"Well," she said, "guess it's just us now."

Figure 12.3 Dorm Room

"Yeah," I whispered. My throat tightened. I felt the tears start to come, but I blinked them back.

Later that night, I walked past Ana's empty room. Her bed was still unmade, a half-finished iced coffee on the nightstand. The air smelled like our dog since he always chose to lay on her bed. I sat on the edge of the bed and picked up a stuffed animal she had left behind. Mrs. Bunny. It was still warm from the sun streaming through the window. I gave it a squeeze as a single tear fell.

I wiped my cheek. I couldn't believe how fast it all went.

Allie is still here. She's not leaving yet. But I know her time with me is growing smaller. She just got her license. Now she brings herself back and forth to work, school, and the gym. She's so independent, so smart. They both are. And yet, they still need me. They ask for hugs, they appreciate little notes, they show their love with small gestures.

But here I am, at a point where I don't fully recognize my life anymore. And that is both exciting and nerve-wracking, all in one little package.

In that quiet moment, sitting alone with Mrs. Bunny, I asked myself: *What now?*

The answer wasn't simple. It wasn't a five-step plan or a box to check. It was a whisper, just an invitation to build a life that feels good to me. A life where I wasn't just responding to "How are you?" with a sarcastic, "Living the dream." I wanted a life where I could keep learning, keep creating, keep growing, right alongside my daughters.

That's what resilience is: not having all the answers but staying open to the questions. Not forcing a perfect plan but trusting the process. It's saying yes to what lights you up, no to what drains you, and always making room for joy, even in the messy, uncertain moments.

And that's the thing about resilience. It's not about pretending you're okay all the time. It's about sitting on the edge of your daughter's bed, bunny in hand, and letting the tears fall. It's about holding your younger daughter close and feeling the weight of change pressing in and still waking up the next day, making breakfast, doing the laundry, laughing at your dog barking at the Amazon truck.

It's about being there for them, even as they grow into their own lives, and learning to be there for yourself, too.

Resilience is not a destination. It's not a perfect plan. It's the daily, quiet choices you make to build a life you want to wake up for.

So keep going. Keep breathing. Keep asking yourself what you need, and give yourself permission to make a life that feels good. Whether that's a cup of coffee in the morning sun, a long walk with your dog, or just a moment to sit in the quiet and remember how far you've come.

Figure 12.4 Last Hug

You are stronger than you know. And you're not alone. This is the journey, and it's yours to shape, one breath, one boundary, one brave step at a time. Keep on going.

Keep Moving Forward

Reference

Harvey, S. (2016). *Jump: Take the leap of faith to achieve your life of abundance.* Amistad.

For Product Safety Concerns and Information please contact our EU
representative GPSR@taylorandfrancis.com
Taylor & Francis Verlag GmbH, Kaufingerstraße 24, 80331 München, Germany

www.ingramcontent.com/pod-product-compliance
Lightning Source LLC
Chambersburg PA
CBHW080730300426
44114CB00019B/2539